THE AMERICAN HUNTING MYTH

Ron Baker

photo by Norman Ives

VANTAGE PRESS
New York / Washington / Atlanta
Los Angeles /Chicago

For all those that have died needlessly
as we slowly progress
toward a more humane world

FIRST EDITION

All rights reserved, including the right of
reproduction in whole or in part in any form.

Published by Vantage Press, Inc.
516 West 34th Street, New York, New York 10001

Manufactured in the United States of America
ISBN: 0-533-06344-2

Library of Congress Catalog Card No.: 84-90300

Contents

Part II: Shooting Down the Myths

Prepublication Praise for
The American Hunting Myth

"There is a message that cries out from within the pages of this book from all the wildlife in the world. Baker has demonstrated great perception and courage in putting this exposition of bureaucratic ignorance into print."

—Joanne Treffs, naturalist, coauthor of
Wildflowers of the Adirondacks

"A multifaceted and wide-ranging indictment . . . The author pleads for a new land ethic and reverence for living things. . . . To an ever-increasing percentage of the civilized world this well-researched and well-written book will have strong appeal."

—William A. Ritchie, Ph.D., anthropologist

Acknowledgments

I am deeply indebted to many people, including many dedicated animal protectionists, for the help that they have given me. Among those who deserve credit for helping to make *The American Hunting Myth* a reality are:

the staff of *Agenda*, who made available some of the information that I have used (and kept my name on the masthead as a contributor while I was working on *The American Hunting Myth* and contributing very little to the magazine);

Rev. Elmer Baker who gave me many insights into Scripture;

the very helpful gentleman who provided additional information about wildlife science programs at Northeastern colleges and universities and the equally helpful gentleman who provided inside information about game management programs on the federal and state levels;

Hope and Cavit Buyukmihci of Unexpected Sanctuary, who offered helpful information;

Dr. George P. Cave, president of Trans-Species Unlimited, who gave me his views on man's ethical responsibility to nonhuman life;

Common Sense magazine, which provided comments made by several ecologists and humanitarians;

Luke Dommer, president of The Committee to Abolish Sport Hunting, who gave me information about the financing of federal conservation programs, and helpful material about Kaibab, and wolves in Alaska.

Rosa Feldman, of Student Action Corps for Animals, who offered hope and encouragement when my manuscript seemed to be at an impasse;

Friends of Animals, Inc., which made available to me information taken from government publications that describe the methodology of wildlife management;

Norman Ives, of Wildlife Acres Sanctuary, who gave me information about turkey hunting in Pennsylvania;

Dick Kenly, a zoologist for the Fund for Animals, who offered much-needed information at a crucial time;

David Lipski, animal rights advocate, who supplied me with information and philosophical insights.

Fred Messerschmitt, animal rights advocate, who gave me copies of *New Jersey Game Regulations* and other helpful material;

Doris Primack, chairperson of the Animals in Politics Task Force of Mobilization for Animals, who gave me copies of proposed hunting bills in New York State;

Dr. William A. Ritchie, a retired archaeologist for the state of New York and active member of thirty-three environmental and animal protection organizations, who supplied me with much-needed statistics;

Sharon St. Joan of the Foundation Faith, who gave me insights about animals from a biblical perspective;

Harriet Schleifer, animal rights activist, who supplied me with additional material about the biological and ecological hazards of public hunting;

David Wolfson, a graduate of Cornell University, who made available to me additional information about the teaching of wildlife science courses on the undergraduate level.

And SPECIAL THANKS TO BINA ROBINSON, New York State representative of the International Ecology Society. Were it not for the many newspaper and magazine articles she sent to me as research aids, this book would have lacked a great deal of important source material.

To all of these people go my most heartfelt thanks.

In Remembrance

A cold, dark morning in early November with a chill breeze blowing from the northwest, a morning typical of late autumn in the Adirondacks. As I strolled quietly through deep woods on the heavily forested 100-acre wildlife sanctuary that my wife and I maintain, I was alert to the sights and sounds of the forest. My destination was a place of special beauty in the hills above our log cabin. On my right, the lower slope of a ridge was covered with picturesque white birches and other tall hardwoods. On my left, a cedar swamp reposed beneath the leaden sky. Beyond, at a distance of about 600 feet, lay the posted boundary that divides our sanctuary from the Adirondack Forest Preserve. Suddenly I became aware of a crackling of brush in the thickly wooded swamp. I froze, as I had been conditioned to do during the long Adirondack hunting seasons. The sound grew louder and closer. Was a hunter or a group of hunters trespassing on the refuge?

Then I saw him coming swiftly toward me. He was a magnificent twelve-point buck, smooth and muscled, at the peak of his autumn health. He was by far the largest deer I had ever seen in our sanctuary. I stood motionless. About fifty feet from me, the buck suddenly stopped. He stared at me for a moment, then sniffed the air and wheeled, galloping back through the swamp. I watched him disappear amidst the tangle of evergreens; then I continued on. After ascending a small rise, I paused amidst a cathedral of tall white pines.

Suddenly four shots thundered in rapid succession on the ridge beyond the swamp. My heart seemed to stop beating momentarily. The buck. . . ! The hunter or hunters were apparently on state land not far from the periphery of the swamp. There was a deathly silence. The hunter's bullets had either missed the buck or killed him. Whichever was the case, there seemed to be no reason to pursue the hunter. There was no way to undo what might have been done, and hunting is legal on Forest Preserve lands.

About half an hour later, I walked dejectedly through the swamp in the direction in which I had heard the shots. I crossed our property boundary and continued for about fifty feet. Then I followed our succession of orange posters up a long hill. I had gone only a short distance when, on my left, on state land about a hundred feet from the refuge boundary, I saw the crimson-stained ground where the large buck had fallen. The dry leaves that littered the forest floor were in disarray where the hunter or hunters had dragged the stag's body down the ridge along our boundary line.

In disgust I retreated to the small bunkhouse that had been built a short distance from our cabin. I shared part of the responsibility for the buck's death. If I had not been there to block his retreat, he would have continued toward the safe interior of the sanctuary. I had unwittingly forced him in the opposite direction—toward the hunter's rifle. Somehow I had to repay for my mistake. But how? I pondered for a moment, and then, in a flash of clarity, I knew what I would do to repay the debt that I owed. I would expose the corrupt system that had been responsible for the death of the buck and for the needless killing and wounding of countless animals before him. I would try to help others develop an empathy with all sentient life. And I would do this pragmatically and unemotionally.

On the table in front of me lay a typewriter. Slowly I wound a sheet of paper into the carriage. I paused briefly to reflect and then began to type. . . .

Preface

This is a book about exploitation; the exploitation of nonhuman animals by the dominant animal, man. It is a book designed to expose widely held myths and educate people about the ecological and social dangers and the moral terpitude of recreational hunting. The hunting of wild animals differs from other forms of animal exploitation (vivisection, factory farming, whaling, the slaughter of harp seal pups, et cetera) in that it is not the province of a relatively small professional clique. In North America, hunting is widely considered to be a legitimate sport. In the United States some 30 million people participate in it, often with disastrous consequences for the individual, society, hunted and nonhunted species, and the ecology. Despite the destructive results of public hunting, specialized government agencies encourage it and help to support it, agencies on both the federal and state levels.

There is nothing secretive about the "management" techniques that are used by state game bureaus and the U.S. Fish and Wildlife Service. Almost all of the information that I have included in this book is readily available to anyone who takes the time to delve deeply into the subject. And herein lies the travesty that is public hunting and commercial wildlife management. The fact that a system such as this can operate openly in twentieth-century America, that it can continue to function in basically the same fashion in every state in the nation, is a sad commentary on the insensitivity to nonhuman life that many of us have been conditioned to accept.

It is not the primary purpose of this book to shock readers with horror stories about atrocities committed by lawless hunters. Essentially, the text reflects this intent. I *have* described a number of these cases, particularly in two parts of this book, simply because they helped to prove a contention. But the main purpose of this treatise is to illustrate the ways in which *legal* forms of hunting adversely affect ecosystems and the biology of hunted species and to disseminate the view that all wild animals should be freed from man's exploitation. Indeed, few tales of lawlessness are necessary. Current systems of wildlife management are in themselves an outrage, an archaic vestige of a time when few people cared about the natural world.

This book has been divided by subject matter into three sections. Part 1 describes the aberrations of commercial wildlife management. This is intended as a general overview of game management. The second section presents seventeen arguments that are commonly used to justify sport hunting and/or game management, along with a very detailed analysis of each. Part 3 catalogues some of the harmful effects that recreational hunting has upon society. Some of the most likely explanations for the continued existence of hunting are given. Conclusions are drawn and a practical method is outlined by which hunting could be phased out in favor of constructive wildlife management practices.

I wish that I felt justified in using only moral arguments to condemn recreational hunting. But while ethics are a valid consideration they are less tangible than empirical facts, so I have concentrated mainly upon the latter.

Throughout much of this book I detail the malpractices of the New York State Division of Fish and Wildlife, a branch of the New York State Department of Environmental Conservation. I have targeted this wildlife bureau simply because, as a resident of New York State, I have had a lengthy familiarity with the practices of the wildlife officials, game managers, and commercial biologists in its employ. However, the reader should not infer that I am singling out members of the New York State Wildlife agency for their insensitivity to wildlife. The methodology employed by the New York State Division of Fish and Wildlife is symptomatic of the wildlife mismanagement practices of state game bureaus throughout the United States.

Historically, man's inhumanity to man has been exceeded only by his inhumanity to his nonhuman brethren. Most individuals of most animal species, if well fed and cared for by a person, will live peacefully with individuals of most other species if they are raised together from birth or soon afterward. The human race is unique in its failure to live in harmony with other species when all of its physical needs have been satisfied. It does not have to be this way.

Fortunately, times are slowly changing. Already there has been progress toward ending some of the cruelties that man has traditionally inflicted upon other creatures. While the path will not be easy, I believe that there will be much greater progress in the future. I hope that, after reading this book, you will feel a much deeper commitment to wildlife.

PART ONE

Game Management:
Root of an Evil

I. / An Introduction to Wildlife Management

THE METHODOLOGY AND POLITICAL BASIS OF GAME MANAGEMENT AS IT EXISTS IN NORTH AMERICA AND SOME TYPICAL EXAMPLES OF THE HUNTER-TRAPPER SYSTEM OF MANAGEMENT, FOLLOWED BY AN INSIGHT INTO THE SERIOUS FLAWS THAT ARE INHERENT IN THIS SYSTEM.

> *The powerful do not design rules which encourage outsiders to take away or share power. In addition, those who make rules can unmake and circumvent their own rules to suit their convenience and interests.*
> —Henry Spira, educator and humane activist

ARE HUNTERS CONSERVATIONISTS?

> *. . . To a certain extent trophy hunting is a form of harvesting. The sportsmen were smart enough to know that if they killed off their own sport by overslaughter, they'd have no sport left, so they have been at the forefront of saving and preserving the game.*
> —Ronald Reagan, lifetime member of the National Rifle Association (from an interview in the October 1980 issue of *Field and Stream*)

In a National Hunting and Fishing Day proclamation on September 23, 1978, President Jimmy Carter said:

I would like to take this opportunity to commend the leadership of the nation's sportsmen in conservation and to call upon all Americans to join with hunters and fishermen in promoting the wise use of our natural resources and in ensuring their protection for the benefit of future generations.

Mr. Carter's speech, like most of those delivered by most politicians, dealt in generalities rather than specifics. Those who heard or read parts of the president's speech and who appreciate the complexity of wilderness ecology no doubt wondered whether the president—or his speech

3

writer—fully understood what he was writing when he composed the "wise use and protection" statement. Those who have studied the destructive results of public hunting and wildlife management know that President Carter's idealistic portrayal of hunters and hunting has little basis in fact. The facts are:

1) As a group, sport hunters (and trappers) are not leaders in conservation, they are impediments to it.
2) Most recreational hunters and trappers do not promote the wise use of natural resources; they promote their "sport," and this often results in serious biological, ecological, and social consequences.
3) Sport hunters and trappers are ensuring the consumptive use of wildlife for future generations only because the hunting-trapping system is perpetuated largely for the benefit of those who profit directly from it.

These and other serious charges will be fully examined and substantiated during the course of this book. The truth about hunting, including its disastrous biological and ecological impact, contradicts the barrage of propaganda that issues from state environmental resource departments; from the National Rifle Association; from public relations people employed by the manufacturers of guns and ammunition; from editorial writers and columnists for hunting-fishing-trapping periodicals; from outdoor columnists whose writings appear in many newspapers; from hunters' groups such as the National Shooting Sports Foundation; from those whose jobs involve the manipulation of wildlife and who are represented by groups such as The International Association of Game, Fish and Conservation Commissioners and The Wildlife Society; from organizations supported by professional game managers, hunters, and trappers and by businesses and industries that have a financial interest in hunting, such as The Wildlife Management Institute and The Wildlife Legislative Fund of America; and from citizen-financed "conservation" organizations whose leaders support the hunting ethic.

According to statistics released by state fish and game departments, approximately 28.5 million people purchased hunting licenses in the United States during 1983. Added to these are the estimated 3 million illegal hunters who hunt without licenses. This means that there are more than 30 million hunters in the United States—enough to decide many federal, state, and local elections. But as impressive as these figures are, hunters comprise only about 15 percent of the United States pop-

4

ulation between the ages of eighteen and sixty-five.* This is a very important statistic. A person might ask why wildlife management continues to be structured around the activities of a relatively small minority of Americans. The answer is *not* that public hunting is a sound conservation practice; in fact, it violates every principle of ecology!

THE WILL OF THE PEOPLE?

For me, being a part of the great outdoors, whether it's hunting, fishing or trapping, is a privileged gift from God.
—From a letter by a Monroe, N.Y. hunter to the Middletown N.Y. *Times-Herald Record* (March 20, 1982)

Wildlife belongs to everybody. We think it is audacious of hunters to say they can shoot animals but we cannot protect them.
—Susan Russell, education director of Friends of Animals, Inc. (from a *New York Times* article by William E. Geist [March 31, 1983])

Is recreational hunting condoned or supported by a majority of Americans? As of this writing, the most recent independent survey of American attitudes about hunting was a 1980 poll by Yale psychologist Stephen Kellert that was prepared for the U.S. Fish and Wildlife Service.[1] Unfortunately, the questions that were asked reflect an ambiguity typical of public opinion surveys that deal with hunting. Kellert concluded that 80 percent of Americans approve of hunting for meat, 64 percent approve of hunting for both meat and recreation, and 40 percent approve of hunting mainly for sport. (Fifteen percent approve of trophy hunting.)

But these figures are misleading. First, let us assume that the survey is a representative sampling. Since about 15 percent of adult Americans are hunters, this percentage must be subtracted from Kellert's figures in order to determine the opinions of nonhunters. When this is done, it indicates that approximately two out of three nonhunting Americans approve of "hunting for meat," while about two in five approve of "hunting for meat and recreation," and only one in four approves of "hunting for recreation."

At this point, one must consider the imprecise terminology used by those who conducted the survey. Anyone who eats parts of the animals he shoots can claim that he hunts for meat. In truth, there are a very small number of subsistence hunters in the United States, mostly people

---

*The inclusion of hunters under eighteen and over sixty-five years of age would make the percentage of hunters approximately the same or slightly less when compared to the *total* U.S. population.

who live primitively in wilderness areas. Most hunters can claim that they hunt for both recreation *and* meat. The important question is whether hunting is necessary or unnecessary. Even subsistence hunters may hunt partly for "recreation." The determining factor would be whether a person is hunting for *necessary* food with "recreation" as a fringe benefit or whether an individual could survive comfortably without subsistence hunting, in which case hunting would be done primarily for recreation. One would have to consider this before one could approve or disapprove of "hunting for meat." Further, in order for a survey of nonhunters' attitudes about hunting to have a reasonable degree of accuracy, it would be necessary to ask: "Would you approve of hunting by a homesteader in the wilderness if food from his or her garden, combined with some purchased provisions, would be sufficient to maintain good health?"[2]

It would be safe to say that the vast majority of hunters hunt mainly for recreation since, for most people, there is no pressing need to hunt for survival. Kellert's survey seems to indicate a widespread lack of knowledge about hunting among nonhunters and a corresponding lack of knowledge about the harmful effects of hunting. It has been my experience that most nonhunters who have no strong feelings either for or against hunting have no clear grasp of either the adverse effects of hunting in general or the adverse effects of *specific types* of hunting within the framework of specific types of game management (for example, pheasant stocking, maximum sustained yield deer management, shooting of predators, et cetera).

Better Dead than Alive?

Those who were questioned by Kellert were asked to agree or disagree with the following statement: "In most cases, wild animals such as deer and ducks would be better off if government officials did not try to control the populations of these animals." Only about half as many respondants agreed as disagreed. The percentages of those who disagreed were even greater among those who belonged to selected groups that Kellert classified as "humane organizations" and "wildlife preservation organizations."[3] Thus this might be interpreted as a public endorsement of game management. But a close examination of Kellert's question reveals its ambiguity. Does it refer to "control" of wildlife populations by government officials *themselves* (that is, government hunters and trappers)? And, if so, by what means and under what ecological conditions? Or does it refer to "control" through public hunting and trapping? And what did Kellert mean by "better off"? Better off alive than dead? The report does not specify. Many respondents may not have fully understood Kellert's statement.

Kellert did *not* ask: "Are you aware of the disastrous biological and ecological consequences of public hunting and game management?" In all likelihood, the most common response from nonhunters would have been "*What* disastrous consequences?" If a person reads between the lines of the responses to many of Kellert's questions, he or she will discern a widespread lack of knowledge about biological and ecological facts as they relate to recreational hunting. If a majority of nonhunters were aware of the hazards of public hunting and wildlife manipulation, the approval rate for all forms of hunting would be only a small fraction of that which was indicated by Kellert's study. At any rate, the survey cannot be construed as an unconditional public approval of game management, even an approval based upon popular misconceptions about this system. Much less can it be viewed as a *potential* approval, assuming that most nonhunters were aware of the facts about commercial wildlife management and its detrimental effects upon wildlife populations and ecosystems.

Sport hunting is an evil that has no redeeming virtues. Regrettably, most people (including many members of environmental organizations) consider public hunting to be a minor ecological issue, or no issue at all. But modern sport hunting, and the system that helps to perpetuate it, is a significant factor, and in some areas the *primary* factor that has destroyed the balance of nature.

There are many arguments that hunters and wildlife manipulators use to justify public hunting. At one time or another I have been exposed to each of these, and *none* of them reflect sound reasoning. Later in this book, the major arguments that hunters use to justify hunting will be analyzed. But in order to fully understand the magnitude of the disaster that has resulted from public hunting, one must first understand the destructive system that perpetuates hunting. How does this system work? Why does it exist? How did it become this way? And how can it be improved?

USE AND ABUSE

Big game hunting is great in New York State. . . . We've opened all the doors for north country bear hunting, creating opportunity during conditions to suit your taste. . . . And if you're looking for BIG racks the north country is your choice. . . . And if waterfowl hunting turns you on the most come to New York. We don't have a waterfowl season. We have five waterfowl seasons.

—Sampling of composite quotes from *I Love New York Big Game Hunting* and *I Love New York Small Game Hunting*. Both are official brochures of the New York State Department of Environmental Conservation.

Webster's Dictionary defines conservation as:

A conserving, preserving, guarding, or protecting; a keeping in a safe or entire state; preservation.

But it can also mean "official maintenance and supervision, as of natural resources." And here we have a direct contradiction, because the "official maintenance and supervision" of wildlife does not mean guarding or protecting animals or keeping wildlife populations in a safe or entire state. It means the opposite: the controlled killing of wild animals for consumption by hunters, which results in economic benefits for a small percentage of Americans.

In theory, wildlife management is the manipulation of wildlife populations and their habitat for the purpose of reducing certain species of wild animals so that they will not become overpopulated and succumb to starvation, disease, parasites, stress, severe weather, or a combination of these factors. The method that is used to achieve this theoretical goal is a system of regulated hunting and trapping in which qualified people are licensed as hunters and trappers. The oft-repeated theoretical basis of game management has led to a common misconception about the purposes of hunting and the manipulation of wildlife and its habitat. The real reasons for the present system of wildlife management are considerably less altruistic than those that are usually cited in public addresses by state and federal conservation officials. Like most other aspects of modern life, government conservation is a commercial enterprise; it is big business, and as such, the principle of profit and loss usually determines operating procedures. Unfortunately, our society has traditionally viewed Nature as an adversary with which to do battle rather than as the Mother of All Life, with which to peacefully and reverently relate. Combine this dominant philosophy with the profit motive that is the basis of our free enterprise system, and the foundation is laid for a procedure in which the welfare of wildlife and ecosystems assumes a low priority.

The United States Department of Agriculture Forest Service brochure *Wildlife for Tomorrow* provides an insight into the procedures that typify the present system of wildlife management. According to this booklet:

There are National Forests in the West where the winter range for deer and elk, and in some instances the summer range, is

8

inadequate to carry the present level of big game populations. The same situation exists in the deer-yard areas of the North Central and New England states. Where this situation occurs, it can generally be corrected through a reduction in animal populations through hunting combined with a habitat improvement program for the ranges of the involved species.

Therefore, many deer and elk are shot so that herds will achieve a better balance with food supplies. Then habitat is manipulated so that greater numbers of fawns or calves will be born in response to improved forage, combined with innate biological factors, thus providing sustained yield "harvests" for hunters, revenue for state game bureaus, and real and imagined benefits for state and local economies.

Dr. Henry M. Weber, the late president of The Committee for Dove Protection wrote:

The original purpose of game management was to insure the adequate regard for the wildlife resource. . . . When "hunting" became a morally questionable commercialized process of "sport killing," game management was forced to become a tool to keep the supply of targets available. As this Frankenstein has steamrollered its way into state and federal government wildlife agencies, habitat for wildlife has steadily deteriorated.

Government wildlife agencies, particularly those on the state level, share part of the responsibility for this deterioration of habitat.

SPECIAL INTEREST RIGHTS AND SYSTEMIC WRONGS

"Commercial" factors do play a role in today's wildlife management practices.
—John E. Wilbrecht, a project leader with the U.S. Fish and Wildlife Service
at the National Elk Refuge at Jackson Hole, Wyoming (from a letter to the
author)

A typical example of wildlife management methodology has been the attempts by the Florida Game and Fresh Water Fish Commission to institute hunting in the Tosohatchee Preserve. This case is emblematic. Variations have occurred many times in many states. Thus it is an appropriate starting place for a study of wildlife management. The preserve, located on the west bank of the Saint John's River, consists mainly of wildlands that were saved from bulldozers at the eleventh hour by the efforts of dedicated conservationists. Early in 1978 the Florida cabinet voted to ban hunting on the preserve. Hunting would be reinstituted only if the Game and Fresh Water Fish Commission determined that

9

hunting would be necessary to ensure healthy populations of one or more species of wildlife. Meanwhile, prior to the cabinet's decision to ban hunting on the preserve, the director of the Game and Fresh Water Fish Commission wrote in a letter to state legislators:

> If a decision is made not to hunt the Tosohatchee area, I think it should be made with the full realization that disease and/or parasites or malnutrition are going to harvest the surplus and the survivors will be on a lower plane of physical health than might be desirable.

The fallacies in the Florida game director's statement will become evident to the reader during the course of this book. Meanwhile, at the time his comments were penned, no study had been made of the effects of hunting on the preserve. But on November 2, 1978, the director announced that the results of a study on the effects of the hunting ban had been completed. He claimed that "biological data derived from the health of the deer herd indicates that the herd has reached its carrying capacity for that particular range." He warned of a "potential die-off of some magnitude." At this time, fifty-five deer had been removed from the preserve (presumably to hunted areas). The director recommended removal of an additional 120 deer. Significantly, the hunting ban had been in effect for only ten months.* There are more than 580,000 acres of land open to hunting within a fifty-mile radius of the Tosohatchee Preserve, compared to only 26,000 acres that have been closed to public hunting. In the entire state of Florida, there are only 120,000 acres of a total of 4.8 million acres of public lands closed to hunting.

Equally important are the comments of citizen-environmentalist Tess Cammack. In a letter to the Saint Petersburg *Times* of December 18, 1979, she wrote:

> If hunting were allowed on the Tosohatchee Preserve, shotgun blasts and vehicular traffic could be expected to seriously disturb and disperse the species which were supposed to be protected. Most vulnerable would be the cougar and black bear.
>
> Hunting could be expected to become increasingly accepted as a tool of deer population control since man would be the only large predator left. With every passing year the balance would be more difficult to reestablish.

Then Cammack pinpointed the fundamental problem: "Hunting on

---

*When annual deer hunting is suddenly halted over a large area, the deer herd in that region will initially experience a population increase. But within several years the herd will decline to a level compatible with the ability of its habitat to support it.

environmentally sensitive land threatens to be a continuing issue as long as the Florida Game and Fresh Water Fish Commission is composed of people who believe that wildlife should be . . . manipulated for the ultimate 'harvesting' by hunters."

The prohunting bias of wildlife officials and game commissioners results partly from greed. The money that finances state wildlife agencies comes mainly from two sources: from the sale of hunting, fishing, and trapping licenses and from matching funds from federal excise taxes on guns and ammunition. Consequently, wildlife bureaus promote hunting and attempt to increase the number of hunters.

Maintaining Hunter Relations

The favoritism that is extended to hunters by state wildlife officials often includes personal contact. High-ranking members of state conservation departments and directors of state fish and game bureaus will sometimes deliver speeches at rod and gun clubs.[4] But most wildlife officials try to avoid face-to-face contact with any group that favors the abolition of hunting and trapping.

State fish and wildlife departments are among the few government agencies on either the state or federal level that are funded primarily or exclusively by special interest monies, while catering solely to the group or groups that they represent. More important, wildlife bureaus, as they are presently structured, exist at the expense of many nonhunting outdoor enthusiasts. Hunting conflicts not only with the would-be right of wild animals to pursue their lives as Nature intended; it also interferes with the rights of nonhunting hikers, backpackers, and autumn campers who wish to experience solitude.

In some states, such as Idaho, Florida, and Pennsylvania, the state wildlife agency is governed by a game commission. These commissions consist of five to eleven members. Almost without exception, members of these commissions are sympathetic to hunters. In fact, most members are hunters or former hunters. There have been nonhunting ecologists who have served on game commissions (as in California and Michigan), but at any given time there have been no more than two ecologists serving on each board. This is the reverse of proportional hunter-nonhunter representation, since only about two of every eleven Americans are hunters. In states where there are game commissioners, they influence their state wildlife department by their power to suggest changes in hunting regulations that are favorable to hunters and to suggest and introduce hunting legislation (for example, lengthened seasons on a hunted species or a hunting or trapping season on a previously protected species).

Wildlife officials and game commissioners have a singular and broad-based authority. Within the limits of legality and the legislative process, they hold the power of life and death over most of the wild animals that exist within their spheres of domination.

THE POLITICS OF WILDLIFE MISMANAGEMENT

The legislature (of a given state) has a great deal of discretion as to the means to be adopted for the conservation and protection of fish and game; and if these means do not violate any constitutional provision, the courts will not set up their judgement as to whether they are the best or most desirable.
—Declaration of the Supreme Court of the United States with regard to the rights of states to manage wildlife (35 *American Jurisprudence 2d, Fish and Game,* Sec. 1)

Sport hunting has been termed one of the most politically riddled, financially backed institutions in America. No other recreational activity is as coddled and protected by bureaucrats and functionaries at all levels of government. The hunting lobby easily outspends antihunters who attempt to block the expansion of hunting through legislation, public referendums, and legal suits. It is not uncommon for hunting opponents to be outspent ten to one during publicity campaigns. Consequently, hunters and government wildlife agencies usually prevail.

But the entrenched system of wildlife management could not continue to function if the legal apparatus were not designed to enforce it. Since state fish and game bureaus are government agencies, our courts, police, and existing statutes are structured in such a way as to insure the exploitation of hunted animals. In view of this, a person can better understand some of the difficulties that must be overcome if constructive changes are to be enacted. But how do state laws that affect wildlife become law? And why is it difficult to pass protective legislation?

State conservation departments and/or game commissions are usually not in complete control of establishing "game" laws. In most states, new hunting regulations must be passed by both houses of the state legislature and signed by the governor before taking effect. Unfortunately, most politicians who serve on state "natural resource" committees are hunter-oriented. This is a result of individual preferences, traditional legislative practices, the prohunting orientation of the government wildlife bureaucracy, the apathy of most nonhunters, the power of the hunter lobby and the arms industry, and the political view that the business economy is of far greater importance than the welfare of the earth and the life that it supports. Most politicians who are not strongly prohunting usually vote for hunting legislation. (Hunters vote

12

but animals do not, and there are usually no sustained massive public protests against most hunting bills.) The decision of the Florida cabinet to ban hunting on the Tosohatchee Preserve was very unusual. In most states (including Florida between 1979 and 1985), more public lands are being *opened* to hunting.

There are many difficulties in seeking to pass bills that would protect hunted wildlife, and some of these difficulties are a result of established lawmaking procedures. On the state level, the procedure for accepting or rejecting a legislative bill has traditionally been: introduction, referral to committee, three readings, and, after final passage, on to the other house for the same procedure. But in many states, including New York, such a large number of bills are introduced during each legislative session that shortcuts have been developed. Bills are usually read by title, not by full text. A bill placed on the calendar might never be voted on were it not for powerful rules committees, which may authorize consideration of a bill or allow it to die. In the New York Assembly, the speaker appoints committees and in the state senate the majority leader performs this task. Thus the real authority is centered in the rules committees and the powerful politicians who appoint them. The system of handpicking committee members is one reason for the strong prohunting bias of state legislators who serve on environmental conservation committees. Party leaders will often discipline any maverick who does not follow the "party line" or majority opinion by assigning him to a less desirable committee.

Sometimes an environmental resource committee chairman will wait until the last days of a legislative session before bringing a bill that he heavily favors to the floor of the legislature for a vote. At this time, many politicians are anticipating their recess and are not anxious to spend time debating the merits of a supposedly "minor" bill that deals with the expansion of hunting. With more "significant" issues on the agenda, they may vote for prohunting legislation simply because they wish to move on to other bills. Identical prohunting bills may be submitted by conservation committees in each house, further increasing their chances of passage.

There are other reasons for the routine passage of most prohunting bills. In most states, bills that are voted on during the closing days of a legislative session are submitted to the full assembly and senate with such rapidity that only a small number of legislators have more than a general idea of the full content of the bills they are voting on. In New York State, most legislators rely on the *Legislative Record and Index*, a weekly publication that summarizes the content of pending bills. The year 1980 saw 19,252 bills introduced in the New York State Legislature, but only 1,033 passed both houses and 903 *(87 percent)* were signed by the governor. As this would indicate, the odds are heavily in favor of a governor signing into law a bill that has been passed by the legislature of his state. And this is equally true of hunting legislation. Hunters not only comprise a significant block of votes; they are a very vocal minority. Naturally, the bills that have been proposed and then pushed through a legislature by the ranking politicians that serve on legislative committees stand the best chances of passage.

Sometimes, if resource committee politicians consider a prohunting bill particularly important (for example, if its passage would result in a much greater flow of revenue to the wildlife agency of their state), it may be *added* to a public assistance bill, an aid to education bill, or other significant legislation to ensure its passage. Thus, even if a governor is not strongly prohunting, he may sign the bill, particularly if he considers the attached hunting legislation to be of relatively minor importance.

How do these established legislative procedures affect the potential for the protection of hunted and trapped wildlife? Even if a majority of protectionists are elected to state legislatures, there is little hope for a quick change in the current system of wildlife exploitation. Hunting is a deeply entrenched system that will not be changed overnight. As long as a few powerful politicians are in control of environmental conservation committees in each state, as long as they are handpicked for their prohunting loyalties, and as long as the economically based system of game management remains entrenched, nothing short of massive public protests that result in proportional representation on game commissions and state wildlife agencies will lead to the evolution of existing procedures.

The Web of Intrigue

There is usually a cliquish relationship between state officials in all branches of government. This includes high-ranking politicians, officials of state conservation departments, and members of game commissions in states where these exist. Any attempt by state legislators to tamper with the authority and established functions of any state agency usually provokes strong protests from the affected officials, who respond by lobbying their friends in positions of power on the legislative committees that introduce and support legislation favorable to their agency. Wildlife officials often make proposals to friendly politicians who serve on wildlife and environmental resource committees, and many of these proposals are written into bills by one or more committee members. Thus, with the exception of minor nongame legislation and endangered species preservation (the funds for which come mainly from voluntary state income tax donations and from the federal treasury), state laws that affect wildlife usually do little more than perpetuate and expand the hunting-trapping system.

The following are typical wildlife bills that passed the New York State legislature during two recent sessions and were signed by the governor:

1) a bill that allowed the establishment of a special gunning season for white-tailed deer in the state's Southern Zone if and when it is determined that deer are causing extensive crop damage;
2) a bill that allowed shooting preserves to extend the waterfowl season by as much as fifteen days if adverse weather conditions during the regular season should result in less than a normal influx of hunters;
3) a bill that extended the deer season in Westchester County from thirty to sixty-one days; and
4) a bill that allowed the Department of Environmental Conservation (DEC) to issue free hunting and trapping licenses to persons over seventy years of age and disabled veterans.

Three primary considerations that govern the programs of the New York State Division of Fish and Wildlife are described in McKinney's *Constitutional Law of New York* (Vol. 17½, *Environmental Conservation Law*). They are a regard for:

"(1) ecological factors, including the restoration and improvement of natural habitat and the importance of ecological balance in maintaining natural resources;

"(2) the compatibility of production and harvesting of fish and wildlife *crops* with other necessary or desirable land uses; and

"(3) the importance of fish and wildlife resources for recreational purposes" meaning hunting, trapping, and fishing.

The problem is that numbers two and three are incompatible with number one (which is seldom a consideration of professional wildlife manipulators). Consequently, the current system of wildlife management is incompatible with a well-balanced natural ecosystem.

The reality of game management *usually* conflicts with game management theory. Game biologists deal mainly with the continuance of individual *species*; deer, bear, grouse, pheasants, et cetera. Their jobs are not to establish healthy populations of all native species, interacting harmoniously within wild ecosystems. By manipulating habitat and restocking some species of "game" birds and mammals and by periodically lengthening hunting and trapping seasons and issuing party permits for antlerless deer "harvests," the primary objective of wildlife management is to expand public hunting and insure a continuing flow of the revenue that results. Sport hunting is *not* used as a tool of wildlife population control, as most wildlife officials claim. The purpose of wildlife management is to insure *high populations* of popular "game" species for "harvesting" by the greatest number of hunters that game bureaus are able to license.

THE ARROGANCE OF POWER

The wildlife species we know today, whether game, non-game, threatened or endangered, receive the conscientious attention of professional resource managers. These people not only work to keep species from becoming extinct, but strive to enhance and increase wildlife populations by applying proper management techniques.
—Carroll Henderson, coordinator of the nongame wildlife program for the Minnesota Department of Natural Resources. (Quoted from the Minnesota *Volunteer*, September-October 1978 issue. The *Volunteer* is the official publication of the Minnesota Department of Natural Resources.)

Most people would probably assume that a rational and ecological explanation of a state's wildlife management practices will be given by any official of that state's wildlife agency. And most people would probably be shocked by many of the comments that such an official would undoubtedly make. But I was too familiar with game management to be shocked when I spoke with a middle-level official of the New York State Division of Fish and Wildlife while compiling information for this book. I was interested mainly in the reasons for the lengthy Adirondack big game seasons. New York State's Northern Hunting Zone, which includes the Adirondack State Park, has the longest combined hunting seasons for black bear and white-tailed deer east of the Mississippi. As of 1984, the Adirondack gun seasons for deer, including a preliminary one-week muzzle-loader season, are seven consecutive weeks, eight weeks once every five to ten years, due to calendar inconsistencies. Adirondack bear hunting, including a special early season, lasts eleven weeks. As of 1984, gun hunting for deer in most of New York State's Southern Zone was restricted to thirty days. (It was twenty-three days at the time of my interview with the wildlife official.) The Southern Zone includes the Catskill State Park, which has a relatively high concentration of deer, a result of management techniques as well as environmental factors. Bear hunting is permitted in the Catskill and Allegany regions and is open for two and a half to three weeks, depending upon location.

Gun hunting for deer in New York's Northern Zone during the autumn of my interview with the wildlife official extended from October 11 through December 7; bear hunting began September 20 and closed on the final day of deer season. Rifle and/or shotgun season for deer in the Southern Zone lasted from November 17 through December 9. Bear season encompassed essentially the same dates, where it was permitted. There are also archery seasons for deer and bear in the Northern Zone and for deer in the Southern Zone. During the autumn of my interview, with the official they lasted from September 27 to October 17 in the Northern Zone and from October 15 to November 17 in the Southern Zone. In addition, there were five extra days of bow and arrow hunting for deer following the close of the Southern Zone firearms season. As a special attraction, there was an "experimental" bear hunt in one section of the Adirondacks using teams of dogs to pursue bears. The area included in subsequent hunts has been gradually increased, as has the length of the season. By 1984 it had been extended to two and a half weeks. (A treed bear makes an easy target.)

For reasons of brevity and in order to discuss the most relevant issues, I decided to confine my questioning mainly to the firearms seasons for deer and bear in New York's two zones. My interview had been purposely unscheduled, so that the wildlife official would not have time to prepare answers to anticipated questions. Nonetheless, he proved to be very blunt. The latter part of our conversation went thusly:

"I'm curious as to why there is such a wide discrepency between the length of the deer-bear seasons in this state's Northern Zone and those in the Southern Zone."

"Well, of course, the longer Northern Zone seasons are partly a result of tradition. But we find that lower (human) population and lower hunter density in the Adirondacks permits somewhat longer hunting seasons. Here deer and bear harvests per square mile are usually somewhat lower per season than in the Southern Zone."

"But three weeks versus seven or eight weeks, including muzzle-loader hunting in the Northern Zone, *is* a substantial difference."

"That's true, but we've found that many hunters like to hunt the Northern Zone from mid-October to mid-November and then hunt the Southern Zone when big game seasons open there."

I suppressed the urge to ask the official whether these hunters allow hunting to totally dominate their lives during two or more months each year.

"I can understand why some hunters might be interested in doing this," I answered. "But Vermont, which is a sparsely populated state, has a rifle season for white-tailed deer which lasts only sixteen days.

Next to Pennsylvania, where deer hunting with shotguns and muzzle-loaders lasts about three weeks, Vermont has, until recently, had the highest deer kill per square mile of any eastern state. So isn't it conceivable that New York's Northern Zone big game seasons could be shortened somewhat without any substantial harvest reductions?"

"Well, no doubt it could. But some hunters like to camp out during the early part of the Northern Zone deer-bear season."

"What about hunters who want to camp in the Southern Zone? It gets pretty cold in the Catskills by the third or fourth week in November."

"There is a somewhat greater ratio of private to state land in the Catskills as compared to the Adirondacks. If we were to lengthen Southern Zone big game seasons, beginning them while the weather was still mild, it could lead to such an increase in hunter use that many more rural landowners would post their property."[5]

I shrugged my shoulders. "Well, isn't this their prerogative? They have a legal right to do this."

The official shot a sharp glance in my direction. "Actually, there are many considerations that wildlife biologists must make in evaluating the relationship of game populations to potential length of hunting seasons. Besides, hunting season length in New York State is established by law."

"I don't doubt what you say," I concluded. "But you told me that harvest percentages could probably be maintained in the Northern Zone if big game seasons were shortened by two or three weeks. Now, assuming that the state legislature would agree to a shortening of the seasons in this region, couldn't this be done without causing an undue hardship for anyone?"

He didn't crack a smile. "Quite possibly it would interfere with hunters' vacation time."

After thanking the official for his assistance, I tried to avoid his steely gaze as I ducked out of the door.

I found it disturbing, though predictable, that the official had avoided mentioning the welfare of deer and bear populations and the establishment of reasonably well-balanced ecosystems. It appeared that the potential for an increase in the amount of posted private lands was the primary factory that was inhibiting those entrusted with plotting the course of game management in New York State from allowing their professional capabilities to be completely guided by their sentiments. (Division of Wildlife officials in New York State have recently developed a solution to the increased posting of private acreage. As in many states, more state lands are now being opened to hunting and greater numbers of hunter access sites are being established in and adjacent to state forests, parks, and game management areas.)

As I walked from the DEC building to the visitors' parking lot, I pondered the comments made by the wildlife official. And I wondered how many of those who exercise power over the life and death of wild animals in America know about, or care about, the ecological consequences of their activities.

A MISDIRECTION OF POLICY

Whereas, there is increasing sentiment developing on a national scale to discredit hunting and the harvest of all wildlife; and . . .

Whereas . . . [hunting is] an absolute necessity for the . . . future well-being of many wildlife populations . . .

Now therefore be it resolved that the International Association of Game, Fish and Conservation Commissioners . . . [shall] cooperate with public and private agencies [and] develop a comprehensive program to "Tell it like it is. . . ."

—From the policy declaration of The International Association of Game, Fish and Conservation Commissioners (quoted from *What They Say About Hunting*, a publication of the National Shooting Sports Foundation)

Did the game official's remarks about New York's hunting seasons and hunting regulations reflect the official DEC policy? I wanted to learn the answer, so I mailed a detailed list of questions to Kenneth F. Wich, New York State director of fish and wildlife. Some of these questions were identical to those I had asked Wich's subordinate. Wich responded with a lengthy letter that explained the official reasons for certain hunting regulations in New York State. Regrettably, despite his professional-sounding discourse, many of his statements were generalities that avoided the biological and ecological repercussions of hunting and left much room for further inquiry. There were a few questions he did not answer directly, perhaps not without good reasons.

For example, in response to my question "Why are New York State's big game seasons, particularly those in the Northern Zone, considerably longer than those of neighboring states?," Wich wrote:

Considering the geographic differences in public sentiments and legislators' response to constituents within states, you can imagine the low probability of ever achieving uniform interstate hunting season dates. Moreover, big game harvest strategies vary considerably among states and hunting season frameworks vary accordingly.

What does public sentiment or legislators' responses to constituents have to do with maintaining optimum deer populations and reasonably well-balanced ecosystems? Nothing at all! But hunter's sentiments and the lobbying of hunters' groups have a great deal to do with the continuing expansion of sport hunting.

19

Wich noted that in New York's Southern Zone his department has the authority to regulate quota "harvests" of antlerless deer, "primarily adult females." (Some states issue a pre-determined number of antlerless deer hunting permits. Other states have deer-of-either-sex seasons. Nevada and the province of Quebec do not permit the hunting of does or fawns; only bucks with antlers at least three inches in length may be legally killed.)

In answer to my question "Why is there a considerable difference in the length of the big game seasons in New York's two zones and could the Northern Zone seasons be shortened considerably without reducing deer and bear harvests?" Wich replied (italics added by author):

> The lengthy Northern Zone big game seasons offer a recreational opportunity that is compatible with northern New York big game populations. Deer population density *is lower* in the Northern Zone than in the Southern Zone. . . . Relatively few hunters take advantage of the interior Adirondack deer resource . . . Shorter deer seasons would *needlessly restrict* people from hunting recreation and taking *harvestable deer*. . . .

It is important to understand the connection between low deer populations in the Adirondacks and longer hunting seasons combined with attempts by wildlife officials to increase (rather than decrease) hunting pressure in this area. The rifle season for deer in northern New York opens one week ahead of deer season in northern Maine, two weeks ahead of southern Maine, a week and a half ahead of New Hampshire, two or three weeks ahead of Vermont (depending on calendar dates), and a month ahead of southern New York. The New York State DEC encourages hunters from densely populated southeastern New York and nonresidents who hold New York State hunting licenses to hunt in the Adirondacks. By doing so, they patronize Adirondack merchants, increase potential hunting days, stimulate greater hunting interest, and thereby generate increases in hunting license revenue. Pittman-Robertson funds are also increased as a result of the lengthy northern New York deer-bear seasons.[6]

Wildlife officials in New York and other states go to great lengths to avoid offending hunters and their lobbying groups. This was reflected in a written comment by Mr. Wich. Responding to a question about the discontinuation of an experimental early muzzle-loader deer season in New York's Southern Zone (a season that has since been reinstated, but that now follows the firearms deer season), he wrote that "relatively high harvest rates forewarned of serious conflicts with deer population management, other hunters, and landowners."

20

Apparently, the majority of Southern Zone deer hunters, who use either high-powered rifles or shotguns, did not want other hunters (those who use primitive weapons) to reduce the number of deer prior to the opening of the firearms deer season. Furthermore, the influx of "specialized weapons" hunters had been accompanied by an increase in the posting of private rural lands. A reduction in the amount of land open to hunting, combined with a loss of "harvestable" deer before the traditional hunting season commenced, was a situation that New York State wildlife officials could not tolerate. Furthermore, if *too many* deer were killed during the hunting seasons, there would be fewer deer for hunters to shoot the following season. (As will be explained later, deer "management" is designed to maximize fawn production and maintain deer herds at artificially high levels.)

PREJUDICE VERSUS PREDATORS

A national park is the ideal natural laboratory because every effort is made to minimize human influence on the ecosystem. . . . There's no better place to study population dynamics.
—Stuart L. Croll, chief forest ranger at Isle Royale National Park, referring to the interaction between wolves and their prey ("Trouble in Wolf Heaven," by Thomas McNamee, *Audubon* magazine, January 1982)

In some areas [of Minnesota] being pro-wolf is equivalent to being anti-American.
—Odean Cusack ("Fear and Loathing of 'the Beast'—Behind Minnesota's Wolf Controversy;" *Agenda,* March-April 1983)

If any proof were needed that the placation of hunters is a primary concern of state wildlife officials and game commissioners, Wich and his subordinate offered some convincing evidence. This prohunting bias, which, as we have seen, is typical of those in state wildlife agencies, has led to a variety of ecological problems, not the least of which has been a decline or disappearance of large predators in most parts of the United States. By wildlife management standards, there must be a sufficient number of deer and "game" birds for hunters to shoot. Therefore, large natural predators, such as timber wolves, mountain lions (panthers) and coyotes, and sometimes smaller predators, such as lynx and bobcats, are a hinderance to management goals. The two main objectives of wildlife manipulators are to keep populations of favored game species at abnormally high levels and to reduce the number of large natural predators if and when predator populations rise above predetermined levels.

This was reflected in one of Mr. Wich's remarks. Asked about New York State's five-month coyote hunting season combined with an additional trapping season, he wrote:

> Coyote hunting and trapping seasons are liberal but not excessive. They are necessary to control increasing coyote numbers and to reach desired population levels.

"Desired population levels" are usually coyote populations as low as possible without the threat of their becoming endangered or extinct. Despite the fact that coyotes feed mostly on small mammals such as rabbits, mice, and squirrels, there is constant pressure from hunters' groups to "control" them since they do occasionally kill deer (most often those that are weakened by age or disease). There is little danger that a healthy, alert adult deer will be killed by coyotes unless it is trapped in deep snow or hindered by an icy snow crust. To some degree, either of these conditions will also impede coyotes.[7]

The State of Maine versus the Coyote

Coyote "control" is being increasingly used as a management procedure in many states. This is true in the state of Maine. In his foreword to the 1978 *Big Game Project Report*, Glenn H. Manuel, commissioner of the Maine Department of Inland Fisheries and Wildlife, stated:

> Our wildlife biologists feel that the primary reasons for these [deer population declines in western Maine] are a period of increasingly severe winters . . . and a decrease in quality of habitat (inadequate winter food and shelter), coupled with an increase in predation on deer by coyotes. Hunting pressure does not seem to be a major factor.

Manuel did not explain how coyote predation could be reconciled with a decline in deer habitat. If coyotes fed mainly on deer or even if they were to kill a modest percentage, they would act as a natural check or balancing factor to offset decline in the quality of deer habitat. Greater numbers of coyotes do not result in fewer healthy deer. But most wildlife officials equate greater numbers of deer with better hunting. When deer are (as wildlife biologists would say) in danger of "exceeding their range carrying capacity" and appear headed for a population decline, the usual solution, as noted in the *Wildlife for Tomorrow* booklet, is to increase deer "harvests" and improve habitat and reduce the number of coyotes if it appears that they are having any predatory effect on a declining deer herd. But the truth is that coyotes, like most predators, will follow the path of least resistance. If smaller prey is abundant, the coyotes will usually leave deer alone, although they *will* often feed on the carcasses of deer that have been recently winter-killed.

In most areas, declines in deer populations are temporary. But coyotes make convenient scapegoats for wildlife officials who are trying to prevent reductions in annual deer "harvests" while employing management techniques that are designed to increase the size of deer herds and insure greater hunter success rates. Manuel did not suggest pesticide poisoning or acid rains and snows as possible factors in the deer population decline in northwestern Maine.

In 1978 a few Maine state wildlife biologists were willing to step onto the firing line and suggest to their superiors that several small areas in the northwestern part of the state be closed to deer hunting for one year in order to gain more accurate information about the causes of the apparent deer population decline—and to allow the herd to increase before the 1979 hunting season! Naturally the locations that were selected for closure were among the least heavily hunted in the state. Incredibly, officials at the Department of Inland Fisheries and Wildlife followed suit, recommending the closures to Manuel. But wildlife officials hastily changed their position when they began to receive angry letters from hunters. After a public hearing that dealt with the proposed closures, Manuel received a petition "bearing about 100 signatures." The petition demanded that deer seasons remain at their usual four week length in northern Maine and that no areas be closed to deer hunting. Manuel added in the 1978 *Project Report* that he did not favor shortened hunting seasons "if there is no evidence to indicate that the deer herd will be increased." (As shall be explained later, when deer are "managed" for hunting their populations may rise with gradually increased hunting pressure and stabilize and then decline if hunting pressure is gradually reduced.) Manuel concluded by noting that "coyote control will be employed when and where it is necessary."

Predictably, the following year, Manuel noted in the *Project Report* introduction that there had been "liberalized trapping seasons on coyotes." There were also liberalized coyote hunting seasons. As of 1980, there was no closed season on coyotes, meaning that they could be legally hunted at any time during the year!

The Coyote Is Vindicated

By the autumn of 1983, it was becoming apparent that Maine's deer herd was declining in the southern part of the state as well as in the north. There are fewer coyotes in relatively populous southern Maine. But there *has* been a *human* population increase of about 15,000 per year in this region since the early 1970s, resulting in a loss of wildlife habitat. There has also been an increase in illegal poaching in recent years. In northern Maine, clear-cutting of timber over wide areas has temporarily reduced browse and cover for deer. Pesticides are sprayed from the air for the "control" of insects such as the spruce budworm. And there has apparently been an increase in the pursuit and killing of deer by domestic dogs.

It was these factors, rather than coyotes, that by early 1984 threatened to bankrupt Manuel's department. Half of his department's annual $11–$12 million budget is directly dependent upon deer hunting. Some Maine hunters, finally convinced of the seriousness of the deer situation, were calling for a three- to five-year moratorium on deer hunting in the state. But Manuel and many others in his department opposed a moratorium because of a potential loss of hunting license revenue.[8]

A BIO-ILLOGICAL SYSTEM

ELK AWAIT AIRLIFT INTO AREA OF GOVERNMENT WOLF HUNT—Sixty-three elk are ready and waiting in Fort Nelson to be airlifted into the Kechika valley in northeastern B.C. next month. The elk airlift is a project of the environment ministry, which has carried out a controversial wolf hunt in the same area this winter.
—From a news story in the Vancouver (B.C.) *Sun* (February 24, 1984)

Moose are suffering in Maine because of the condition of that state's deer herd. Moose, although relatively few in number, had been in great demand by many hunters. Particularly since the mid-1970s, the Department of Inland Fisheries and Wildlife had sought an annual moose hunting season. In 1979 the Maine legislature passed a bill making moose legal game during a six-day season in late September. Wrote Manuel in his 1980 report: "I hope that the 1980 [moose] season will prove successful and the Department will be allowed to manage this resource for the benefit of all Maine people."

Why did the Department of Inland Fisheries and Wildlife choose this time to push doubly hard to persuade the Maine legislature to establish moose hunting, particularly since the state had a herd of only 20,000? Fewer deer, combined with a parallel decline in Maine's overhunted black bear population and a necessary reduction in the length of the bear season from six to three months, meant a potential loss of hunting license revenue. Management rationale dictated that some other form of hunting had to be implemented to take up the slack. The moose was a logical choice to those who were perpetuating an illogical system.

Therefore, in September 1980 the first moose hunt since 1935 was held in Maine. But before the moose season was four days old, a few state politicians in this hunter-dominated region were considering introducing legislation that would end moose hunting in the state. One hundred moose were killed on the opening day of the hunt. State senator Gerard P. Conley (D-Portland) claimed that moose had become so tame that "you can have your picture taken with them first, then take ten steps backward and shoot." By the end of the season, only 65 of 700 moose hunters had failed to kill a moose. Some moose hunting was conducted illegally. News reports told of moose that had been shot from the windows of camps, from the back of pickup trucks, and even from rowboats.

Late in 1980, opponents of the hunt formed an organization known as SMOOSA (Save Maine's Only Official State Animal), whose goal was to stop the hunts. Members circulated petitions, which received more than 20,000 signatures—enough to force the issue to a vote in a public referendum. The referendum was held on November 8, 1983 (during Maine's hunting season for deer and bear), and the moose lost by a 3–2 margin.[9]

Despite continuing protests over the moose hunts, wildlife officials in Maine by early 1984 had planned the biggest moose hunt yet for the following September. The Department of Inland Fisheries and Wildlife was expected to issue at least 1,100 moose hunting permits, including 110 to out-of-staters. During the 1983 hunt more than 900 moose were killed.

An Alternative

As exemplified by the Maine moose hunt, state wildlife officials and game commissioners seek to implement new forms of hunting in an effort to keep copious amounts of hunting license revenue rolling into their departmental coffers. Kenneth F. Wich, New York's director of fish and wildlife, alluded to this in his response to one of the questions that I had mailed to him:

> The revenue from the sale of fishing and hunting licenses is vital for the Department of Environmental Conservation to manage New York's fish and wildlife resources. Inflation has greatly increased the costs of fish and wildlife management while license fees have remained the same for several years. Increasing the number of licenses sold does help; however, the real solution to the dilemma is to increase license fees commensurate with inflationary costs.

However, the best solution to the gross mismanagement of North American wildlife would be a complete restructuring of the system of wildlife management, one that would accentuate the concept that animals are not "renewable resources" for man to use or abuse, but sentient beings with the right to live unmolested in natural surroundings.

ENVIRONMENTAL HARM VERSUS ENVIRONMENTAL HARMONY

. . . Wildlife management generally is man's last-ditch attempt to restore some semblance of order to an ecosystem in disarray from his own mismanagement. . . . Whenever possible, the goal of wildlife managers should be to return the disturbed ecosystem as close to the condition it was before humans upset the balance.
—Ecologist Edward Flattau ("Nature Is [the] Best Wildlife Manager," Elmira, N.Y. *Star-Gazette*, March 31, 1980)

The serious biological and ecological consequences of the current system of wildlife management have resulted because those who perpetuate this system disregard two of the most basic laws of nature.

Law 1: When an ecosystem or a part thereof is managed for reasons of materialism or self-interest, with little or no concern for the welfare of the environment, the result will be a seriously imbalanced ecosystem.

Law 2: When wildlife is managed according to a system of favoritism, insuring large numbers of game species while excluding large predators and demonstrating a disproportionate lack of interest in the welfare of nongame and endangered wildlife, hunted species will generally reproduce in greater than normal numbers with larger litters and/or greater birth and fertility rates, thereby maintaining artificially high populations.

The second practice, like the first, can have disastrous consequences. When abnormally high populations of a small number of frequently hunted "game" species are combined with a scarcity of predators, the result is usually a decline in the amount of natural plant food that could otherwise be utilized by infrequently hunted animals and nongame wildlife. Serious ecological imbalance often results because the populations of large herbivores (such as those of the white-tailed deer) have become ecologically top-heavy. Competing nongame species and minor "game" species will not maintain optimum populations, and there will not be the wide variety of species that would be found in a well-balanced ecosystem. (This will be explained in much greater detail later in this book.) Nature is an extremely delicate balance. As in the case of Damocles' sword, when the thread is cut, there can be serious consequences to wildlife and the environment.

The disruption of wildlife populations and ecosystems in America has resulted mainly because of the mismanagement of our environment. In fact, *with the exception of very infrequent natural disasters, which result only in temporary ecological disruptions, there has never been a serious ecologically related wildlife problem in modern times that has not been a direct result of human interference in the normal processes of Nature.* This is true whether interference has taken the form of habitat destruction or deterioration, environmental contamination, destruction of predators, significant habitat manipulation over large areas, or public hunting.

The basic environmental pitfall of the current system of wildlife management is that rather than restoring ecosystems to a more primitive natural state and seeking to establish a heterogeneous mixture of native animal species, game managers manipulate wildlife and its habitat within the framework of the *existing* imbalanced ecostructure, which is characterized by an overabundance of a few commonly hunted species.

Game management is an unscientific practice. True *science* is environmentally sound; it deals with observable natural phenomena, ideally the way that Nature would be if man had not upset its balance. But the current system of wildlife management is a perversion of Nature's laws, a design that is motivated not by an environmental ethic but by avarice and a desire to exploit. More than three centuries ago, the famous astronomer Francis Bacon wrote: "In order to control Nature we must first obey her laws." Commercial wildlife management does not conform to this principle, and it is ineffective unless practiced on a continuing basis. In a normally structured ecosystem, Nature gives equal consideration to all native species of animals. But this is not true of wildlife managers who do not conduct their programs in accordance with normal natural patterns.

The *underlying* reasons for the current system of wildlife management are numerous, but they may be grouped into three main categories: 1) Philosophical, 2) Economic, and 3) Educational. Historically, North Americans have relied upon hunting and fishing as partial sources of sustenance. The production of food has slowly become the province of a relatively small professional group. But while this has been occurring, many people have learned to hunt as a pastime, rather than as an essential practice. Traditional American concepts continue to pervade both our economic and educational systems. As evidenced by Dr. Kellert's study, a significant percentage of nonhunting Americans have no strong antihunting feelings; they accept hunting as a fact of life. The reason for this is that people living in the Western hemisphere have traditionally held the view that nonhuman animals exist for human use, whether for consumptive purposes, as beasts of burden, or for various "recreational" purposes—hunting, zoos, circuses, rodeos, bullfights, et cetera. Fortunately, people's attitudes are slowly progressing. Many people are now beginning to question and openly criticize traditional homocentric values. However, the proponents of equality for all species of animals remain in a minority.

There is another factor that may help to explain the evolution of present methods of wildlife management: that is the widely held but seldom professed belief that self-gratification is of greater importance than the welfare of the earth and the life that it supports. This often repressed view has resulted in serious flaws in the economic and educational structures of our society. And it is likely that these flaws are aggravated by unbridled greed.

II. / The Roots of Wildlife Exploitation

THE CULTURAL AND SOCIOECONOMIC UNDERPINNINGS OF AMERICAN WILD-
LIFE MANAGEMENT AND HOW OUR EDUCATIONAL SYSTEM AND THE POWER
STRUCTURE WITHIN STATE GAME BUREAUS HELP TO PERPETUATE IT.

*Man was long considered above or outside of nature—first as a spectator, then
as a manipulator of it. . . . Our collective "folie de grandeur" has led us to the
brink of disaster in our modification of the natural order.*
—Professor Ervin Laszlo (from a paper presented at the Institut de
L'Environment, Ministry of Cultural Affairs, Paris, in 1971)

THE HISTORICAL VIEW

*Only to the white man was nature a "wilderness" and only to him was the
land "infested" with "wild" animals and "savage" people. To us it was tame.
Earth was bountiful and we were surrounded with the blessings of the Great
Mystery.*
—Chief Luther Standing Bear of the Oglala Sioux (Courtesy of Kootenay
Environmental Institute Ltd., Galena Bay, B.C., Canada)

How did wildlife management evolve in North America, and why
does it continue to involve the exploitation, rather than the protection,
of wild animals? There are cultural reasons for this, and the three major
ones (philosophy, our money-based economy, and our educational system) will be examined in this section. At its root, the exploitation of wild
animals stems partly from ignorance and superstition and partly from
materialism, self-interest, and a lack of empathy with nonhuman life.

Let us briefly trace the development of wildlife exploitation in North
America from its origin—an origin that, like modern game management,
was based on a desire for material wealth.

The accumulation of material wealth from the killing of wild animals
is almost an American tradition, although certainly not a *native* American
tradition. It originated two and a half centuries ago, when French and

English settlers in the New World began to use fur as a medium of exchange. There was a demand in Europe and the American colonies for fur—especially for beaver pelts to be used in the manufacture of coats. During the 150 years that followed, beavers were trapped to the brink of extinction in both Canada and the Eastern United States.

The philosophy of the early American settlers and their successors was diametrically opposed to that of most American Indians. The settlers, partly because of a traditional misinterpretation of Judeo-Christian religious doctrine, which supposedly taught that God had given man "domination" over Nature, considered animals to be renewable natural resources whose lives were of no consequence and who existed solely for man's consumptive or material use. Most of the settlers had come from cities and towns, and, although they learned to live in the wilderness, they never gained an understanding or appreciation of ecology.

Unlike the white settlers, most members of most Indian tribes lived basically in harmony with Nature. They took from the land only what they needed for survival and believed that the Great Spirit had ordained them to be *responsible* caretakers of the Earth.[1] They believed that animals, in a biocentric sense, were their brothers and sisters. Most Indians could not understand the English common law concept of public ownership of resources. To them there were no such things as renewable or non-renewable resources. The Earth, along with its animals, plant life, water, soil, and minerals, belonged to the Great Spirit. These creations were sacred, and it was sinful to defile them. Members of many Indian tribes prayed for the spirit of each animal they killed to provide their simple needs—food and clothing and, in some cases, basic shelter. The Indians were true conservationists. Significantly, they dealt in bartered goods; they did not have a system of currency. Their medium of exchange may have been either a cause or a result of their simple life-style. But it was a factor that contributed to their appreciation of Nature.

The "Sports"

During the nineteenth century, increasing numbers of pioneers moved from the wilderness to cities and towns. Towns and villages were built in what had once been wilderness. Many pioneers gave up hunting, trapping, and fishing and began to rely on professional farmers and the developing commercial food industry to provide their consumptive needs. This resulted in a steady decline in the percentage of American subsistence hunters. But during the decades after the Civil War, a new breed of American hunter began to proliferate. These were city and townspeople who hunted mainly for recreation. As the effects of the

Industrial Revolution created increased amounts of leisure time, recreational hunting became an increasingly popular pastime. Railroad travel was becoming cheaper and faster, allowing many city people access to rural and backwoods areas dozens or hundreds of miles from their homes. Most of these recreational hunters, who came to be known as "sports," were seeking trophies. The "sports" killed many deer, elk, bears, wolves, mountain lions, and other large mammals in order to have their heads stuffed and mounted. Often the carcasses were left to rot.

During this period, "market hunting" was also becoming increasingly popular. Bison were killed for their hides, passenger pigeons for meat, herons, egrets, ibises, and other birds for plumes and feathers. It is estimated that the last buffalo in Pennsylvania was killed about 1800, the last elk in New York in 1845 and in Pennsylvania in 1867. By this time the wild turkey had become nearly extinct in the northeastern United States. The last moose in the Adirondacks was shot about 1860.* Large predators were killed not only for trophies but because they competed with trophy hunters *and* market hunters for deer, moose, elk, and other commonly hunted herbivores.

It soon became obvious to some of the "sports" that something would have to be done if there were to be any major hunted species left for their recreational and consumptive use. Thus, during the late 1800s, many private game preserves were established in the Eastern United States. Before this, in the late 1870s and 1880s, some states and territories had established regulations restricting the numbers of wild animals of certain species that each hunter could kill during a given year. In 1878, Iowa established the first legal "bag limits" in the United States. Closed seasons on buffalo were legislated in several Western territories. Deer were illegal game in Vermont from 1865 to 1897, giving the deer herd a chance to increase. But there was widespread poaching in states and territories that had enacted game regulations.

Groups of recreational hunters concerned about the potential loss of their wildlife "resources" organized to encourage stricter enforcement of game laws. In 1887, the Boone and Crockett Club was formed, and it soon became well known for the trophy hunting of its members. The League of American Sportsmen was formed in 1898. In 1900, the Lacey Act placed restrictions on market hunting, including penalties for violators. A handful of early conservationists, including Teddy Roosevelt

---

*Moose are making a comeback in the Adirondacks, having extended their range from Canada and northern New England. There have been several confirmed moose sightings in the Adirondacks in recent years.

and Gifford Pinchot, urged the federal government to purchase wild lands for forests and parks—in most cases not to preserve them in a primitive state forever, but to regulate their recreational and commercial use. Meanwhile, the number of game bureaus increased as more states began to issue hunting licenses, establish "bag limits," and introduce potential "game" species into areas where these species were low in number or nonexistent. The basic concept of game management had become established. Gradually many seriously threatened species began to repopulate wild lands and extend their ranges.

The Anti-Nature Ethic

An enlightened public could have demanded legislation and the establishment of government agencies that would have insured the protection from sport hunting and trapping of all species of wild animals. (Wilderness subsistence hunting could have been allowed to continue on a controlled basis.) In order to understand why this was not done, one must consider the philosophy that prevailed during the late nineteenth century. The word *ecology* had not yet been coined. Most people were unaware that there is an intertwining web of cause and effect between man's activities and the natural environment. Indeed, the predominating philosophy held that man was not a part of Nature, but was separate from it and superior to it. The object of culture and civilization was to push back the wilderness and establish cities wherein people would have more leisure time and physical comfort. Wild creatures were not one's biocentric brothers and sisters; they were utilitarian entities to be used or abused as desired. Of what consequence would it be if half of the species of animals native to North America were exterminated or the wilderness were decimated? Protesting the destruction of the natural land and the killing of its inhabitants was the furthest thing from the minds of most of those living in a culture that held that the *raison d'être* was to acquire status, prestige, and material wealth. In fact, the rapid exploitation of "natural resources" was *necessary* in order to perpetuate this ethic. And at that time most people believed that these "resources," including wildlife, were inexhaustible. There was a market for fur, feathers, and hides, and passenger pigeon pie was a delicacy! So, in the context of these times, even the establishment of a few closed seasons and the legislation of hunting regulations, game preserves, and state and national parks and forests were somewhat radical measures, entailing foresight, a willingness to oppose powerful industrial lobbies, and a desire to partially awaken the public from its apathy.

In contrast to nonhunters and nontrappers, the "sports" had a vested interest in the perpetuation of wildlife. If wild animals were to be indiscriminately slaughtered by market hunters, then sooner or later the sport hunters' supply of live targets would be depleted. The only way to ensure the future of sport hunting was to protect many rare and threatened species and establish stricter hunting codes.

The Business of Exploitation

As the American population rapidly increased during the early twentieth century, so did the number of people who hunted for sport. More hunting regulations were passed as hunting pressure increased and wild acreage declined. The reduction in privately owned natural acreage resulted in greater hunting pressure on state and national forestlands. A great amount of tax money has been spent for the purchase and maintenance of government lands. However, since these lands are publicly owned, it became necessary for both the federal government and state governments to find other ways to generate revenue from these lands both for the sake of regional economies and to help to pay the salaries of federal and state game wardens, forest rangers, park rangers, fire wardens, et cetera. Three basic methods evolved:

1) A system by which people pay a fee for the use of a state or national park. (There are variations of this, such as payment for the use of public facilities such as campsites and bathing beaches or admission for public tours of museums or historical sites.)
2) Logging operations on government forestlands by which the federal government or a state government receives payment from a private logging contractor.
3) Public hunting, trapping, and fishing, in which state governments and the federal government receive money from those who engage in these activities. (The federal government, in addition to receiving excise taxes from the sale of guns and ammunition, receives funds from the sale of duck stamps, which are required to hunt waterfowl.)

As the number of consumptive users of wildlife increased, it became necessary to increase not only the number of hunting regulations, but also the number of people employed by government fish and wildlife agencies, due to additional field and administrative work and the need for game law enforcement. As greater numbers of hunters paid increasing amounts of money to increasing numbers of people in government wildlife agencies, wildlife officials (most of whom were hunters or former hunters) became increasingly beholden to "sportsmen" and their lobbying groups. In the process, wildlife management became essentially a commercialized operation designed to maintain a steady supply of live targets. It became prudent to manipulate wildlife and its habitat to insure that a modest percentage of outdoor recreationists killed legal "game." (After all, empty-handed hunters might become dissatisfied and this might result in fewer license sales and an increase in the illegal killing of wildlife.)

Since the mid-1960s, inflation has cut into government operating expenses to an increasing degree. The result has been that, on a widening scale, wildlife agencies in most states have actively sought to *increase* the numbers of hunters, trappers, and fishermen in order to insure increases in revenue for their departments. This has been done primarily by the use of public relations activities involving state publications, printed leaflets, information disseminated to the media, and speaking engagements by wildlife officials. (Many of these enterprises are partially subsidized by taxpayers' money.) Hunting has become, to use the words of one humanitarian, "a big, bloody business." A person needs only to examine the hunting/government, bureaucracy/economic growth complex a bit more closely to learn where this has led.

THE ECONOMIC CONNECTION

This is a money economy we live in—not an economy that places ecological considerations first—or humanitarian, or ethical, or moral considerations first.
—Eve Smith (for British Columbia Voice for Women, South Pender Island,
B.C., Canada)

The exploitation of American wildlife continues partly because of avarice, which is encouraged by our free enterprise system and its monetary medium of exchange. Profiteering is the basis of this system, and in order to swiftly create the greatest amount of revenue for the greatest number of people from the "utilization" of wild animals it becomes *expedient* to exploit them—to *kill* them for consumption, animal products or trophies.

Why is killing wild animals the fastest and surest method of creating wildlife-related revenue? The answer is that "natural resources" generate economic wealth. These resources are considered to be anything in Nature (animal, plant, or mineral) that can be put to some form of *human use* and for which a market either exists or can be created, and that can then be traded to the public for cash, in the process accumulating greater material wealth for the producer. In this sense, hunted and trapped wildlife are much like cattle, hogs, sheep, and chickens; they represent a cash crop for a segment of our society. But there is a variation: in the case of wildlife exploitation, hunters pay cash to wildlife agencies for the privilege of "harvesting" wildlife. Hunters then generate revenue

34

for a small sector of the private economy by purchases that indirectly result from the act of hunting.

The profit-making system is based upon the conversion of natural resources into processed forms. As long as there are adequate "resources," this will result in a steadily increasing production of products. The conversion of the natural into the artificial and its subsequent cash sale insures that a specific "resource" (which according to prevailing marketing theory has no inherent value in its natural form) becomes economically "productive."

Commercial wildlife management is an outgrowth of our economic system. Like trees in a forest, animals living in the wild, independent of human interference, are commercially "nonproductive." Existing in their natural state, they do not generate revenue. The present system of wildlife management creates a commercially productive, artificially manipulated environment from a wild, naturally balanced, economically nonproductive environment. The catalysts for this transformation are public hunting, fishing, and trapping. The method that is used to insure the sustained flow of revenue that results is the periodic manipulation of wildlife and its habitat and the structuring of hunting regulations in such a way as to insure a perennial supply of living targets. Those reaping profits include, among others, state conservation departments, the U.S. Fish and Wildlife Service, the arms and munitions industry, and, particularly in rural areas and isolated villages, motels, restaurants, service stations, sporting goods stores, and real estate brokers who sell camps and land to hunters. These people represent only a small percentage of Americans. But in the absence of widespread protests about wildlife exploitation, they are a large enough percentage to insure the perpetuation of public hunting and game management. Furthermore, state and local governments receive operating revenue from employer taxes and from state sales taxes, which are bolstered by hunter's purchases. It is for these underlying reasons, and the more evident reasons mentioned earlier ("The Politics of Wildlife Mismanagement") that most government officials encourage the existing system rather than making an effort to curtail it.

But isn't there some way to make wildlife *protection* economically profitable? There *are* ways to do this. Several methods of reforming wildlife management while maintaining a flow of revenue for government and the private economy will be suggested later in this book. But at the present time, none of these alternatives would fit into the established system, in which the physical destruction of wild animals generates material wealth for a portion of our society.

THE EDUCATIONAL CONSPIRACY

Teach your children that whatever befalls the Earth befalls the sons of the Earth. . . . This we know—the Earth does not belong to man, man belongs to the Earth. . . . Man did not weave the web of life; he is merely a strand in it. Whatever he does to the web, he does to himself.

—Chief Seattle (1854)

If a society is to develop a set of wholesome values, then these values must first be acknowledged by academics and then taught to the young people of that society. Likewise, if we are to progress toward a higher level of culture in which compassion and reverence for life triumph over materialism and the profit motive, then children, adolescents, and young adults must be taught to respect all forms of life. Unfortunately, when young adults are "educated" about wildlife at colleges and universities in North America, their training usually reflects predominating attitudes, which include the concept that wild animals are insentient beings that must be managed for their own good and for the good of the environment and human society. This educational procedure is also a result of flaws that are inherent in our educational system. Education mirrors social and cultural standards, and the reverse is equally true. Prevailing methods of managing forests and wildlife are ecologically unsound; likewise, there are serious imperfections in the educational process that help to insure the continuation of these practices. The defects within our educational system are also found within the educational systems of most other technological nations of the Western hemisphere. In part, the officially sanctioned system of wildlife management in North America may be traced to some of these imperfections.

What is wrong with education? The most fundamental problem is that education does not encourage a respect for the earth and the life that it supports. Education teaches young people how to earn a living but not how to foster a sense of responsibility toward their environment. Today, even more so than in the past, the American educational system prepares young people for a self-oriented, profit-making life-style, precisely the type of life-style that, in North America, has resulted in 250 years of wildlife exploitation.

Technical education, in particular, reflects these qualities. Skills are taught to a student so that he may obtain the highest-paying job for which he is qualified. Young people are taught how to manipulate their environment for pecuniary gain. The study of agriculture, for example, is hardly a process by which a student learns self-sufficient or cooperative organic farming. A modern agricultural education is centered around the principles of "agri-business"; the use of machine technology, soil-depleting chemical fertilizers, and environmentally degrading poisons to obtain the greatest margin of profit on one's investment (in the process helping to feed, and slowly poison, humans and nonhumans).

Avarice Strikes Again

Our educational system must share part of the responsibility for the materialistic self-orientation that exists within our society. With few exceptions, education in North America is not designed to develop an awareness of conservation and a sense of restraint in one's relationship to one's environment, and this is evident from grade school through graduate school.

We have seen that our economic system is based upon the utilization of so-called "natural resources" and that the natural environment and the plants and animals within it are generally considered valueless unless exploited for profit. The "use" principle is emphasized either directly or indirectly in most technical subjects that are taught at educational institutions in America. But this concept is probably most evident in forestry and wildlife science courses on the undergraduate and graduate college levels because these courses teach the *direct* exploitation of plants and animals living in their natural state.

The chairman of the wildlife biology department at a state university once said that his department "endeavors to train students so that they are qualified to obtain employment with fish and wildlife agencies." And *this* is the problem. The study of wildlife is basically a mechanistic procedure. The purpose of college training in wildlife science is not to nurture an empathy with wildlife and an appreciation of all plants and animals that interact within natural ecosystems. The purpose of a wildlife "education" is initially to bombard a student with various facts and technical data and then to illustrate how these facts and figures apply to the subjective methodology of wildlife management. In this fashion, a student becomes qualified as a manipulator of wildlife and its habitat. Some students find employment with state wildlife agencies and the U.S. Fish and Wildlife Service, thereby helping to perpetuate the commercial exploitation of wildlife and its environment.

THE PATRON SAINT

We abuse land because we regard it as a commodity belonging to us. When we see land as a community to which we belong, we may begin to use it with love and respect.

—Aldo Leopold (*A Sand County Almanac,*
Sierra Club/Ballantine Book Ed., 1970)

Wildlife science programs at most American colleges and universities have been in existence only since the 1930s or thereafter. Prior to that time, most of those employed by state wildlife agencies (those who were college-educated) had majored in biology or zoology. Then, in 1933, something happened that sent shock waves rippling through the biological science community at many leading universities and led to the eventual establishment of forest zoology, wildlife ecology, wildlife biology, wildlife technology, and wildlife management curricula at most American universities. This was the publication of Aldo Leopold's *Game Management*. Leopold (1887–1948) also authored the more widely known *A Sand County Almanac*, which is considered by many to be an ecological classic. But while Leopold was well versed in woodlore and the natural sciences and voiced many lofty concepts about man's responsibilities to the natural world, his epitaph as a renowned ecologist is not fully justified. For one thing, he was an avid recreational hunter. As a youth in Burlington, Iowa, he often carried a shotgun as well as notebooks into the woods and he relished duck hunting during autumn. As a young man employed by the U.S. Forest Service, he preached and practiced the eradication of predators. ("They kill our game.") But he later changed his views after lamenting the death of a wolf that he had shot.

So while Leopold had a basic appreciation of ecology, his awareness of man's responsibility to the land and the animals that inhabit it was narrow and dulled by his own hunting experiences and his view that man has not only a right but a responsibility to manipulate wildlife and ecosystems for their own good as well as for the benefit of hunters.

A brief passage from *Game Management* summarizes the practices that Leopold advocated: ". . . Game can be restored by the creative use of the same tools which have heretofore destroyed it—axe, plow, cow, fire, and gun." The serious fallacies in this concept and the disastrous effects of its application will be thoroughly examined in a later chapter. For now, suffice to say that this pseudoecological approach is the result of an archaic misconception that was formulated at a time when it was commonly believed that people must manipulate and ultimately control Nature for their benefit. Leopold was not the first to advocate habitat manipulation as a partial cure for wildlife problems, but he was the first to write a book about it and teach it to university students. Leopold served on the Wisconsin Conservation (Game) Commission and was awarded America's first chair in Game Management at the University of Wisconsin, where he taught wildlife ecology.

Leopold's views formed the basis of the teachings that followed. So, from the beginning, university courses in wildlife science have been based upon traditional homocentric cultural concepts and the belief that since most people do not respect the natural land, the manipulation of wildlife and its habitat is necessary for the enhancement of ecosystems as well as a prerequisite to the consumptive use of wildlife. Not coincidentally, wildlife science professors usually stress that this manipulation should favor commonly hunted species.

At best, the widespread manipulation of wildlife and its environment is a false cure for ecosystems that have been adversely affected by man's activities. The Leopold strategy deals with *effects* rather than *causes*, the ultimate causes being human overpopulation, habitat development, environmental contamination, public hunting, and the absence of an environmental ethic that would include a sense of individual and social responsibility to the natural world. At its worst, the application of Leopold's habitat manipulation principles can result in ecological disasters, as will be detailed during the course of this book. Today, wildlife science is usually taught more as a business than as anything resembling a true science, which it is not. As with most businesses, the primary emphasis is upon the *human* benefits that are supposedly derived from manipulating Nature. It is doubtful whether Leopold, hunter and habitat manipulationist that he was, would have approved of the profit-oriented direction that modern wildlife management has taken and the educational methods that have since been developed.[2]

PROGRAMMING THE COMPUTERS

If a constant percentage of the [deer] population is harvested each year, the percentage applying to the standing crop of that particular year, the population will decline to and stabilize at a level at equilibrium with the rate of harvesting. The level may be either above or below that generating the MSY (Maximum Sustained Yield). . . . The two methods of estimating offtake operate on the trend of yield against equilibrium standing crop of animals.
—From *Applied Biology*, edited by T. H. Coaker (Academic Press, 1976). This is used as an advanced wildlife biology textbook at the University of Vermont.

What is taught to wildlife science students at American institutions of higher learning? Consider the course descriptions that are contained in the catalogues of several universities located in the northeastern states:

—From the catalogue of the State University of New York, College of Environmental Science and Forestry, which is affiliated with Syracuse University. (Italics are the author's):

"WILDLIFE ECOLOGY AND MANAGEMENT I—A study of the ecological principles governing wild animal populations and the relationship of these to *manipulation of said populations.*

"WILDLIFE ECOLOGY AND MANAGEMENT II—A study of wildlife management techniques, *schemes* and programs."

From the undergraduate catalogue of the University of West Virginia (1982–83):

"WILDLIFE MANAGEMENT I—Basic principles of handling wildlife *as a forest crop,* including . . . habitat manipulation and game administration.

"PRINCIPLES OF WILDLIFE MANAGEMENT II—*Major game animals* and problems and principles involved in their management."

From the catalogue of the University of Vermont (1982–83):

"GAME ANIMALS (A Sophomore course)— . . . introduction to specimen collection and preservation, sex and age determination."

"PRINCIPLES OF WILDLIFE MANAGEMENT (A Junior course)—Plant and animal ecology applied to *control of wildlife populations. . . .*"

"WETLANDS WILDLIFE ECOLOGY (A Senior course)—Life histories and management emphasizing N.A. waterfowl and *furbearer resources. . . .*"

Cornell University offers a course in its "Natural Resources" division titled "Introduction to Consumptive Wildlife Recreation." This is described as a "brief history of trapping and hunting; role of consumptive recreationists in conservation; firearms and archery nomenclature, function, ballistics, and safety; content of New York State hunter training, bowhunter education, and trapper training courses; discussion of current methods, laws, ethics, basic shooting instruction with rifles and shotguns."

The catalogue of the University of Maine at Orono briefly describes the activities of the Maine Cooperative Wildlife Research Unit, which "provides for a cooperative wildlife program sponsored and financed by the University, the Maine Department of Inland Fisheries and Game [sic], the U.S. Fish and Wildlife Service, and the Wildlife Management Institute." Members of the Cooperative Wildlife Research Unit, which includes wildlife management professors, help to compile information for the annual big game project reports published by the Maine Department of Inland Fisheries and Wildlife.

College catalogues give only a general overview of subject material. Let us consider some specifics, beginning with the type of textbooks that are used in wildlife science courses. A text that is often used as a guide to wildlife management is *Big Game of North America*, a Wildlife Management Institute Book compiled and edited by John L. Schmidt and Douglas L. Gilbert (Stackpole Books, 1978). In a section dealing with the management of large ungulates, the authors assert that "with sound management programs opportunities will continue to be available to those persons wishing to hunt, observe or listen to elk in their natural habitat." But the management of elk and other ungulates is designed to maintain their populations at artificially high levels—not for the purpose of wildlife observation, but to provide hunters with living targets. The authors mention nothing about those who might wish to observe or listen to large predators such as cougars (panthers) or wolves in their natural habitat, but they *did* include a section about predator control. On page 373, the student will find a picture of a man setting a steel coyote trap. But the student learns that "the most efficient and effective way to reduce coyotes and wolves over broad geographical areas is the use of toxicants." On page 375 is a photograph of a man aiming a high-powered rifle from the cockpit of a helicopter. The caption states: "When coyotes or wolves are to be reduced for the benefit of wild ungulates, aerial shooting is usually the technique of choice." The authors do not claim that these and other "management" procedures are undertaken to establish well-balanced natural ecosystems. But by citing prevailing practices and accurately portraying them as methods that are approved by professional game managers, even the most open-minded students will often conclude that these procedures are not only environmentally sound, but are the *only* intelligent way to deal with wildlife and its habitat.

Mechanistic Teachings

Most wildlife science texts contain at least one or two chapters of material similar to that found in *Big Game of North America*. For example, in chapter 24 of *Wildlife Management Techniques*, edited by Robert H. Giles, Jr. (Wildlife Society, 1971) the student finds an illustration of a "stem of decision tree," with options branching out that will help to "formulate a set of regulations and laws that will accomplish desired population and harvest" of deer. The options include five main factors, which are correlated in the diagram. They are the starting date of the hunting season, season length, weapons to be used, sex restriction (in this case deer of either sex would be legal game), and finally the price of hunting licenses!

Applied Biology, edited by T.H. Coaker, quoted earlier, is widely used as an advanced wildlife biology text at many colleges and universities. It includes a section titled "Wildlife Management and the Dynamics of Ungulate Populations." Here are found many sets of complicated equations that supposedly can be used to insure sustained harvests of ungulates under certain habitat and animal population conditions. Some

41

of these mathematical calculations would boggle the mind of a college calculus professor or a professional game manager. One of the more interesting inclusions in this section is a graph that correlates sustained annual yield (numbers of animals killed by hunters) with the "standing crop herbivores" (numbers of living deer, elk, moose, et cetera). The student is informed that "sustained annual yield against population size in equilibrium with the offtake, according to the interactive model. A curve of the form $bx^2 + cx^4$ is fitted to the right flank."

This textbook also includes a chapter on various methods of controlling bird "pests."

Other examples:

—In *Wildlife Biology* (Second Edition), by Raymond F. Dasmann (John Wiley and Sons, 1981) it is asserted that with the many game laws and regulations that exist throughout the United States, wildlife populations appear to be protected from the effects of hunting. According to Dasmann: "Sport-hunters and fishers are rarely a part of wildlife problems—usually they are a part of the solution."

Ironically, Dasmann later admits that since ecosystems are completely interrelated, hunting by a species that is not a part of the ecosystem will take food away from predators, parasites, scavengers, and all other forms of life that are affected by hunted species. Dasmann concludes that continued hunting changes an ecosystem.

—If a student reads *Wildlife Ecology*, by Aaron N. Moen (W. H. Freeman and Co., 1973), he or she will learn that since a significant percentage of animal watchers do not care whether they see a small underweight deer or a larger specimen and since more small deer than large deer can exist on a given amount of forage, "a program aimed at a higher population of small deer may be more desirable from a human sociological point of view." (And, not coincidentally, from a hunter's point of view, since more deer—even small deer—will increase hunter success rates.)

—In *Furbearing Animals of North America*, by Leonard Lee Rue III (Crown Publishers, Inc., 1981), the student is informed that the trapping of muskrats is "a necessity." According to Rue, "at least 75 percent of the muskrats of any given area should be removed annually to curtail disease and destruction of habitat that occurs because of their overpopulation." (The fallacy and subsequent consequences of this nonecological practice will be fully examined later.)

—From *Waterfowl Ecology and Management: Selected Readings*, compiled by John T. Ratti, Lester D. Flake, and W. Alan Wentz (Wildlife Society, 1982), comes the following revelation: "The use of dynamite to open dense marshes has been common (Provost

1948). . . . Blasting with ammonium nitrate or other less expensive explosives and bulldozing have revitalized this effort (Mathiak 1965)." Blasting and bulldozing aren't the only forms of habitat manipulation that are outlined in this textbook. For example, a student learns how red foxes, striped skunks, raccoons, and badgers were "controlled" in one area in order to reduce predation on waterfowl eggs and nestlings. This was done for the unstated purpose of increasing the number of waterfowl for hunters' guns.

—A supplementary text that is sometimes used in wildlife science courses is *Waterfowl Tomorrow*, edited by Joseph P. Linduska (Bureau of Sport Fisheries and Wildlife, 1964). In one chapter, the student learns how natural habitat is destroyed by dredging and digging for the purpose of constructing artificial marshlands for waterfowl breeding.*

Included among the reading material that was required for wildlife science students at one college in 1982 was an article by wildlife pathologist Bill Vogt titled "The Kaibab Comes to New Jersey." This appeared in the June 1976 issue of *Outdoor Life*. Vogt included a great deal of prohunting sentiment and very few concrete statistics to support his claim that the annual deer hunts conducted at the Great Swamp National Wildlife Refuge in New Jersey are necessary to keep the deer herd well within the carrying capacity of its compact natural habitat. More will be written about the Great Swamp deer hunts later in this book. But for now it will be enough to note that the hunts have resulted in no long-term deer population declines at the swamp.

Harvest Orientation

What are some of the activities in which wildlife science students participate? At one college, wildlife biology students are encouraged to receive job experience by helping state biologists gather statistics at local deer checking stations during deer season. At a state university, students collect simulated data about deer and "game" bird populations based upon "harvests" by hunters in a region of that state. The object of this data collection is to correlate it with hunting pressure in order to maintain populations of these species at a level high enough to insure sustained annual "harvests." At many colleges, commercial biologists and game officials give speeches about wildlife management from a harvest perspective.

*Let me emphasize that I did not deliberately choose these books or their authors for critical review. The books that I have cited are emblematic and typical of the vast majority of wildlife biology and wildlife ecology texts.

But this is not all. At one northeastern college, field trips in wildlife technology include a demonstration by wildlife technicians of pheasant release shortly before hunting season. And at another college—incredible as it may sound—a wildlife management professor asks his students to trap and collect the skins of four different animals—if possible rare specimens! Even zoology courses that do not deal exclusively with wildlife often require the student to commit inhumane acts. Teresa Nelson, a field representative for Defenders of Wildlife, abandoned a zoology program at the University of Minnesota when she learned that she would be required to trap animals. Unfortunately, not all wildlife science students have been gifted with Ms. Nelson's sensitivity.

At most colleges and universities, not every wildlife course is slanted toward hunting and habitat manipulation. Some courses deal exclusively with facts about wildlife and its relationship to ecosystems. But the objectivity of these courses is a drawback rather than an asset, because little or no emphasis is placed upon an ethical responsibility to the natural world. Seldom do professors openly advocate a responsible stewardship of the earth and the life that it supports. Almost without exception, students receive information about wildlife either from a habitat manipulation–game management perspective or from a nonsubjective but mechanistic orientation. The message that is imparted during the educational process is the antithesis of an environmental ethic. Professors seldom if ever teach that all life is of equal value or that nonhuman animals are sentient creatures that should be allowed to pursue their natural lives with a minimum of interferance and man-made disruption. But this is little more than might be expected, since the wildlife science programs at most colleges and universities have been "accredited," or approved by The Wildlife Society* and the Wildlife Management Institute.† Until this connection can be broken there is little hope for widespread educational reforms.

Negativism

Despite the methods that are often used to "educate" potential wildlife pseudoscientists, it would be wrong to assume that most wildlife science professors are villains who care little or nothing about wildlife

*The Wildlife Society, a strongly prohunting organization, consists of state, federal, and privately employed biologists, state and federal game managers, wildlife science professors, and those in related professions.

†The Wildlife Management Institute, another strongly prohunting group, is a private membership organization that lobbies for the preservation of hunting and game management. It is funded partly by industries that profit as a result of hunting.

and ecosystems. As in any other profession, all types of people work in this field. A small percentage of enlightened professors advocate natural or restored ecosystems. (A few of these educators will be quoted in later chapters.) And many of those who advocate the manipulation of wildlife and its habitat for hunting purposes are sincere, dedicated people. While it is often not their fault, their instruction mirrors the narrow framework of accepted wildlife management practices. And the result is a vicious cycle whereby the system of training continues, largely unaffected by constructive change.

In far too many cases, a student who has undergone the educational conditioning process and received a B.S. or M.S. in wildlife science more closely resembles a wildlife management "computer" than a sensitive, enlightened person. Like a computer, the graduate is able to recite myriads of technical facts about wildlife. He or she can apply any number of management principles to a particular wildlife situation, whether it involves the manipulation of habitat, the restocking of hunted animals, or the "cropping" of a certain percentage of an animal population in a certain area. Like the computer, a graduate often feels little or no empathy with the natural world around him.

Even worse, the training that students receive often creates *negative* attitudes about wildlife, including an insensitivity to nonhuman life. Wildlife science treats animals as *groups* rather than as individuals. Since no emphasis is placed upon a respect for the lives of individual animals, the future manipulator of wildlife will often consider animals to be automatons with no inherent perceptions beyond a dim instinct for self-preservation. The student who is busily compiling "harvest" statistics has little time to seriously consider the ways in which *individual* animals contribute to the welfare of natural ecosystems. The root of the insensitivity that continues unbroken from teacher to student to the next generation of teachers is the presupposition that man has a divine and/or biological right to use anything in Nature in any way that he deems expedient.

SUPPRESSION OF THE INTELLECT

Just one year ago, I was invited to speak to the student chapter of the Wildlife *Society of Kansas State University. . . . I asked how many of the students were hunters: about 99 percent of them were.*
—Hunting writer John Madson ("What About This Anti-Hunting Thing?," published in *Maine Fish and Wildlife*. Reprinted in *The Conservationist*, September-October 1976 issue).

45

Wildlife science students are *individuals,* and two to as many as five or six years of study have varying degrees of negative effects. If a student has hunted and/or trapped before entering college, the study of wildlife science may have little or no additional impact upon his or her thinking. But the sensitivity of an open-minded freshman may be diminished unless he or she has an unshakable commitment to wildlife.

Many, if not most, of those who major in wildlife science turn out similar to the bearded graduate student who informed me with an air of indignation that *of course* deer and game birds are being managed for hunters as well as wildlife observers. "That's what our forests and wild-life *are for*—multiple use!" Why had he entered the wildlife science program? Did he like animals? Was he interested in life in the outdoors? "I'm really not sure *why* I entered the program."

There are a small number of wildlife students like the pleasant, smiling young woman who told me that she was writing her master's thesis on the subject of deer habitat. Did this have anything to do with game management or habitat manipulation for the purpose of enhancing hunting opportunities? Oh, no, she was simply interested in deer and their habitat. But if she did not connect the subject of her thesis with the way in which this information would be used if she were a game biologist, then she was either incredibly naive or else she had sublimated everything that she had been taught about the prevailing system of wildlife management.

There are a very small number of students who did not agree with the hunting-trapping ethic when they entered college but wished to learn about wildlife, recognizing the fact that there are as yet no practical alternatives to the existing educational system. These students include a small number of idealists who advocate reforms in the wildlife management system. One of them is Bob Thomas.* In the spring of 1983, Thomas was a forty-year-old honor student in his second year of a wildlife technology program at a two-year agricultural and technical college affiliated with the State University of New York. Thomas, who had previously held two jobs, neither of which were associated with conservation or wildlife management, became involved in wildlife technology partly because he wished to acquire the information that he believed would be necessary to become a useful contributor to the con-

---

*A pseudonym used to protect the student's identity. A letter from Thomas that contains the quotes that have been used here is in the author's files.

servation movement. But he was often depressed by classroom instruction:

> "Sometimes it is very saddening and a little lonely to sit in a classroom with 45 students (the majority of whom hunt and trap as a 'hobby') while an instructor fills their heads with the rationalizations about the need to 'harvest' wild animals for their own good."

At the time of this writing, Thomas plans to seek employment with a wildlife sanctuary or a protectionist organization. The commercialism that has permeated his education has led him to a greater awareness of the exploitive nature of game management:

> "I realize now that many instructors will preach as gospel those same old nostrums . . . as a justification for sport-hunting simply because they were themselves so instructed in the past. There is a very great need now for a frontal assault upon that rationale which forms the foundation for the ediface of current mismanagement practices."

Constructive wildlife education programs are desperately needed at American colleges and universities. What qualities would characterize a constructive wildlife education? There would be a strong emphasis upon the interrelationship and interdependence of all life and the fact that people are a part of nature—not apart from it or superior to it. There would also be a strong emphasis upon a love of Nature and an empathy with all life. Unfortunately, before this occurs, constructive changes will have to be made in the way that wildlife is managed. And before *this* happens, the way that we perceive animals must evolve, along with the way that we view our role in Nature.

In the meantime, the current system of training will continue, along with the utilitarian views that prevail within wildlife science departments, the political structure, and the government conservation bureaucracy. Michael Frome, the well-known conservationist and author, learned this while lecturing at the University of Vermont in 1979. Despite the fact that Frome has never advocated the abolition of recreational hunting, he was strongly criticized by some wildlife science professors, wildlife biology students, Vermont game biologists, and the outdoor writer for a local newspaper for his views about coyote and bobcat protection and his belief that state wildlife agencies should be responsive to ecologists and not merely to hunters and trappers. In an issue of *Defenders*, the magazine of Defenders of Wildlife, Frome responded to this criticism. Alongside his column was a cartoon of a group of sheep wearing graduation caps. He wrote: "It was great being a professor while it lasted. I learned a great deal. But, I wonder, what about the students going through the mill? Where is their higher education to be found?"

ECOLOGICAL DEMOCRACY ON THE DEFENSIVE

I believe we should utilize as many plant and animal resources as possible, as long as we don't jeopardize the species' perpetual existence.
—Gary B. Will, senior wildlife biologist for the state of New York (from a letter to *New York Birders,* the newsletter of the Federation of New York State Bird Clubs, Inc., December 1982 issue)

Only a very small percentage of wildlife science graduates find employment with state game bureaus. But the process by which wildlife biologists, game managers, wildlife technicians, and public relations people are hired by these agencies is noteworthy. In most states, those who seek employment with their state wildlife agency must first pass a civil service examination in the field that they expect to enter. While some of the questions on these exams test one's general knowledge about wildlife, others often deal with the management practices that are taught in wildlife science courses at colleges and universities. When a job opening exists, the three top candidates are usually screened by a wildlife official. (There have been exceptions in which applicants have been hired on the basis of political connections, although this is usually denied by state officials.) Interviews are often conducted with an applicant's background information at hand and are structured in such a way as to determine his or her philosophical compatibility and willingness to embrace accepted practices. As the applicant has already graduated from a duly accredited wildlife program, there is usually no conflict. But the degree of latitude often given to interviewers who select from a number of high-scoring test applicants usually assures that those who are hired agree with the prevailing system of wildlife management. Thus, in terms of philosophy and attitudes about wildlife, these people are usually among the *least* qualified to deal with wild animals in a sensitive and ecologically sound manner.

Most game biologists and other representatives of state wildlife agencies appear to be congenial and sensitive people until they begin to discuss hunting. I remember a typical instance during the summer of 1981 when I had a conversation with a wildlife biologist who holds a Ph.D. in ecology and is employed by the New York State Division of Fish and Wildlife. I was interviewing this seemingly pleasant person

48

because I was seeking information for an article that I planned to write for a magazine. Although the article had nothing to do with the management of "game" species, this subject happened to surface during our conversation. The biologist admitted that "some people out there are opposed to trapping," but claimed that it is a much sounder practice to trap beavers, raccoons, and other fur-bearing animals than to use petroleum for the manufacture of synthetic furs. "Wildlife are renewable resources," I was told, "while petroleum is a nonrenewable resource. The public should understand this."[3]

On the subject of deer hunting, the biologist told me that for purposes of "nuisance, accidents, and their own protection, deer *must* be harvested. So why not allow people to recreationally utilize this renewable resource?" Then the biologist smiled and in a low voice confided that "the only way to effectively get the deer herd under control is to really shoot the hell out of them!" Making a fist, with rapid arm movements for emphasis, the biologist beamed self-assuredly. "We hit the antlerless deer hard last year; we're going to hit them hard again this year, and next year, and the year after that, for as long as it takes to get the state's deer herd down to a desirable level!" If you find this story difficult to believe, let me assure you that I was *doubly* shocked by the young woman's insensitivity. Afterward, I found myself thinking of the pleasant graduate student who was composing a thesis about deer habitat. Would she turn out to be a carbon copy of the DEC biologist? Or was she *already* a carbon copy?

THE INDICTMENT

This . . . report is a compilation of the most up-to-date statistics we have on the [deer] herd and contains a lot of "meat."
—Benjamin Day, chief wildlife Biologist for the state of Vermont (in a letter to Edward F. Kehoe, at that time Vermont Fish and Game Commissioner. This letter was included in the 1978 *Vermont Deer* [Hunting] *Prospects Report.*)

It would be difficult, if not impossible, to swiftly reform the wildlife management system from within either the educational or the professional establishment. Why? Because of the same factors that throughout history have hindered reformers from enacting constructive changes in unjust systems. First, game management is a solidly entrenched practice. Second, as noted by Henry Spira, those in positions of power are usually unwilling to share power with those of opposing viewpoints. Third, those in positions of power and influence usually uphold the status-quo because they have risen to power by faithfully executing their "responsibilities." (A person who disagrees with a system can hardly be expected to rise through that system's ranks!)

Most state wildlife agencies employ biologists who work exclusively in nongame and/or endangered wildlife programs. Some of these biologists were hired for these positions because of their interests. Others were hired because job openings were available. State conservation departments often laud their efforts in monitoring pesticide levels, seeking solutions to the regional acid rain problem, reintroducing bald eagles or peregrine falcons, or pinpointing the cause of a disease that affects a certain species of bird or mammal. (Often the cause may be man's environmental contamination—acid rains, pesticide poisoning, et cetera.) But these seeming altruists would not advance very far if they did not believe in public hunting and trapping or at least if they did not give occasional lip service to this system. In addition, nongame programs are usually undertaken in conjunction with game programs. While there has been some progress in nongame management and endangered species protection in North America during the decades of the sixties and seventies, there has been no corresponding progress in abolishing or reducing the length of most hunting and trapping seasons, decreasing the number of hunted species, or decreasing the amount of public land available for use by hunters. (As previously noted, they have all been on the *increase* in most states.)

The Conservative Reformers

Despite the many factors that usually insure the harvest-orientation of government wildlife personnel, there *are* a very small number of relatively progressive state and federal wildlife biologists who quietly offer their alternatives to existing methodology, even if to little or no avail. But most of those who have been gifted with even a small degree of sensitivity eventually must either desensitize themselves or break away from the system. And there *are* wildlife biologists who have left state game agencies because of an increasing distaste for game management practices. The small number of wildlife professionals who have placed ideals above self-interest and have left the system to pursue other careers are worthy of respect, as are the smaller number of state and federal biologists who have had the courage to openly question their superiors and make independent recommendations, often at the risk of unpopularity and job stagnation or reassignment.

But the majority of those within the system, those who work to perpetuate it for their benefit and for the benefit of those who profit from it, deserve the vigorous criticism of humanitarians who harbor a deep commitment to wildlife and the natural land. The Fund for Animals has published a pamphlet titled *Wildlife Mis-Management*. It concludes:

> When the state biologists are paid directly from [hunting] license fees, as they now are, the only ones the biologists are really accountable to then are the 'sportsmen,' in effect their employer, and the biologists' decisions and 'studies' reflect this bias.

Public hunting and the current system of wildlife management have created many more problems than they have solved: more biological, ecological, and agricultural damage and more suffering—much more suffering. This will be thoroughly documented in the pages that follow.

PART TWO

Shooting Down the Myths

HUNTERS' ATTENTION— . . . Do you know that hunting often is important to the environmental picture and why? . . . Do you know that hunters were the first to promote sound conservation? And they still do. No species is currently endangered by legal hunting.
—From *The Vermont Guide to Hunting* (a publication of the Vermont Fish and Game Department)

Commercial wildlife biologists and game managers have many arguments that they use to justify the hunting-trapping system. Likewise, hunters have adopted some of these arguments and have contrived others to bolster their image and defend recreational hunting. Many nonhunters believe these popular myths, and this is one reason there is not a greater percentage of people actively opposed to public hunting.

How would a wildlife protectionist respond to these arguments? Many nonhunters are unaware that there are potent and well-grounded counterarguments that can be used to disprove popular prohunting rationalizations. And it is for this reason that each of the most significant hunting justifications is presented here, followed by a critical analysis.

The more important prohunting arguments may be grouped into four categories: 1) Pseudobiological Arguments, 2) Pseudoecological Arguments, 3) Conservation Arguments, and 4) Pseudoethical Arguments. I have tried to achieve continuity by this categorization. At the beginning of each section I have included a brief description of the arguments that are analyzed in that section.

All of the prohunting arguments that are presented here have either been voiced to me by a hunter or hunters or have appeared in print, either in newspapers, in hunting magazines, in literature published by hunters' organizations, in books that were written by hunters and dealt with hunting, or in "conservation" periodicals published by state game agencies or environmental resource departments.

All prohunting arguments are extremely vulnerable to legitimate criticism. Those who believe that wildlife should be freed from man's domination should be aware of this and should know how to effectively answer them.

III. / Pseudobiological Arguments

THESE ARE ARGUMENTS THAT HUNTERS USE TO JUSTIFY HUNTING ON THE GROUNDS THAT THE CURRENT SYSTEM OF WILDLIFE MANAGEMENT IS NECESSARY TO MAINTAIN HEALTHY POPULATIONS OF BOTH HUNTED AND NON-HUNTED WILDLIFE SPECIES. A RELATED JUSTIFICATION IS THAT HUNTING IS NECESSARY TO MAINTAIN A SYSTEM OF "CHECKS" ON GAME POPULATIONS. THE MOST OFTEN USED ARGUMENT IN THIS SECTION IS THAT MANY MORE WHITE-TAILED DEER AND OTHER LARGE UNGULATES WOULD STARVE OR DIE AS A RESULT OF DISEASE OR SEVERE WEATHER IF A CERTAIN PERCENTAGE WERE NOT "HARVESTED" ANNUALLY.

THE HABITAT MANIPULATION ARGUMENT

The person who thinks that an animal which escapes death by hunting will live happily ever after is frightfully naive in the ways of nature. The four scepters of death are always hovering nearby and, more quickly than most people suspect, bring about a "natural" death, usually slower and more painful than that inflicted through hunting. . . . It is the sincere desire of every sportsman to make a kill as quickly and cleanly as possible—one that is probably more merciful than would have been in store for the individual animal had it survived to die a "natural death."
—Paul M. Kelsey, "conservation educator" for the New York State DEC
(from a column in the Ticonderoga, N.Y. *Times* December 7, 1982)

Hunters' Argument: THE SCIENTIFIC MANIPULATION OF HABITAT, WHEN PROPERLY APPLIED, BENEFITS NOT ONLY GAME SPECIES BUT *ALL* SPECIES OF ANIMALS NATIVE TO THE MANAGED AREA.

Analysis: In an editorial in the November 1979 issue of *Field and Stream*, Jack Sampson commended some of the habitat manipulation techniques that are commonly used to manage wildlife. His editorial deserves a detailed study—not for the purpose of singling out Sampson or *Field and Stream* for overstatements, but because the views expressed by Sampson are no doubt shared by a majority of American hunters. On the surface, many of Sampson's remarks may seem valid. But as with most prohunting arguments, it is necessary to dig beneath the surface to gain an accurate perspective.

Sampson uses the Federal Aid in Wildlife Restoration Program, otherwise known as the Pittman-Robertson Act, as the basis for his observations. This is the program that is funded by an 11 percent excise tax on firearms and ammunition and helps to subsidize state wildlife agencies and the U.S. Fish and Wildlife Service. It was enacted in 1937, ostensibly to pay for the purchase and preservation of wildlife habitat. Today habitat is often manipulated with these revenues. The federal government allocates Pittman-Robertson (P-R) monies to the states on a 75-25 cost-sharing basis for various projects, described by Sampson as "research, land acquisition, habitat development and outdoor education."

Research includes activities such as obtaining information about bears by tranquilizing them and outfitting them with signaling devices to monitor their movements—for the purpose of game management. Certainly it is not necessary to engage in this type of activity to prove that ecosystems are poorly balanced or that many species of wild animals are being crowded out of their normal range; that natural food sources are diminishing because of habitat development; that animals are succumbing to air, water, pesticide, and in some areas, noise pollution; and that many species are low in number and otherwise in serious trouble. These are established facts. Furthermore, "wildlife research" usually has little to do with maintaining optimum populations of bears or other hunted species within well-balanced natural ecosystems. Most often its purpose is to help to determine those methods that will be used to stabilize, increase, or decrease the number of bears and other "game" animals in certain areas to a level compatible with the number of hunters and average annual "harvests."

"Land acquisition" means, almost without exception, hunted lands—in some cases public game lands. According to a biologist with whom I spoke, some Pittman-Robertson funds that have been designated for land acquisition and wildlife restoration have, in addition, been used for such purposes as road and trail construction and hunter access sites. Money spent for these purposes is not being used for conservation, if one uses Webster's primary definition of the word.

Outdoor education refers mainly to training programs for prospective young hunters and trappers and the dissemination of information about wildlife and its habitat that is usually oriented toward hunting and trapping. This includes lectures given by state wildlife biologists at

56

public schools and the distribution of printed material about hunting and game management, some of it intended for young people. In addition, some P-R monies have been used to build target ranges for use by hunters-in-training.

In 1981, $14 million of an $83 million P-R allocation to states from the federal government was used for hunter safety programs. Some states, such as New Jersey, received more money for hunter training than for "wildlife restoration"!

On the subject of habitat development, Jack Sampson claims that while most Pittman-Robertson funds are used for the perpetuation of game species, these programs do not discriminate against nongame animals:

> The reason is simple. Certain groups of wildlife prefer certain types of habitat. For example, annual burning in a southern pine forest to stimulate the growth of low vegetation for food and cover for bobwhite quail automatically helps mice, rabbits, bobcats (which eat mice and rabbits), and at least twenty species of songbirds. The mice, rabbits, and songbirds need the same type of food and cover as do the quail, and, therefore, the bobcat's dinner table is set, too.

(Naturally, the human hunter's dinner table is also set!) Sampson's remarks are an oversimplification. Bobcats may be trapped in most states, and in order to ensure the survival of the bobcat, it is necessary to provide it with a source of food. Furthermore, rabbits are legal game in most states. As for mice and songbirds, these nongame species are necessary for the semblance of a balanced ecosystem, an ecosystem that would support the maximum number of each game species that is intentionally managed—in this case, quail, rabbits, and bobcats. Therefore, in order to insure the greatest number of quail, rabbits, and bobcats compatible with the altered environment, it is expedient to maintain an ecosystem in which mice and "at least twenty species of songbirds" are found.[1] However, the *primary* purpose of the "management" described by Sampson is the creation of a habitat favorable to the bobwhite quail and rabbit, both of which are hunted, and the bobcat, which is hunted *and* trapped. The fact that mice and songbirds fit into the scheme is coincidental, and the program is not a humanitarian act specifically designed to benefit these nongame species. (Presumably, *some* of the field biologists who practice nongame management—the few idealists—are involved because of a personal commitment. But the high-level officials who prescribe these activities usually have much less altruistic motives!)

Contrary to the pontifications of some forest managers, annual or periodic controlled burning usually has a harmful effect upon the ecology of a forest—*any type of forest*. It can deplete soil quality. It kills shrubbery and the lower branches of fruit producing trees. It can have disastrous effects upon territorially inclined animals such as red squirrels, gray squirrels, chipmunks, and mice (those that survive the fire). It may harmfully alter the composition of aquatic life in brooks, if any small streams are in or near the burn area. It adversely affects the normal succession of flora and fauna. And what will happen to early-nesting birds that are in the path of the smoke-producing fire? (Much burning is done in the spring.) Will they all return to the same area? Periodic burning may eventually provide a suitable habitat for some animals, but what about its immediate effects? A charred ground surface isn't an ideal habitat for any animal. What happens to toads and salamanders and to the insects that many birds would feed upon, particularly those that live at or just below the ground surface? Even the burning of low underbrush often kills low-bush blueberries and other kinds of low-growing berry bushes, upon which many species of birds and small mammals depend.

The Hazards of Habitat Manipulation

Wildlife biologists Steven C. Wilson and Karen C. Hayden commented on the use of "controlled burning" as a wildlife management tool in the February 1981 issue of *National Geographic* ("Where Oil and Wildlife Mix"). The article concerns the Aransas National Wildlife Refuge, on the east coast of Texas. According to Wilson and Hayden (italics added by author)

> . . . controlled burnings, now part of the refuge management plan, kill shinnery oaks and other scrub. The scrub encroaches on the prairie grass ecosystem upon which the Attwater's* and other indigenous creatures depend. Fire is *the most economical way to undo the destruction from decades of domestic abuses.* By favoring small rodents, it also benefits the coyote, a rodent controller in nature's plan.

Not mentioned is the fact that burning temporarily destroys the tall grass that coyotes in this relatively open area would normally use as cover. Furthermore, small rodents that are unable to escape the fire and those that are trapped in shallow burrows will not survive to be "favored." The *Geographic* article includes a photograph of a dead prairie

---

*The Attwater's prairie chicken is an endangered species.

king snake that, according to the authors, "died only inches from its underground home, which offered safety from the momentary heat." The controlled burn covered several hundred acres.

The *Geographic* article quotes Aransas biologist Steve Labuda, who contends that "the primary purpose of a refuge is to create or maintain existing habitats for the benefit of the indigenous species—the critters that live there naturally." It is true that natural succession will result in *slow* ecological changes, including new and different species. These changes occur over a period of decades. The animals that are "natural" or native to an area are those that would live in a climax ecosystem, one that has been undisturbed for one to three or four centuries, depending on geographical area, elevation, average annual rain- and snowfall and type of habitat. Regular habitat manipulation, especially the use of fire, creates adverse conditions for *all* wild animals until grass and low growth can regenerate. As might be expected, hunting is permitted at Aransas Wildlife Refuge.

Forestry and wildlife personnel are human and prone to occasional errors in judgment. Accidents involving "controlled burning," while infrequent, sometimes happen. In 1976, a fire intended for "habitat development" in Michigan's Manistique River Forest raged out of control when a strong wind suddenly developed. Before the fire was contained, at the cost of one firefighter's life, thousands of animal's lives, and over $3 million in federal tax money, it had ravaged 70,000 acres of Manistique Forest and neighboring Seney National Wildlife Refuge.

Sometimes the *intentional* results of prescribed burns can be worse than the results of habitat manipulation fires that burn out of control. In the autumn of 1981, a "controlled" burn ravaged 5,000 acres of California's Yosemite National Park, charring and destroying pine, cedar, and fir trees. The fire had been set in order to destroy bushes, branches, dead trees, and low growth. Six additional burns were conducted in Yosemite during the summer of 1982. Even worse, lightning-set fires on interior tracts of federally owned forestlands in the Western states are now sometimes allowed to run their course!

Death by Poisoning

The U.S. Fish and Wildlife Service, as a wildlife management procedure, is using Pittman-Robertson funds to finance the spraying of toxic herbicides and pesticides on federal lands. Herbicides are used to destroy unwanted vegetation and promote the growth of low-level browse to encourage large numbers of deer for hunter's guns. In 1983, more than 40,000 acres were treated with toxicants for this purpose.

Chemicals are also used to kill "rough" fish and encourage the

59

growth of "sport" fish populations. According to the 1978 *Draft Environmental Impact Statement: Federal Aid in Fish and Wildlife Restoration Program*, between 1975 and 1985, $2.6 million would be used to treat 2,112 miles of streams. The Fish and Wildlife Service also projected $374,000 for herbicide application to control aquatic weeds on 4,461 acres. Poisons are nonselective, and they often kill nontarget fish and other aquatic life, further upsetting the balance of nature.

Hunted waterfowl are "favored" by encouraging the growth of plant food through the poisoning of carp and other "nuisance fish" and by poisoning some types of plant life in marshlands and along coastal areas. Between 1975 and 1985, the Fish and Wildlife Service projected the use of toxicants on 520,000 acres.

Logging Destruction

Like burning and poisoning, logging has serious effects upon wildlife. Animals are stressed and dispersed by the noise and environmental disruption that is created by logging machinery and chain saws. Many wildlife homes may be destroyed by wheeled or tracked machinery as a result of ground compaction and the demolition of low, rotting stumps and small decaying logs. Other homes and potential homes for red or gray squirrels, flying squirrels, raccoons, owls, hairy woodpeckers, and other animals are destroyed when trees are cut, since there is sometimes a percentage of undetected rot in the lower and mid portions of trees that are removed. Not all logging that is related to wildlife management is conducted during the fall and winter. If logging operations are conducted during spring or early summer, innumerable birds' nests are lost, along with the eggs or nestlings that they contain.

Skidders and other machinery crush or uproot low-growing bushes and small shrubs that would produce berries for many species of birds and small mammals. If too many white pines, hemlocks, maples, hickories, beeches, ashes, and other cone-, nut-, or seed-producing trees are cut over a wide area, primary food sources are lost and the result will be the starvation of many small mammals and drastic reductions in the populations of many species that depend upon these trees for food and/or homes. The ecosystem is drastically and often disastrously altered. If logging is a regular activity, periodic destruction of wildlife and ecosystems occurs.

Clear-cutting is sometimes employed as a deer management practice. In hilly areas this causes erosion of hillsides. Silt may wash into streams, killing aquatic life and adversely altering aquatic ecosystems. Naturally, *some* commercial logging is necessary on privately owned timberlands. But less destructive methods need to be developed. Logging done solely for "game habitat improvement" on state and federal forest and parklands is completely nonessential and is usually very destructive to established ecosystems.

Threats against Predators

Even the removal of a few key trees in ecologically sensitive areas can adversely alter ecosystems. Paul M. Kelsey of the New York State Division of Fish and Wildlife has suggested the removal of good perch trees from hedgerows or from key pheasant wintering areas in order to reduce predation by owls and hawks. Pheasants are stocked in six counties in southwestern New York. In 1981, 4,308 of these birds were released by New York State wildlife technicians. Approximately 65 percent were stocked one week to ten days before the start of pheasant hunting in southwestern New York State. The remainder were released *during the first two weeks of the hunting season.* Most stocked pheasants are killed by hunters. Many of the remaining birds die from a lack of food or cover or from severe weather during the winter following their release or are killed by foxes, hawks, or owls. However, the birds that remain after hunting seasons are usually dispersed rather widely and probably suffer relatively *light losses* as a result of predation. But these light losses worry game manipulators much more than heavy *hunting* losses because pheasants are not stocked to provide food for natural predators. Kelsey, writing in the Olean (New York) *Times-Herald* (October 8, 1981) admitted that predators have some merit and managed to solve this problem with the following suggestion:

> The known value of predators as rodent destroyers, and thus as benefactors to the farmer, puts the stress of predator control work on eliminating habitat favorable to the predators, and increasing favorable escape cover for the birds [pheasants].

Kelsey, you will remember, lamented the loss of wildlife as a result of "the four scepters of death" (starvation, disease, severe weather, and predation). He might have added a fifth: hunting. Pheasants that are stocked for hunting in artificially large numbers are either shotgunned or die "natural deaths." With fewer predators, more pheasants will die during winter as a result of the first three factors, ultimately much slower and more painful ways to die than from the quick and relatively sure talons and beak of a hawk, eagle, or owl. Naturally, most of the pheasants would not be around to endure the "five scepters" if they had not been artificially propagated and released. (The ring-necked pheasant is not a native of North America. It was first introduced to Oregon from China in 1882—for hunting purposes.)

In summary, the main purpose of habitat manipulation is to insure maximum numbers of hunted animals.

A Precarious Quasi-Balance

Returning to the remarks made by Jack Sampson in his *Field and Stream* editorial:

> Wildlife managers can name the game and nongame species planned for in any one area simply by looking at a habitat.

One might question the goal of such planning unless it is specifically designed to aid an endangered species native to a particular geographical area. Habitat manipulation, especially when it drastically alters the character of natural land, is not conducive to environmental harmony. Why not allow Nature to balance itself, while wildlife biologists stock only those rare, threatened, or endangered species that need restoration and whose presence would not cause drastic changes in established ecosystems? The answer is that the system does not work this way. The reason it does not work this way is because game officials believe that helping wildlife for the sake of wildlife would not generate a maximum revenue yield for their departments and state economies.

Sampson continues:

> When P-R funds are used to create a certain type of habitat, the results are not increases in game and decreases in nongame. The land becomes more attractive to those wildlife species that prefer that type of habitat and becomes or remains less attractive to animals with different needs. That is why the P-R money is used to burn in one place, impound water in another, cut timber in another, plow and cultivate in another, and provide complete protection to vegetation in another. And the record shows that it works. The number of nongame species benefited invariably exceeds the number of game species.

Once again, this is an oversimplification. If the purpose were not to increase the numbers of game animals, or at least to perpetuate them for the benefit of hunters, there would be little reason to manipulate habitat—unless this were intended to reestablish an endangered species, *while safeguarding the quality of the habitat for other native animals.* But the alteration of established ecosystems is seldom done for this purpose, and even when it is, many animals often suffer because the quality of the habitat has been rendered unsuitable for them.

The word *game* is used by some to denote *hunted* species. But many species of animals not commonly considered game species may be trapped. (Examples are the marten, fisher, beaver, otter, mink, muskrat, opossum, weasel, red fox, and bobcat.) In many states, the latter two species may be both hunted *and* trapped. Thus most of the species that "benefit" from wildlife management are those that may be either hunted or trapped or both. They benefit either from habitat manipulation that is designed to "favor" them, from activities that are intended to increase the populations of the animals they prey upon, or from favoritism shown to true nongame species, such as certain types of songbirds, that happen to prefer the kind of habitat on which the other species are found. This creates what might be termed an "ecological quasi-balance," in the short term benefiting the game animals whose management is the primary concern of wildlife officials. Furthermore, there are nongame species that may be reclassified as game species if their numbers increase to a certain level, although game species are seldom reclassified as nongame even when their populations decline substantially.

The type of activities that Sampson advocates are prime examples of synthetically created habitats. The system "works" simply because man is *altering* the environment in a way that may appear to benefit certain species. But how many songbirds and other small animals are killed or displaced by timber cutting and other management activities? What happens to members of those species to whom the altered habitat has "become less attractive," particularly those with strong territorial incentives? A dispersal of foxes, raccoons, squirrels, chipmunks or other territorially motivated animals to more favorable locations can create a temporary overabundance of these species in some areas, resulting in stress, aggressive behavior, food shortages, and ecological imbalance. But even if no animals were to *suffer* from this type of management, an artificially created habitat is the product of a nonenvironmental outlook. Burning, impounding water, cutting timber, and plowing and cultivating do not complement established ecosystems. These ecosystems, which normally evolve over a period of two or three centuries, can be altered by man in a relatively short time. And who benefits the most? Hunters and trappers.

According to Sampson:

> . . . the beaver, pronghorn, bison, elk, whitetail deer, wild turkey, trumpeter swan, wood duck, sea otter, and several species of egrets and herons were in dire straits during the early 1900's. Today, all these animals are abundant. And it does not cost the federal taxpayers one penny. . .

As will be fully documented later, the last sentence is grossly inaccurate. All of the species that were mentioned, except for the egret, heron, trumpeter swan, and sea otter (the latter governed by the Marine Mammal Protection Act), are legal game in some states. As for the other species cited by Sampson, their continued existence is largely a result of the pressure that was exerted upon federal legislators by groups that Sampson terms "the big protectionist and environmental lobby in Washington." This includes, among many others, the National Audubon Society, Defenders of Wildlife, the Sierra Club, and Friends of the Earth. This is not to mention the animal protection groups such as Greenpeace, Friends of Animals, The Fund for Animals, and the Animal Protection Institute, all of which have helped to insure protective legislation for some species of wildlife. (Incidentally, by so labeling the opposition, Sampson implies that most hunters are antienvironment. As will be shown later, this is an accurate assessment, although many hunters would disagree.)

Sampson concludes his editorial by asking readers to write to their congressman or senator: "Tell him to stick with the Federal Aid in Wildlife Restoration Program. Don't let the uninformed dreamers ruin nearly half a century of fine conservation." Naturally, this is the type of "conservation" in which the hunting-trapping ethic predominates. While this typifies management procedures, it demonstrates confused priorities. Economic considerations notwithstanding, wildlife management should respect the needs of all species that are normally found within undisturbed natural ecosystems.

The Bitter Fruits of Land Mismanagement

During 1975, game management on state and federal wildlands included the following activities:

- —422,868 acres burned.
- —18,094 acres clear-cut.
- —35,415 acres sprayed with toxic chemicals and defoliants.
- —126,375 acres bulldozed.
- —599,526 acres flooded to created duck breeding habitat.

The acreage included in these management plans has been increasing annually. Projections for 1985 include more than 2.4 million acres slated for habitat manipulation. This includes 715,000 acres scheduled for burning.

One example of a disruptive "conservation" practice that is much less environmentally destructive than most other forms of habitat manipulation may be seen by a wilderness hiker who backpacks to remote Branch Pond in the Green Mountains of southern Vermont. If he or she hikes to the west side of the pond, he or she will notice a large area of hardwood trees that are conspicuously leafless on a hill to the south. This tract is about one square mile in size. A close examination will reveal that all of the large and medium-sized trees in this area have been killed by girdling. The purpose? One reason was to provide low-growth browse for deer.

The management of this tract, which is public land belonging to the Green Mountain National Forest, included a logging operation during 1964–65. Many of the trees in the logged area contained a high percentage of rot. Rather than cut the partly decayed trees, foresters decided to kill them by girdling—in the process regenerating the girdled area with spruce, yellow birch, and hard maple (trees with a potentially high commercial value). In the meantime, the low growth would act as browse for deer and provide more healthy whitetails for hunters' rifles.

According to W. F. Schumann, who is a district forest ranger stationed in Manchester Center, Vermont, girdled trees that were near the Stratton Shunpike, a narrow gravel road that passes a short distance from the logged area, and Forest Road Number 70, a gravel road constructed for access in case of a forest fire, were removed for firewood. (There are many large girdled trees still standing along the latter route.) The vast majority of the trees that were girdled were in the interior forest and were left to rot on the stump. Said Schumann: "The [trees] still standing provide cover and nesting sites for many species of wildlife. . . . We feel that our activities in this area have been successful."

Which animal species benefited from the girdling? Perhaps the four species of woodpeckers native to the Green Mountains. Maybe ovenbirds and a few other species of songbirds that require low cover or build their nests on or near the ground. Maybe raccoons, red squirrels, and flying squirrels, which were provided with potential homes. But these three species of mammals rely heavily upon beechnuts during late summer and autumn, and nearly all of the beech trees three to four inches D.B.H.* and over were killed by girdling!†

---

*D.B.H. is a forester's term meaning "diameter at breast height." It denotes the diameter of a tree 4½ feet above the ground.
†The American beech is in danger of extinction in the Eastern United States as a result of *Cyptococcus*, a tiny scale insect, and *Nectria ditissima*, a small red fungus. This combination, known as the beech bark disease, is a European import.

Did any other animals benefit from the girdling? Perhaps red foxes and snowshoe hares, grouse, and maybe a stray bobcat or two, all of which often favor dense foliage and all of which may be hunted and/or trapped.

By the mid-1970s, the low growth hardwoods had become three to four feet high. Such a tangle of underbrush had been created that hikers who used the Branch Pond trail that traversed the main girdled area found walking almost impossible. In places the trail was nearly obliterated.

Admitted Schumann: "I agree that the girdled, dead trees do pose a visual eyesore. For this reason, the Green Mountain National Forest has discontinued this practice. . . . As the trees grow up, all signs of logging will disappear." Most of the girdled trees are at an elevation of 2,500–2,800 feet. In this cold climate, it will take one to two *centuries* for the forest to attain its premanaged growth. All in all, Nature is the loser.

I do not doubt that, like many other hunters, Jack Sampson honestly believes that disruptive land and wildlife management practices are a necessity. But one wonders who the uninformed dreamers are. How many more years will it take forest and wildlife managers to realize that many of their economically motivated "conservation" practices are ecologically destructive, that most are antienvironmental, and that virtually all should be reevaluated in favor of natural ecosystems?

THE ARTIFICIAL ECOSYSTEMS ARGUMENT

Hunters' Argument: IT MAY BE TRUE THAT ECOSYSTEMS ARE ARTIFICIALLY MANIPULATED IN SOME LOCATIONS, BUT IT IS ALSO TRUE THAT GAME MANAGEMENT IS EFFECTIVE IF PRACTICED ON A CONTINUING BASIS. THUS IT CANNOT BE PROVEN THAT PUBLIC HUNTING DOES ANY HARM TO WILDLIFE POPULATIONS WITHIN THE FRAMEWORK OF THE ECOSYSTEMS THAT ARE FUNCTIONING WITH MAN'S AID.

Analysis: This depends upon what a person considers "harm" and how much proof he or she needs. Nature is a very delicate balance, and even minute changes in the established metabolic processes may result in long-term disruptions.

Hunting and trapping have contributed to changes in the behavioral patterns of many species of wild animals. Animals such as foxes, coyotes, and raccoons, which are believed to have been diurnal in North America two or three centuries ago, are now mainly nocturnal. Deer forage in open areas mainly at night and during twilight and predawn, as a result of human population pressure, development, and hunting, some of which is done out of season. One can only speculate what long-term effects this might have. But, at best, it prevents people from observing or photographing many species of wildlife during the daylight hours.[2]

Hunting alters the makeup of family units and, particularly in the case of social animals such as wolves, coyotes, deer, elk, caribou, bighorn sheep, and seals, disrupts social structures. Animal societies are very well ordered. The loss of a dominant member or the leader of a family unit can result in lessened survival expectancies for remaining members that had depended upon the leader's superior strength and intelligence for direction and social stability. When a new group leader emerges, he or she may not have the superior qualities of the previous patriarch or matriarch. (This may be one factor that contributes to population fluctuations of social "game" animals.)

Doesn't the premature loss of group members occur naturally through accident, malnutrition, disease and—in a balanced ecosystem—natural predation? Yes, but it occurs at a considerably slower rate than during relatively short hunting seasons. Except in rare cases of severe natural disasters such as tornadoes, hurricanes, lightning-set forest fires, or volcanos, natural decimating factors, including predation, remove a few animals at a time. But hunting seasons, which often result in mass invasions of hunters and the loss of correspondingly high numbers of animals in a two- or three-week period, can have a devastating impact upon "game" populations.

Then why not substantially lengthen hunting seasons or establish year-round hunting in order to spread the "harvests" of legal game species over a longer period of time? For one thing, this would probably result in the hunting-related deaths of a much greater number of animals, particularly the ungulates, due to higher hunter success rates. (It was because of a lack of hunting regulations that many species of animals became almost extinct during the ninteenth century.) Of equal importance is that the abolition or weakening of most hunting regulations would be very biologically destructive because pregnant and nursing mothers and very young animals would be killed. Fortunately, from a logistical standpoint, hunting seasons, especially "big game" seasons, can continue to be extended only so far, after which the task and the associated cost of policing hunters would make the work of conservation law enforcement officers much more difficult. Moreover, hunting seasons are a means of regulatory leverage for state wildlife bureaus. If limited seasons were abolished in favor of year-round hunting, the power of wildlife agencies would be weakened and many more hunters would be tempted to hunt without purchasing licenses.

Returning to the negative biological effects of hunting: By substituting unnaturally large numbers of recreational hunters for much smaller optimum numbers of natural predators, people are creating an additional decimating factor upon heavily hunted species such as deer, ruffed grouse, pheasants (where this exotic has become established), and all species of hunted waterfowl. Where predators and prey coexist, members of prey species usually become aware of the existence of predators and have little difficulty adjusting their lives and behavioral patterns. But hunting by large numbers of people creates additional stress on hunted birds and mammals. Thus hunters are adding to, rather than subtracting from, the problems faced by animals living in the wild.

Intensive recreational hunting may adversely affect nongame animals and out-of-season "game" animals. If there is sufficient hunting pressure during big game seasons, the resulting gunshots, combined with the loud shouts of hunters driving deer, will inevitably result in increased stress upon nonhunted animals. Deer hunting usually occurs during late autumn, when individuals of many species are still storing food for winter. Furthermore, some irresponsible deer hunters have been known to use a wide variety of nongame and illegal game species for target practice. In the short term, more effective "hunter management" is needed; stricter controls on *who* can hunt, *what,* and *where* they can hunt and the establishment of maximum hunter density levels per given area, which are well below those that now exist in most intensively hunted locations. Unfortunately, these reforms will not be implemented in most areas in the near future unless there is a strong public outcry.

Hunting Is Dangerous to Environmental Health

Hunting has other adverse effects on wildlife:

—In some parts of the United States and Canada, large numbers of ducks and geese are crippled by debilitating, poisonous lead shot. In 1975, the U.S. Fish and Wildlife Service estimated that 25 percent of all waterfowl that are shot escape wounded. Many of those that are not badly wounded suffer a slow death from lead poisoning. Those that have been seriously incapacitated will soon die. From 1975 through 1977, the U.S. Fish and Wildlife Service found that 26 percent of a sampling of 4,942 canvasback ducks had lead shot embedded in their flesh. This is particularly shocking because hunting seasons on this species were closed during those years! Dick Kenly, a zoologist for the Fund for Animals, researched the effects of duck hunting in the Brigantine National Wildlife Refuge in New Jersey during November 1979. Kenly learned that 24 percent of a large sampling of several species of ducks had sustained crippling wounds. One species, the bufflehead, had been crippled at a rate of 39 percent! The lead poisoning of bald eagles that have preyed upon wounded ducks is a serious problem. (This is in addition to the estimated 200 bald eagles that are illegally shot each year.) Many hunters are opposed to a conversion from lead to steel shot because steel shot would be more expensive and does not have the spraying effect of lead.

—There are no official statistics on the annual numbers of deer, bears, and coyotes that are seriously wounded, but not taken by hunters. However, *The Michigan Journal of Wildlife Management* estimated that as many as 35 percent of the deer in that state that are hit by hunter's bullets may escape wounded. The percentage may be even higher during bow hunting seasons.

—Intensive deer hunting often results in smaller and weaker deer, since most hunters shoot large, healthy bucks, leaving the younger and smaller bucks to breed. The late ecologist Edwin Way Teale called this "evolution in reverse." Furthermore, reproductive patterns are drastically altered because of a numerical imbalance of does to bucks—as much as five to one in some areas. (Under normal browse conditions and optimum deer population levels, there are about 52 males and 48 females for every 100 fawns born, or about a one-to-one ratio.) Large bucks *do* exist, but are found mainly in very lightly hunted areas. Generally the large bucks are found either in rugged, trackless wilderness where accessibility is limited, or in wooded areas adjacent to districts that have a relatively high human population and that because of their close proximity to development, are shunned by most hunters. On November 11, 1981, a twenty-two–point, 250-pound buck was shot in an outlying area of Albany County, New York, five days before the opening of firearms deer season. (The hunter was fined $1,255.) The buck was believed to be the fifteenth largest ever shot in the United States. In most areas it would have been shot long before it had reached this size.

—In some states, threatened predators such as the timber wolf, cougar, and lynx may be legally shot and/or trapped. Montana is attempting to legalize grizzly-bear hunting. Some normally abundant species have become rare as a result of habitat destruction combined with overhunting. In 1982, the state of Rhode Island (which has a human population density of about 800 per square mile) was experiencing a shortage of rabbits in some areas. In order to ensure an abundant supply of targets for rabbit hunters, the Division of Fish and Wildlife of the Rhode Island Department of Environmental Control imported *snowshoe hares* from the province of New Brunswick. Vocal protests by animal preservationists, led by the Animal Protection Institute, were unable to prevent the implementation of this plan.

—In an increasing number of states, more and more species

of animals are becoming legal game; new seasons are initiated and existing ones are extended to satisfy hunters and increase revenue for state game bureaus. (New and longer seasons may result in greater license sales due to increased numbers of legal game species and a greater number of hunting days per year. A fringe benefit for wildlife agencies may be increased support for their game management programs from those who profit as a result of hunting.)

Examples of "liberalized" hunting and trapping seasons have become numerous in recent years. During the mid-1970s, the firearms season for deer in the state of Pennsylvania was lengthened from six to twelve days. In addition, a six-day muzzle-loader season was added.[3] In 1983, gun seasons for deer in Pennsylvania (excluding nonhunting Sundays) stretched from November 28 through December 17.

In New Jersey, gun seasons for deer were lengthened from six to twelve days in the late 1970s with the inclusion of a muzzle-loader season. In 1983, five more days were added. Holders of special permits were allowed to shoot one deer of either sex during this period. There were also two days of special permit shotgun hunting during the muzzle-loader season. Total deer season during 1983 (excluding Sundays) was December 5 through 23.

During the late 1970s, a ten-day "black powder" season (another name for a hunt with muzzle-loaders) was added to the deer season in New Hampshire. This increased the length of gun seasons for deer in that state from three to four and a half weeks.[4]

One might ask whether a wilderness is simply a huge experimental game farm. Hunting preserve rationale is the basis of the present wildlife management system. While game management "works," provided that enough sentient creatures are moved and countermoved across the ecological chessboard, hunters should seriously consider both the hazards and the Draconian morality of this system.

THE STARVATION ARGUMENT

Hunters' Argument: HUNTING IS NECESSARY TO KEEP GAME SPECIES IN CHECK. WITHOUT ANNUAL HUNTING, MUCH GREATER NUMBERS OF DEER, ELK, MOOSE, AND CARIBOU WOULD STARVE DURING WINTER. HUNTING ALSO HELPS TO KEEP POPULATIONS OF SMALL GAME ANIMALS SUCH AS RABBITS AND SQUIRRELS IN BALANCE WITH AVAILABLE FOOD SUPPLIES. PHEASANTS, GROUSE, AND OTHER GAME BIRDS SOMETIMES HAVE AN ANNUAL MORTALITY RATE PER CLUTCH AS HIGH AS 75 PERCENT AS A RESULT OF DISEASE, PARASITES,

MALNUTRITION, WEATHER FACTORS, AND PREDATION. IF HUNTERS DID NOT CROP THE SURPLUS, NATURE *WOULD* AND THE RESULT WOULD BE DECIMATED HABITAT AND WEAK, UNHEALTHY ANIMAL PUPULATIONS.

Analysis: During one of New Hampshire's deer seasons, a Granite State game biologist said during a radio news interview, "Some people think that the hunters have killed Bambi. They should see the starved deer lying dead in the woods during late winter and early spring." The biologist's statement is probably the most frequent rationalization that hunters and game managers use to justify public hunting.

Hunters have convinced many people that we would be overrun by wildlife, especially deer, if it were not for annual "thinning" by humans. A typical remark is found in Charlie Dickey's *Deer Hunting* (Oxmoor House, Inc., 1977). According to Dickey, "Hunters are the only control we have for keeping the [deer] herds checked in balance with the habitat. Certainly hunters are the most economical way. They're glad to do it for free, or even pay to hunt."

Is public hunting really needed in order to keep deer and other large ungulates in balance with their food supplies? This question can be answered in part by a description of some of the "management" programs that have been undertaken in the United States and the results of these programs. The first major "deer management" experiment was conducted in 1908 on the Kaibab Plateau in Arizona. This area of about 1 million acres is bounded by canyons, plains, and arid regions. A relatively stable herd of about 4,000 mule deer was confined to the plateau, which offered good seasonal habitat. Game officials wanted to learn whether the elimination of large predators and the improvement of deer habitat would result in a substantial deer population increase. So a systematic program of wolf, coyote, and cougar extermination was undertaken by government hunters. At the time, the Kaibab region was a prime sheep grazing habitat. Game officials removed 195,000 sheep and 20,000 cattle from this area, thereby allowing grass on these partly open, partly forested lands to be utilized by deer as a major source of food during spring, summer, and early autumn. Hunting and trapping were forbidden. The result was an ecological disaster. During the next decade and a half the deer population in the Kaibab region increased astronomically—to approximately 100,000! An estimated 60,000 died of winter starvation and malnutrition. The Kaibab debacle is often cited by hunters as an example of what may happen in the absence of public hunting. Hunters usually neglect to mention that the Arizona disaster resulted from an ecologically destructive management program that had been *deliberately* designed to increase the size of the deer herd. Eventually the herd stabilized at around 10,000, but not before its habitat had been almost destroyed and its supply of natural food had been nearly exhausted.

Even without "habitat improvement" projects, the killing of natural predators can have serious effects upon populations of large herbivores. During the late 1940s, the U.S. Fish and Wildlife Service began an extermination of wolves on the Melchina Range south of the Arctic Circle in northern Alaska. The result: From 1947 to 1957 the caribou herd in this area increased from 4,000 to 42,000 and starvation rates rose markedly. Finally, in 1957 the Fish and Wildlife Service reversed its policy, designating the Melchina Range a "wolf management area" rather than a "wolf control area." Shooting wolves was prohibited, and by the close of the decade the caribou herd had begun to decline.

During the 1970s, another wolf control program was initiated in Alaska, largely because of pressure that was exerted by hunters on the Alaska Fish and Game Commission. Moose had been declining in three management areas totaling 9,000 square miles south of Fairbanks. This was due in part to the fact that for ten years the Alaskan government had allowed the shooting of cow moose. During the 1973 hunting season, hunters killed 710 of an estimated herd of 3,000 moose in the region south of Fairbanks. In 1976, then commissioner James W. Brooks ordered the elimination of the approximately 175 wolves that were believed to exist in this area. In March 1978, the Alaska Fish and Game Department authorized the elimination of 60 percent of the wolves in the Innoka Nowitna region so that the moose population could grow. As of this writing, Alaskan wolves are still being killed by sport hunters and trophy hunters *and* the Alaskan government. Approximately 1,000 Alaskan wolves are "harvested" each year by hunters from foreign countries, principally Germany. Wolf hunting in Alaska is a profitable enterprise, especially for guides, who are somtimes paid as much as $10,000 for a single expedition. Three hundred wolves are killed annually in Alaska by state and federal game officials. This is an incredible statistic when one considers that biologists for the Alaska Fish and Game Department have estimated that only 8,000 to 12,000 wolves are left within the state's 400,000 square miles. This means that there is about one pack of eight wolves over each 250 square miles of suitable habitat (an area about 16 miles on each side). One of many criticisms of the Alaska Fish and Game Department's recent "wolf control" policy was delivered by the *New York Times* in an editorial titled "Perverted Technology vs. Wolves" (December 24, 1982). The editorial writer noted that game managers in airplanes and helicopters have often followed wolf pups that have been captured and outfitted with special collars that emit radio signals. The pups eventually return to their pack, alerting government hunters to the location of the pack, which otherwise might not be discovered.

Horror stories about chronic deer overpopulations in deliberately manipulated and/or ecologically imbalanced areas notwithstanding, the population of any species of wild animal can never increase beyond the capacity of its habitat to support it. There are biological limits on the numbers of deer that, under a given set of ecological conditions, can exist in a habitat of a given size and quality. A deer herd cannot continue to increase indefinitely. When a deer herd expands beyond an ecologically ideal level (meaning a much lower population density than is found in most hunted areas in the United States), stress will result in die-offs even if there is adequate forage and an absence of severe weather such as drought or cold and snow. This is a cumulative process and does *not* occur suddenly as a result of an intolerable combination of adverse habitat and weather conditions. The term "range carrying capacity," often used by wildlife biologists, is a subjective determination, particularly since deer populations fluctuate in response to the amount of forage and other environmental factors.[5] However, a real or imagined "range carrying capacity" is not likely to be approached under certain habitat conditions and is not likely to be reached or "exceeded" unless deer populations are managed for hunting, as they now are in most parts of the United States.

In many extensive areas of mature forest, such as those that are found in parts of the northeastern United States, ideal conditions usually exist for *low* deer populations even in the absence of large predators. For example, as previously noted, deer population density is much lower in lightly hunted sections of the Adirondacks than in southern and southwestern New York State, which, with the exception of the Catskill Park, is characterized by open agricultural lands interspersed by woodlands. Most of these woodlands, with the exception of those in hilly, sparsely populated areas, are 500 acres or less. One reason for low deer populations throughout much of the Adirondacks may be light hunting pressure. Another reason is a lack of low-growth browse as a result of heavy forestation. My experience indicates that one annual fawn per fertile doe is common during many years in parts of the Adirondacks—particularly during those springs that have been preceded by a severe winter. This is in contrast to two, or very rarely, three fawns per doe in more heavily hunted areas, such as parts of Vermont and sections of agricultural southern New York. Furthermore, in the latter areas, a greater percentage of does may mate, leading to higher birth rates.

73

Hunting Alters Deer Reproduction

Why are there usually higher deer reproductive rates in areas where hunters "harvest" a substantial percentage of the herd each year? Deer populations, and the populations of most other species of wild animals, are usually cyclic. Their numbers in a particular geographical area will increase to a certain point and then decline, apparently as a biological reaction to decreasing food supplies and stress resulting from too many members of their species inhabiting a limited area. Occasionally, when food is scarce, the population of a species will "crash" as a result of die-offs and low birth rates and remain low until food supplies become reestablished. (This is particularly true of "game" mammals in intensively hunted areas.) In addition, when deer are at a high population level, a greater percentage of male fawns will be born. A study by wildlife biologists on the George Reserve in Michigan during the late 1940s indicated a fluctuation in the birth of male fawns from 70 to 45 percent depending upon the quality of winter forage. Does with restricted or low-quality forage produced the highest percentage of male fawns. It was found that only 38 percent of the does gave birth when the deer population was at its highest concentration. (It is now known that does will reabsorb embryos if they have mated during times of low food supplies or if food becomes scarce during winter.)

After a wildlife population has reached a low point in its cycle, there are usually greater fertility and reproductive rates to begin building the population to optimum levels. In areas where deer kills by hunters are heaviest during hunting seasons, the result is an abnormally rapid deer population "crash." Where this occurs on an annual basis, if there is adequate food for a deer herd, the surviving bucks will impregnate most of the ovulating does, which in turn will usually conceive two fawns rather than a single fawn with their first and subsequent pregnancies. (This is apparently a genetic characteristic that has evolved. In a balanced ecosystem, does would usually give birth to a single fawn on their first attempt and twins thereafter, at least in those areas where browse is plentiful.)

Game managers determine how many does and fawns may be killed during a hunting season while insuring as large a number of deer as possible the following season as a result of increased breeding rates, coupled with the condition and the amount of browse that would be available for surviving deer and other deer population and habitat factors. In congested areas in some states, such as New Jersey and Connecticut, that have a high human population density, the numbers of hunters that are allowed into a particular area may be limited, thus reducing buck "harvests." (But this is rare!) As detailed earlier, food supplies are often increased through habitat manipulation, including "controlled burning" and timber cutting. Maximum fawn production is abetted by the gradually increasing annual "harvests" that usually result from increasingly lengthy hunting seasons. By this means, does will mate at an earlier age than would be true if there were no hunting. Under normal conditions, does do not begin breeding before their second or third year, but studies have indicated that intensive hunting may trigger an innate survival mechanism that may cause fawns to ovulate and breed during their first autumn. In addition, greater numbers of does will ovulate when there is hunting. This is apparently an emergency reaction to the loss of large numbers of deer during a short period of time. It is Nature's way of ensuring the replacement of herd members. It is no coincidence that deer hunting seasons usually coincide with the rutting season for bucks!

When a large number of deer are killed during a short period of time, there is more food for remaining deer; this may be one factor that helps to trigger increased reproductive rates in the presence of hunting. (Naturally there would be a population decline if food supplies were to become dangerously low.) This increased reproductivity in heavily hunted areas usually results in an abnormally high deer population year after year. Habitat factors such as the abundance and quality of food and the percentage of wooded as opposed to cleared land, along with climatic conditions and biological characteristics of the herd, also play a part in determining deer population levels. But it should be remembered that under a specific set of conditions a deer herd cannot exceed a maximum population density before stress, malnutrition, and disease lead to a temporary population decline. (Disease is usually not a direct result of population density. It is the end result of a combination of adverse environmental factors.) Naturally there are high deer populations some years in unmanaged areas and in unhunted areas, but in nonhunted, unmanipulated wild areas that have an optimum number of predators, deer populations tend to cycle around or just below the maximum number that the habitat can safely support. While there is some population fluctuation, there are usually not the population "crashes" (such as those that are artifically induced by hunting) and the abnormally high reproductive rates resulting in high deer populations that characterize deer herds in areas were there is intensive hunting—and particularly in those areas where deer habitat has been "improved" by manipulation.

The population principles that apply to deer herds also apply to herds of moose, elk, and caribou. For example, the 1983 edition of *New Hampshire Hunting and Trapping Seasons*, published by the New Hampshire Fish and Game Department, in a reference to that state's non-hunted moose herd, noted that "Intensive management [would] keep the population at a higher level than would occur without management."

Changes in reproductive patterns are typical of most species of mammals and "game" birds that are killed in moderate or large numbers. For example, when large numbers of foxes were destroyed in Europe, larger litters resulted, and instead of the normal balance of males and females, up to eight females were produced in a family of ten. All wild animals have evolved means of limiting their populations in relation to the food and territory available to them. When combined with decimating factors, such as predation, disease, and severe weather, this helps to prevent serious overpopulations of animal species where a slow natural succession of plant life has been allowed to occur.

There are many examples of wildlife populations adjusting naturally to prevailing environmental conditions. Communal birds are limited in breeding by the number of available nesting sites. The breeding of other birds and territorial animals such as wolves is limited partly by the amount and quality of territory open to them. Even rabbits, which have a high reproductive rate, will reabsorb embryos when their populations are at high levels. There is also evidence that trees and plants have evolved means of preventing excessive browsing. For example, the snowshoe hares of Alaska depend on the availability of tree shoots as a primary source of food. Every ten years the population of Alaskan hares increases dramatically. The large number of hares severely damage their food supply of twigs and small branches of birch, poplar, aspen, and alder. John P. Bryant, a biologist at the University of Alaska, conducted studies of the snowshoe hare and the availability of its food sources during the late 1970s and early 1980s. He found that shoots produced by heavily browsed trees contained exceptionally large quantities of terpene and phenolic resins, which makes them extremely distasteful to snowshoe hares. He also found antibiotics and methylated compounds in some of the shoots. These chemicals contribute to sodium loss, which is a factor in the fatal shock syndrome that brings about the cyclic decline in hare populations.

Like many other mammals, the kangaroos of Australia have the ability to reabsorb embryos during times of high populations. In addition, embryos of kangaroos will remain in a state of arrested development during a dry season when food is scarce. Kangaroos will begin to mate more frequently when grasses appear after a long drought. Dr. Edward Sanders, the leader of a University of Utah research team, found that a chemical in the grasses of spring (6-methoxybenzoxazolinone) tends "to define" when a high-quality food supply will be available to a new generation. Mammals in warmer climates often rely upon the lengthening of the days to begin reproducing. Animals such as voles and lemmings live in climates where the coming of warmer weather does not necessarily mean a rapid increase in food supplies. But the chemical that was isolated by Sanders's research group apparently triggers the reproductive mechanisms of many mammals, particularly those living in cold or dry climates.

More Deer for the Gun

In view of natural population limiting factors, it is apparent that hunting by humans is not needed to maintain relatively ideal populations of any species of wild animal. There have been many excellent books written about natural population limiting factors. Margaret M. Stewart, a professor in the Department of Biological Sciences at the State University of New York at Albany, has compiled a bibliography of forty-five references concerning social control of animal population size and population stress and related phenomena.* Three of the best books about natural population controls (one of which appears in Stewart's bibliography) are *A Natural Regulation of Animal Populations*, By Ian A. McLaren (Lieber-Atherton, 1971), *Growth and Regulation of Animal Populations*, by Lawrence B. Slobodkin (Dover Books, 1980), and *The Natural Regulation of Animal Numbers*, by David Lack, a pioneering book published by Oxford Press in 1954.

R. D. Lawrence, a Canadian naturalist and wildlife biologist, described one form of natural population controls in his book *Paddy*,† a story of an orphan beaver that he raised while camping in the Ontario wilderness. Lawrence cited population control among wolves. If wolves are left undisturbed by man, during times of a high wolf population the dominant (or alpha) female will prevent other females in the pack from mating. She will also have fewer pups than if there had been starvation that resulted in a low wolf population, but where prey species were becoming reestablished, creating a greater potential food supply. If a pack should become too large in relation to its food supplies, young wolves will either leave the pack and join a smaller pack or find wolves of the opposite sex and establish new packs. Lawrence notes that all

---

*Stewart's bibliography has been included in an interesting pamphlet titled *Some Things You're Not Supposed to Know About Hunters, Hunting and "Wildlife Management,"* published by Friends of Animals, Inc.

†*Paddy, A Canadian Naturalist's Story of an Orphan Beaver* (Avon Books, 1977). Discussion of natural population controls, pp. 205 and 206.

species of animals are sensitive to population fluctuations and this leads to the natural regulation of animal numbers. The rule, he says, seems to be birth control during good times and increases in reproductive rates during difficult times when a species has declined. This is Nature's way of ensuring the survival of each species. Lawrence concludes: "These population checks and balances are found among all wild animals, even though they do not always work in the same way."

Dr. Michael Fox is another writer who has studied natural population regulation. Fox, a veterinarian and ethologist who has written more than half a dozen books about wildlife and pets, founded the Institute for the Study of Animal Problems, a division of the Humane Society of the United States.

In an essay titled "Man and Nature: Biological Perspectives,"* he wrote the following about wild animal populations:

> One of the most delicately balanced relationships in nature is that of prey and predator populations. All natural systems are self-regulating, all interspecies relationships (as between moose and wolf, caribou and wolf) and social groups (wolf packs) have naturally evolved self-regulating systems.

Fox explained that without a system of natural checks and balances, prey species would soon exhaust their food supplies. Meanwhile, predators such as foxes, bobcats, and wolves are territorially motivated. By remaining in their respective territories, they prevent a depletion of prey, which would result if there were a large concentration of predators in a certain area.

Fox added:

> Prey and predator species are essentially interlocked, and thousands of generations of evolution bind them in total dependence and harmony. Any form of human intervention (by hunting or poisoning) may have disastrous consequences.

David S. Favre, a professor of wildlife law at Detroit College of Law, has authored an interesting scientific report titled *Surplus Population—A Fallacious Basis for Sport Hunting*.† In it he states:

---

*On the Fifth Day, Animal Rights and Human Ethics, edited by Richard Knowles Morris (Acropolis Books, Ltd. 1978) Chapter 6, "Man and Nature: Biological Perspectives" was contributed by Fox.

†Surplus Population—A Fallacious Basis for Sport Hunting, by Favre and Gretchen Olsen (a researcher with a B.S. in biology from Trinity College, 1979). Copyright 1982 by Society for Animal Rights, Clarks Summit, PA.

. . . while an annual cycle does exist for most game animals, this cycle has existed since the beginning of time and there is no basis to support the claim that sport hunting is required to keep wildlife populations under control.

Wayne Evans, Ph.D, a former assistant director of the State of New Mexico Department of Fish and Game, was more blunt. In a letter to Brandon Reines dated July 26, 1978, he wrote:

> Hunting has never been a necessary adjunct to population control and it is highly dangerous to assume that hunting can act as a "substitute" for any mortality factor. It produces its own set of population characteristics distinct from any other type of mortality factor. Those that claim hunting is a necessary "management tool" for population control are actually referring to its theoretical role in managing a population to achieve a specific goal (i.e., hunting). No one will ever be so rash to claim that if there is no hunting, the population will grow to infinity or sink to extinction. In fact, hunting maximizes fawn production. . . . More animals are produced for the gun.

What did Evans mean when he wrote that hunting "produces its own set of population characteristics distinct from any other type of mortality factor"? This question was answered by Douglas Chadwick, a Montana wildlife biologist and former hunter who spent many years researching wildlife in the Rocky Mountain states. Chadwick, who was quoted by Lewis Regenstein in a position paper titled *The Case Against Hunting*, noted that even where the populations of hunted wildlife remain abundant, intensive hunting may have serious biological repercussions. According to Chadwick:

> Animals are changing in response to our many activities. They are learning, modifying their habits, moving their ranges, and even undergoing physical alteration. Large-scale hunting is a potent agent of biological change. . . . Whenever we kill more members of a population than any other single cause, we become the dominant selective force. This means that the animal will begin to evolve largely in response to us. . . .
> We already know, for example, that heavy hunting pressures on large, palm-antlered moose in Europe led to the appearance of thin cervine, or deer-like, antlers on males within a short time. . . .

A biologist for the Montana Department of Fish and Game, with which Chadwick was once employed, once mentioned to him that a moose herd he had been studying had shown characteristics of increased reproduction as a response to hunting pressure. He also said that mating was being done mostly by young males since there were only a few bulls in the herd more than two or three years old. Chadwick wondered:

What are the genetic consequences of this sort of herd structure? And what becomes of the elaborate social structure? When does an elk herd lose the qualities that make it an elk herd and become something else?

Hunting versus Natural Balance

What would happen if hunting were eliminated in an area that had a high ungulate population? Jack E. Hope, a former hunter, wrote in the January 1974 issue of *The Smithsonian* that the immediate results of a cessation of deer hunting would be "overbrowsing, damage to agricultural crops, starvation and a general deterioration in the health of the herd." But within a few years "the population would stabilize at a new level in balance with the available food supply." Hope wrote that the new herd would probably be genetically superior to that of the hunted herd because nature is more selective in thinning the unfit than the hunter. Hope stated that other native species of animals would move in to fill the vacuum created by the lower deer populations, resulting in a wider variety of species and a better ecological balance.

It is true that *elk* herds have sometimes reached high levels in non-hunted Yellowstone National Park. This has been largely a result of low predator populations and winter feeding programs. (The greater the availability of winter food, the more elk will congregate in areas where food is abundant, leading to less winter mortality and larger herds than would otherwise be the case.)

As a rule, there are greater percentages of starvation among deer and other large herbivores when they are existing in areas with low or nonexistent predator-prey ratios. This is a condition that would at least partially be remedied by the reintroduction of timber wolves and/or panthers and/or cougars. Timber wolves have been reintroduced on a very limited scale into a few wilderness areas of the Rocky Mountains. Experience has shown a decline in winter-killed elk and deer. Furthermore, wolves have kept deer and elk herds on the move, thus contributing to better herd health and a reduction in the number of highly browsed areas.

Hunting Often Does Not Reduce Starvation Percentages

But wouldn't some hunting cause a reduction in the percentage of deer to die of starvation and malnutrition during an ensuring winter? There are times when it might reduce the *number* of potential starvation deaths, but not necessarily the percentage of winter-kill. (The number of winter deaths may be curtailed by hunting simply because a large number of over-populated deer are being removed, leaving more food for those that remain. However, an invasion of hunters for a relatively short time during late autumn increases stress on deer and causes deer to pre-maturely use critical fat reserves that would normally help them to survive during winter.)

Hugh Fosburgh, writing in the July 1972 issue of *Audubon*, noted that winter-kill during the very severe, snowy winter of 1970–71 on the 7,000-acre Baker Tract in the central Adirondacks was about 50 percent, approximately the same as on adjacent state land. But deer are protected on the private tract, and it is estimated that no more than twelve to fifteen deer per year are killed here, mostly as a result of out-of-season poaching. Meanwhile, on state land "deer are shot legally during the hunting season, sometimes by hordes of hunters." Logging on the Baker Tract has created an abundant supply of browse, and this, in combi-nation with other factors, probably including the migration of deer from unprotected lands onto the Baker Tract, has produced a much higher deer population density here than on equal acreage on nearby state land.[6] But while it is true that *more* deer starved per given area on the private preserve, it is *not* true that a greater percentage of the *total number* of deer succumbed to winter-kill.

If there were no such thing as pseudoscientific wildlife management and increased fawning rates, plus different sex ratios of fawns in re-sponse to hunting, then several hunting seasons that resulted in a 40 or 50 percent annual decimation of a herd, when combined with natural deer mortality would seriously endanger the survival of the herd. Yet in some parts of the northeastern United States, there are high deer kills by hunters year after year, with no attempts by state wildlife agencies to drastically reduce the number of hunting licenses they issue. Antler-less deer hunting permits usually *are* regulated, and this is part of the design to keep deer populations at abnormally high levels. A buck sur-viving the winter means one animal for the next hunting season, but the survival of an impregnated doe may mean two or three deer the following fall, depending on whether the doe gives birth to a single fawn or a pair of fawns.

In the Southern Zone of New York State, about 60 percent of the deer herd is killed annually by hunters. This includes approximately 70 percent of the bucks and 30 percent of the does. (Example: Before hunting seasons in a certain area—300 does and 100 bucks, for a total of 400 deer. After hunting seasons—210 does and only 30 bucks, for a total of 240 deer.) This results in an unnaturally large ratio of does to bucks, even taking into consideration the production of a larger percentage of male fawns in areas of high deer population.

According to an article by C. W. Severinghaus and Robert W. Darrow ("The Philosophy of Deer Management"), which appeared in the September-October 1976 issue of *The Conservationist*, the official magazine of the New York State Department of Environmental Conservation:

> Ideally, if the desired number of antlered and antlerless deer are taken each year, the population will comprise the highest number of breeding females and lowest number of adult males that collectively can be supported on the critical winter range. As a result, a maximum fawn crop will be produced each summer.

On this basis, among others, deer management is far from a biologically sound procedure. A single buck may mate with six or eight does, thereby helping to maximize fawn production, in the process insuring deer populations that are higher than would otherwise be the case. But intensive hunting alters the reproductive and behavioral patterns of deer, sometimes drastically.

The Great Swamp Boondoggle

The deer population characteristics that have resulted from the annual hunts at the Great Swamp National Wildlife Refuge in New Jersey are a relatively conservative microcosm of the population trends that result from regulated hunting conducted over much larger geographical areas. During the early 1970s, resource managers began to urge the institution of deer hunting at the refuge. There had been complaints that deer were destroying seedings that had been planted adjacent to the refuge and that "overbrowsing" had resulted in the disappearance from the refuge of the native short-eared and saw-whet owls. Thus, in 1974, over strong objections by animal protection groups, hunting was established in the refuge on a permit basis. Since December 1974, there have been annual deer hunts at the refuge. Each hunter has been allowed to kill one deer of either sex during each hunt.

A person who is unfamiliar with the effects that carefully regulated hunting has upon wildlife populations would probably believe that a substantial permanent reduction in the size of the deer herd at the Great Swamp has occurred as a result of the annual hunts. The actual results have been tabulated by the U.S. Fish and Wildlife Service and appear on the chart on page 85. Note that before hunting was instituted in the Great Swamp, the deer herd, which had peaked at 650, had declined in 1973 and then had risen the following year, but to a level considerably below the high point that had been reached during 1971 and 1972. How did hunting affect the deer population? In the three years after the first hunt, the deer population declined to a prehunt low point of about 375. Then, from 1978 through 1980 the deer herd in the swamp increased dramatically to about 650, the same population level that had been reached during the "peak" years of 1971 and 1972. The following year (1981) saw a decrease in the size of the herd to about 600.

What do these figures indicate? First, they illustrate that deer populations are cyclic. They show that the deer herd in the Great Swamp, both before and after hunting was instituted, would rise to a certain level and then decline, partly in response to lessening food supplies and more crowded conditions. Weather was probably a factor, but not to the extent that it would be in colder climates. Three sets of figures are particularly worthy of note. Both the winter of 1979-80 and the winter of 1980-81 were relatively snow-free. But the deer population increased by only fifty from 1979 to 1980 and *decreased* by about fifty from 1980 to 1981. This is in contrast to the substantial increases in the deer population from 1977 to 1978 and from 1978 to 1979. Both the winters of 1977–78 and 1978–79 were characterized by normal snowfalls. In addition, there were severe ten-day cold spells both in February 1978 and February 1979. The latter was the worst prolonged cold period in almost a decade. There was a period of very severe cold from December 15, 1969 to January 28, 1970. Note that the deer population increased by eighty from the autumn of 1969 to the autumn of 1970. This was before hunting was initiated. Note also that despite an unusually snowy winter during 1970–71, the deer herd remained stable at 650 during both 1971 and 1972. This would tend to suggest that the habitat was in good condition at this time.

There are many factors that influence the population cycles of deer and other wildlife and the Great Swamp deer population table tells many different stories. But anyone who carefully studies the chart will reach a few inevitable conclusions about controlled hunting and its effect upon the deer populations at the Great Swamp Refuge:

1) The maximum number of deer that the Great Swamp will support under most conditions is approximately 650.
2) The sharp rise in the deer population, from a posthunt 269 in December 1977 to a prehunt 500 in 1978, was Nature's way of filling the vacuum created by available territory and plentiful food. These conditions resulted from a low deer population, one that had been declining during the three previous years.
3) The average deer population in the six years prior to the institution of hunting at the Great Swamp was about 585. The average deer population from 1978–81 inclusive was 588! This was after the deer in the swamp had begun to increase their reproductive rates in order to offset the hunting factor. It is not simply that there was more food for *fewer* deer during the winters following hunts in the Great Swamp, and therefore less starvation and a greater percentage of does to bear fawns the following spring, although this was no doubt one factor contributing to higher reproductive rates. Note that the Great Swamp wintered higher deer populations in the years preceding the hunts, years in which there apparently were good browse and favorable habitat conditions and therefore low malnutrition rates. Yet, average population levels were approximately the same as those that occurred *after* hunting had been initiated. It becomes apparent that 585–590 deer is the midpoint in deer population cycles in the Great Swamp *whether or not* the herd is "managed" for hunting! It is important to note that deer of either sex have been legal game during hunts in the Great Swamp. Naturally, most hunters seek out large bucks, but if any type of controlled hunting (aside from shooting does only or killing a larger percentage of does than bucks) resulted in dramatic long-term deer population decreases, it would be the non-selective killing of both bucks and does. (Note that the hunt was *shortened*, rather than lengthened, by two days in 1981, when the deer population had reached a high point the previous year. The number of daily hunters allowed in the refuge remained at 250.)
4) The inescapable conclusion is that deer, like other species of wildlife, will adjust their populations to available food and territory. Hunting alters the innate population controls of wild animals and increases their reproductive rates. Thus regulated hunting succeeds mainly in accomplishing one goal: the perpetuation of hunting.[7]

At the time of this writing in the summer of 1984, wildlife officials are attempting to institute bow hunting of deer at the Great Swamp. This would begin in late September or early October and extend until

Deer Population Statistics at The Great Swamp National Wildlife Refuge
1969–81

(Researchers: Dick Kenly and Bina Robinson)

Year	Approx. Prehunt Population	Number of Deer Killed	Percentage of Herd Killed	Approx. Posthunt Population	Season Length	Number of Daily Hunters
1969	520	NO HUNT				
1970	600	NO HUNT				
1971	650	NO HUNT				
1972	650	NO HUNT				
1973	520	NO HUNT				
1974	570	127	22%	443	6 days	150
1975	456	106	23%	350	6 days	150
1976	385	128	33%	257	6 days	150
1977	375	106	28%	269	6 days	150
1978	500	104	21%	396	6 days	150
1979	600	178	30%	422	10 days	250
1980	650	149	23%	501	10 days	250
1981	600	150	25%	450	8 days	250

early November. The result would be to allow hunters to dominate the "recreational" use of the refuge during autumn. Predictably, a news brief in a 1980 issue of *Sports Afield* claimed that "In few places is a harvestable surplus [of deer] more evident than in the Great Swamp National Refuge." New Jersey is largely metropolitan, with more hunters than can easily utilize public hunting grounds and state forests. Much of rural New Jersey is rapidly being bulldozed for development.

The Vermont Deer Disaster

"Economic expediency" is the term that best describes the underlying reasons behind the decisions of those in charge of state wildlife agencies. But there are times when a person who is unaware of this might believe that the welfare of wildlife populations is sometimes the primary concern of game officials and commercial biologists. This illusion is deceptive. As an example, take the case of the Vermont Department of Fish and Game versus the state's legislature. Traditionally, Vermont hunters have opposed doe hunting, in most cases not because of humanitarian considerations, but because, like hunters elsewhere, they realize that by killing a large percentage of does, the size of a deer herd will be reduced, thereby reducing their chances of hunting "success." Consequently, the Vermont legislature, which until 1979 regulated deer hunting in that state, had established mainly "bucks only" hunting seasons. Since the mid-1920s there had been only six years in which antlerless deer hunting had been allowed during or following the sixteen-day firearms deer season, which is held each November. Four of these years were from 1966 through 1969, when Vermont's deer herd had swelled to an estimated 235,000 animals, or about 28 deer per square mile of suitable habitat, a high population density. During these years the legislature had allowed the Department of Fish and Game to take control of the deer herd on an experimental basis. Archery hunters have been allowed to kill one deer of either sex during years with "bucks only" gunning seasons. But there are only about 13,000 archery hunters in Vermont, and archery hunting has resulted in the annual deaths of less than 1 percent of the total number of does in the state. (This figure is based upon Vermont Department of Fish and Game statistics and does not include does that are wounded by arrows and die of their wounds, but are unclaimed by hunters.)

During the 1970s officials at the Vermont Department of Fish and Game, departing from the friendly relationship that exists in most states between wildlife manipulators and hunting-oriented politicians, engaged in a public relations and lobbying campaign to wrest control of the state's deer herd from the state legislature and be given the authority to reestablish antlerless deer hunting. Biologists cited a deteriorating physical condition of the deer herd, which they said had resulted from traditional "bucks only" hunting. It is true that the killing of bucks exclusively is the most biologically destructive form of controlled deer hunting. Even if does were to adjust their birth rates to 75 percent male fawns in order to compensate for buck losses (there was apparently no evidence of this in Vermont, if one believes biologists' reports), there would still be deleterious biological effects that would result from the hunting of bucks combined with a protection of does. Since as many as 80 percent of mature bucks were killed each season in Vermont, reproductive rates genetically designed to adjust the sex ratio of the herd to one buck for each doe would not be able to keep pace with heavy buck losses. Thus, with "bucks only" hunting, there will be a much greater distortion of the ratio of bucks to does than would be true where hunters annually kill a certain percentage of antlerless deer.

This greatly distorted sex ratio occurred in Vermont. During the 1970s, it was estimated that bucks made up less than 15 percent of Vermont's deer population. According to game biologists, the large number of does in the herd were depleting food reserves during winters. Biologists claimed that the quality of winter browse had been steadily deteriorating. Many does had died of malnutrition and stress, and fawns had been much smaller and weaker than normal. Since hunters had killed mature bucks, younger bucks had mated with does and this also contributed to smaller deer. During the 1970s, mature bucks in Vermont weighed about twenty-five pounds less than those in most other states and antler growth was retarded. Fertility rates of does had dropped because of poor health. This resulted in a smaller deer herd since the deer population had decreased to a level compatible with the existing food supply. There had been high fawn and doe mortality during winters. Doe deaths were due in part to the fact that many does had to feed both themselves *and* their developing embryos. This was Nature's harsh way of reducing the deer population and helping to balance the sex ratio. But annual hunting deaths of a large percentage of bucks will retain a greatly distorted ratio of does to bucks. As the percentage of bucks in a herd slowly decreases, the opportunity for hunters to kill a buck during hunting seasons decreases correspondingly. If hunting were slowly phased out (particularly if a hunting formula were employed that insured increasing doe kills and decreasing buck kills), there would be fewer buck losses, a greater percentage of doe losses, and therefore a gradual return to "normal" reproductive rates and a deer herd approaching a one-to-one sex ratio. (Naturally there would still be annual population fluctuations.)[8]

In view of the aforegoing, it is little wonder that the deer herd in Vermont was in very poor physical condition during the mid- and late 1970s. By the late 1970s, the deer herd had decreased from the high point of a decade earlier to about 120,000. State game biologists said that they had a long-term solution to the problem: the regulated hunting of antlerless deer. Was this a legitimate concern for the welfare of the deer herd or simply a desire to control deer hunting procedures in order to increase the number of reasonably healthy deer for hunters' rifles? In order to find out, let us continue the story as it unfolded during the late 1970s.

During the spring and early summer of 1978, Vermont game biologists prepared a detailed report that predicted gloomy deer hunting prospects for the coming November. Winter-kill had taken a high toll during the cold, snowy winter of 1977–78. In one area, biologists surveyed 2.7 square miles of deer range and claimed to have found 307 dead deer, 70 percent of which were first-year fawns. About half were believed to have starved; the remainder died of the prolonged effects of malnutrition, disease, parasites, or pneumonia—or a combination of these factors. As many as 50,000 deer, or more than 35 percent of the previous autumn's herd, had been decimated. This was the highest rate of winter die-off ever recorded in Vermont.

The high rate of winter mortality was partly a result of geophysical factors. Much of rural Vermont (that which is not within the Green Mountain National Forest) consists of land that has been partly cleared for agricultural purposes, principally dairy farming. There are many idle hay fields, with apple orchards scattered throughout, and many "wild" apple trees at the borders of woodlands. This results in abundant food for deer during the spring, summer, and early autumn. But winter creates completely different conditions. The mostly wooded hills in this agricultural country are of a gently rolling nature, and with an abundance of cleared land, including some partly open plateau areas, there is little protection from strong winter winds. As a result, deer congregate in sheltered areas, often marshes and swamps. In comparison to the rugged forested areas of the Adirondacks, White Mountains, and central and northern Maine, there is little winter shelter for deer in Vermont's agricultural regions. Large groups of deer often crowd together in confined winter yards. Combine this with the largely selective "harvests" of adult bucks, and it is easy to understand the reasons for the abnormally high doe concentrations and unusually high winter die-offs in these areas.

The 1977 Fawn "Crop" Failure

The introduction to the 1978 Vermont Deer Prospects Report states (author's italics):

> Most of the 1977 *fawn crop* is dead. . . . Because yearlings represent nearly half of any season's buck kill . . . the buck kill will drop. Does and the current year's (1978) *fawn crop* form 80% of the archery season kill. Older does represented 30% of the winter loss and *will not be available to archers* in high numbers either.

Lamented Commissioner of Fish and Game Edward F. Kehoe: "The [deer] herd's situation has never been more crucial." Chief Wildlife Biologist Benjamin Day wrote: "We lost the best opportunities to assist the herd to recover during the 1960's; and the job of management, if we are ever given that responsibility, will be a long and hard one."

Statistics in the report cited record "harvests" by hunters during the peak deer populations of the mid-1960s of 18,500, 17,300, and 21,300. The latter figure, for the year 1967, included 4,900 antlerless deer. (It should be noted that even in 1970, after four consecutive years of antlerless deer hunting, does still outnumbered bucks in Vermont by about a five-to-two ratio—evidence of high reproductive rates.) During the years of high deer populations and high "harvests," hunter success rates increased to as high as 13 percent. Since 1967, both the number of bucks killed by hunters and the success rates, while fluctuating, had shown a definite downward trend. In 1973, only 8,500 bucks were killed, with a success rate of 6.2 percent. It becomes apparent that when only bucks are "harvested," increased reproductive rates will compensate for these "harvests" only so far and then something must give, usually the amount and quality of forage, usually the size of the herd, and often herd health. Yet even during population low points, herds in heavily hunted areas of Vermont were probably larger than would have been true most years if there had been well-balanced natural ecosystems and no deer hunting.

The biologists' report contained the following revelation:

> . . . It is interesting to note that the [reproductive] rates observed for 3 year and older does were higher in 1972 than those found in the 1960s. [When the size of the deer herd had been considerably larger.—R.B.]. These does produced fawns at a higher rate even though forage conditions had not noticeably improved, but the total wintering deer population was much less due to mass starvation in the winters of 1969 through 1971.

89

The year 1969, it will be remembered, was the last of four years in which there had been regulated hunting of antlerless deer in Vermont. If anyone believes that this form of hunting is a panacea for decreasing winter mortality rates, he or she might be surprised to learn of "mass starvation" during one winter of the period when antlerless deer hunting was being undertaken and an additional winter that followed this management procedure. The report writer surmised that the increase in reproductive rates of older does may have been due to "the lessened competition for food, even poor quality food." The increased reproductive rates at a time of lessened winter deer populations *was* an interesting observation—interesting and rather obvious in view of deer reproductive characteristics—but not a hopeful sign for a department whose members are seeking the regulation of deer hunting. Therefore, it should come as no surprise that the report writer hastily followed by stating that (authors italics) *"preliminary information* from reproductive surveys *currently under way* indicate that Vermont does have dropped back to the lower fawning rates found in the mid1960s." If this had been true, it would have indicated a potential for further decline in the size of the deer herd at this "crucial" juncture in the management of Vermont's herd.

There was sufficient evidence to indicate that the record deer dieoff during the winter of 1977–78 had resulted in a relatively small, if unhealthy, herd during the summer of 1978. Alluding to this, Senior Wildlife Biologist Lawrence E. Garland concluded in the report:

> Hunting season results are expected to be poor enough to cause widespread hunter dissatisfaction. A call for remedial action by the Department and State Legislature is likely.

The army of hunters versus the small number of bucks resulted in the outcome that had been predicted. During November 1978, fewer than 8,300 bucks were "harvested." This proved to be the second lowest deer kill in Vermont in twenty-five years. According to a news report on Burlington radio station WVMT, "Vermonters were shocked by this year's low deer kill."

Many hunters wanted to know why there were so few [buck] deer.[9] Fish and Game officials blamed it on "the years of mis-management by the state legislature." According to a state game biologist, "Naturally we would have liked to have seen a much greater harvest, but considering what the state's deer herd has been through during the past decade, we're lucky to have harvested eight thousand."

90

Milford K. Smith, an outdoor writer for the *Rutland Herald*, wrote in his column of November 27, 1978:

> The deer herd in Vermont has suffered a tragic loss in numbers. . . . Deer need just as much management as a herd of cattle in a farm pasture. . . . The first step that should be taken is to return the management of deer to the experts in the Fish and Game Department.

Where, he might have added, they would receive the conscientious attention of professional resource managers. Smith stated that hunters should rethink the "limited doe season question." And he wrote that Vermont was slowly becoming reforested, creating less than ideal browse conditions for deer, which theretofore had lived mainly on habitat consisting of a combination of woods and open land. According to Smith:

> Proper management can result in a stabilization of the deer population, possibly of smaller size than at present but with large individuals. Otherwise, we could expect to see more deer dead of starvation in the spring, and less deer to hunt in the fall.

Smith did not mention that deer annually suffer tragic losses in numbers as a result of unnecessary hunting. A person might wonder how deer as a species had managed to survive quite well in natural surroundings for at least several hundred thousand years prior to their decimation by hunters during the Nineteenth Century, prior to man's habitat destruction, environmental contamination, and economically motivated deer management schemes. Other facts worth considering: Forested terrain may not be "ideal" habitat for large numbers of deer. But reforestation, either by man or Nature, usually results in smaller deer herds, whose numbers are determined by the ability of their habitat to support them. Naturally, many hunters would be interested in "larger individuals." As for deer starvation, there are no wolves or panthers known to exist in Vermont. (There have been a few unconfirmed sightings of "catamounts.") Coyotes are usually shot on sight by hunters, particularly if a hunter happens to be a sheep farmer.

The *Herald* quoted Commissioner Kehoe, who said, "We have got to manage the deer herd the same as anything else. It is up to biologists to determine areas where there might be overcrowding and grant permission to hunt does."

Forty-two Million Dollars in Humanitarian Aid

After much lobbying and after many heated discussions among hunters who opposed doe hunting, those who favored it, members of the Vermont legislature, and wildlife officials, the legislature in 1979 voted to relinquish its control of the state's deer herd. Now the responsibility for developing a theoretically sound deer management plan was in the hands of the Vermont Fish and Game Department. During the winter of 1978–79, snow depths in Vermont were not as great as they had been the previous winter. The size of the deer herd, while still much smaller than during most years, was estimated to be larger than in 1978. Thus, if the recovery of the deer herd was the foremost objective of the department, one would expect the issuance of a very limited number of buck hunting licenses. Combined with a correspondingly large number of anterless deer hunting permits, closures in some areas of low deer population where there was sufficient browse to last the winter, and possibly a shortened hunting season for bucks, this would have been a management scheme that would have been relatively selective and would have resulted in a more equal sex ratio within the deer herd.

But the Fish and Game Department attempted to do none of these things. What were the reasons? First is the obvious fact that the department obtains much of its operating revenue from the sale of hunting licenses. Equally important is the fact that there were and, as of 1984, still are *no big game licenses* in Vermont. The Department of Fish and Game issues a resident hunting license, which entitles the holder to hunt *all* legal "game" species. It also issues a nonresident hunting license (for all legal game) and a nonresident small game license. This means that, even if game officials had wanted to do so, they could not have reduced the number of licenses sold to "bucks only" deer hunters as an effective management procedure, since there was no way to regulate hunting license sales without affecting the hunting of small game. (The vast majority of resident hunters in Vermont who hunt small game also hunt deer.) With the issuance of anterless deer hunting permits, this meant that game officials were able to *increase*, but not decrease, the potential number of deer to be killed during 1979 (unless, by some very unlikely circumstance, the sales of combination big and small game hunting licenses had decreased drastically from 1978 to 1979). In fact, the sales of resident hunting licenses *had* been steadily declining during the five years prior to 1979. In 1974 about 155,000 were sold, and by 1978 the number was down to approximately 130,000. The hunting of anterless deer assures a greater chance of a "kill" for those who want to place their name in the Vermont state lottery, which determines who will receive permits on a priority basis at ten and fifteen dollars a permit for resident and nonresident hunters, respectively. If a hunter is opposed to doe hunting, he need not apply. And why change the license system to restrict sales when hunting license fees are a major source of revenue?

But is it not true that since hunting is an entrenched practice, wildlife biologists have no choice but to operate within the confines of hunter-oriented game management, that even if they wanted to do so they could not phase out hunting and substitute natural predation? This is very true, and this lies at the root of the biological and ecological problems that result from the present system of wildlife mismanagement! But a desire to return to unhunted, natural ecosystems is not one of the "weaknesses" of wildlife officials and most commercial biologists! To the dubious credit of those concerned, no one was so brash as to suggest that the proposal to kill antlerless deer in Vermont had been motivated by a concern for the welfare of the deer herd.

Naturally, if there had been buck hunting licenses in Vermont, there would have been the usual economic arguments against a decrease in the issuance of such licenses. A reporter for the *Rutland Herald*, commenting on the low 1978 deer kill, claimed that the recovery of the deer herd "is an important economic [issue]. About $84 million is estimated to be spent by hunters for licenses, food, liquor and other goods during the 16-day season." Edward W. Cronin, Jr., an independent research biologist, combined humanitarian considerations with economics. In an article titled "Doe Harvest" in the November 1979 issue of *Country Journal*, he summed up the case for doe hunting in Vermont with the following observation (author's italics):

> For the most basic humanitarian reasons, our society has a responsibility to stop the needless suffering the deer endure. In addition, deer hunting brings in an estimated 42 million dollars into the state's economy each year and the deer herd *must be protected* to insure this important monetary contribution.

Apparently the *Herald* reporter and Cronin obtained their economic statistics from different sources, but in all probability both figures are inflated many times over, since they were presumably compiled by state agencies, which have, as their first priority, the perpetuation of activities which bring revenue into Vermont.

Notwithstanding the fact that hunting is an established practice, it is significant, at least from an ecological perspective, that everyone that has been quoted with respect to the condition of the deer herd in Vermont during the late 1970s (a game official, two state biologists, an independent biologist, a newspaper reporter, and a hunting-fishing-trapping columnist) apparently *assumed* that some form of deer hunting would be the only possible solution to the condition of Vermont's deer herd. This is no more than might be expected, but one would be justified in asking whether *any* form of hunting would have been a sound solution to the health of the deer herd in Vermont or anywhere else. Ethical considerations aside, and despite the certitudes uttered by game managers, a person might ask whether it is intelligent, or even logical, to advocate continued annual hunting as a solution to a problem that has been caused by hunting. One form of hunting, the killing of bucks, had been responsible for the Vermont deer disaster. To support another form of annual hunting as a cure (in which a certain percentage of does and fawns of either sex would be killed) is not unlike calling in Satan to perform a series of exorcisms. One dangerous practice is done away with, and another potentially dangerous practice is initiated. We have seen how deer management by the use of antlerless deer hunting permits perpetuates recreational hunting. The fact that surviving deer may be in slightly better physical condition when deer of either sex are killed is a matter of expediency, not a concern for the welfare of deer.

Apparently it occurred to few people that a phasing out of hunting combined with a reintroduction of large predators in nonagricultural areas where there is sparse human population would have been the ultimate solution to the deer situation in Vermont during the late 1970s. At least if anyone suggested this, it was not taken seriously by those in positions of power. It should be noted that approximately 47 percent of male Vermonters between the ages of eighteen and fifty are hunters, and most are deer hunters. The percentage is much higher in rural areas.

The Herd Declines

Two relatively snowless winters during 1979–80 and 1980–81 helped to increase the size of the deer herd in Vermont. The first of these winters was unusually mild. As a result, the 1980 "harvest," including antlerless deer, totaled nearly 25,000. Then the deer kills began to decline. In 1981 the Vermont kill dropped to 17,000 despite relatively light snows the previous winter. The following year, only 8,000 deer were killed by Vermont hunters. Many hunters blamed the shooting of does for the low 1982 deer kill. Officials at the Vermont Fish and Game Department blamed other factors: mild, snowless weather during all but the final three days of the hunting season; an estimated 27,000 deer that had starved (that's right, *starved!*) during the previous winter; increasing forestation in parts of Vermont; increased commercial development; and the large number of deer that were believed to have been killed by dogs the previous winter. (Trails that have been compacted by snowmobiles make excellent runways for dogs, and snowmobile use is rampant in rural Vermont.) It is possible that stress resulting from the noise of nearby snowmobiles contributed to the large number of winter deer deaths in Vermont and what has been, despite annual population fluctuations, a generally declining herd since the early 1970s. As for starvation, antlerless deer hunting had been in effect for two seasons prior to the high 1981–82 winter-kill. Like the high starvation rates reported by game biologists during the late 1960s and early 1970s at a time when the deer herd was supposedly in better balance with its habitat because of antlerless deer hunting, the 1981–82 die-off is evidence that this type of hunting has little effect on percentages of deer to succumb to malnutrition-related ailments.

On December 19, 1982, Gary W. Moore, who had replaced Edward F. Kehoe as Vermont fish and game commissioner, said in a televised interview that it would be unfair to blame antlerless deer hunting for the poor "harvest" of November 1982. Moore said that two counties in which there had never been antlerless deer hunting had shown a decline in "harvests" of 50 percent from the previous year. He also stated that there had been low deer kills in Vermont even before the institution of antlerless deer hunting. (This was an interesting comment because during most years of "bucks only" hunting in Vermont legal bucks were outnumbered by protected does by at least four or five to one.)

What were the real reasons behind the decreasing deer kills during three years of antlerless deer hunting? No doubt some or all of the factors that were cited by the Fish and Game department were partly responsible. It is equally likely that other, perhaps more significant, factors were at work. One possibility is that game biologists overreacted and that too many antlerless deer hunting permits were issued, resulting in doe kills that were too great for the herd to easily sustain. A second possibility is that the Vermont deer herd in 1979 was already in such poor condition that the additional doe and fawn kills resulted in a drastically reduced deer population due to hunting losses and winter mortality. A third possibility is that as of 1982, the deer herd in Vermont had not had sufficient time to begin readjusting its reproductive patterns to compensate for doe "harvests." You will recall that the deer herd in New Jersey's Great Swamp declined for the first three years after hunting had been instituted and then began to increase during the fourth year. Under good browse conditions, pseudoscientific deer management through the issuance of antlerless deer hunting permits will result in abnormally high deer populations. Game biologists in Vermont claim that winter browse in that state is still in poor condition—little wonder in view of the deer disaster of the late 1970s, a condition that was caused in no small part by recreational hunting!

A spokesperson summed up the sentiments of those in the Vermont Fish and Game Department when he said that "we are very disappointed by the low [1982] deer kill." Meanwhile, Commissioner Moore expressed opposition to antlerless deer hunting in 1983.* Whether or not his department's solution to the poor health of Vermont's deer will prove to be a cure worse than the disease remains to be seen. The only way to describe the deer situation that exists and has existed for many years in Vermont is that it is a colossal mess. Any form of deer "management" that is designed primarily to provide hunters with live targets will not have beneficial effects either for deer or their environment. Considering the biology of deer and experience at other locations such as the Great Swamp, it is doubtful whether a permit system for hunting antlerless deer will ever contribute to substantially improved health of deer in Vermont. But if it does there will be slightly healthier deer only *for hunters' guns*.

The State Parks Giveaway

Sometimes the starvation argument is used in ways, and under circumstances, that make it particularly suspect. During 1976 the New York State Department of Parks and Recreation and the Environmental Conservation Department, after nine public hearings, which were attended mostly by organized hunters, opened sixty parks to deer hunting. These represented roughly a third of New York's parks. Soon afterward a suit was filled by Friends of Animals, Inc. But in September 1981, New York State Supreme Court justice John Jones ruled that all legal requirements had been met. He also decreed that Friends of Animals had no legal right to sue since it could not prove that it was an "aggrieved" party. (In July 1981, the U.S. Supreme Court had issued its infamous "clamming decision," which ruled, in effect, that individuals or groups cannot sue federal or state governments, or private industries, to protect wildlife.)

A spokesman for New York State parks commissioner, Ohrin Lehman, said that hunting in some state parks had been undertaken on the premise that it was more humane than allowing hundreds of deer to starve in areas of high deer concentration. "Where there is a deer management problem and where it is safe, we will continue to use hunting as a way of limiting the deer population," Lehman's spokesman said.

Interestingly, it was during 1976 that the New York State DEC added an extra weekend to Northern Zone deer seasons. (During most years

*The Vermont Fish and Game Department did not issue antlerless deer hunting permits for the 1983 deer season.

there are seldom more than twelve to fifteen deer per square mile in much of the Adirondacks—more during summer and early autumn, fewer during winter and early spring.) In 1975 the DEC had instituted an early Northern Zone bear hunting season. This had increased bear hunting in this part of the state from six to eleven weeks.[10] In 1977 an early Northern Zone muzzle-loader season for deer and bear was established. (Only about 3,000 to 4,000 bears exist over a 16,000 square mile area.)

What was curious about the timing of these events? The years 1974–77 were a period of rampant inflation and layoffs of state employees in many states—including New York. These included layoffs and threatened layoffs of Fish and Wildlife personnel. The economy "bottomed out" during the winter of 1975–76, when New York State's unemployment rolls swelled to more than 11¼ percent of the work force, the highest state unemployment rate since The Great Depression. This was preceded and followed by frantic attempts by state agencies in New York and elsewhere to increase their revenue. In New York there was little lengthening of hunting seasons, establishment of new seasons, or opening of new lands to hunting before the spiraling inflation of the early 1970s and the gasoline "shortages" of 1973–74, which helped to fuel the rate of inflation. (The continual lengthening of hunting seasons "mandates" increased management activities and creates more work for employees of wildlife agencies—in this case the New York State Division of Fish and Wildlife. The result is increased job security, since wildlife officials can point to the "important" work that is being done. Meanwhile, hunters are satisfied and the killing continues.)

The period 1974–77 was a time of increasing controversy in New York State over the granting of $10,000 bonuses, or "Lulu's," to senior members of the state senate and assembly. These Lulu's were never abolished. While it would be difficult to conclusively prove, it is not unlikely that the increased hunting opportunities granted in New York, and in many other states, during the early to mid-1970s and thereafter were attempts to increase revenue and shore up state economies on the backs of white-tailed deer and other wildlife. After all, taxpaying citizens, including hunters, have a recourse. They can vote politicians out of office. Deer and other animals do not have this option. Neither can deer use the courts to gain freedom from harrassment by humans. But they may wish that they could.

The Harriman Park Battle

Officials of the New York State Parks Commission and the Division of Fish and Wildlife have continued their campaign to open state parks

97

to hunters. They have usually succeeded but they lost the battle of Harriman Park. In 1981 the DEC received permission from the state legislature to conduct the first deer hunt in the history of the park, which is thirty miles northwest of New York City. Since the late 1970s, DEC officials had been attempting to open the park to deer hunting. As usual in such cases, biologists had cited high deer populations and an increase in deer-automobile collisions. But before the first hunt began in 10,000 acres of the 52,000-acre park, Glenn Cole, a biologist for the Division of Fish and Wildlife who helped to implement the deer-management plan for the park, said that the number of does that would be killed would be only about half the number of bucks killed—a poor way to reduce a deer population!

Shortly before the hunt was scheduled to begin in November 1981, volunteer lawyers for Luke Dommer's Committee to Abolish Sport-Hunting sought a court order barring the hunt. They argued that there had been inadequate research into the potential environmental impact of hunting at the park, which already had been receiving very heavy recreational use, especially during the summer months. An appeals court granted an injunction that interrupted the hunt and called the hunters out of the woods on the afternoon of the first day. One week later the appeal was lost and the hunt resumed for two weeks, with a total of seventy-four deer killed. Most of the deer that were taken were large, and few showed any outward signs of malnutrition or poor health. According to Dommer, a wildlife biologist at a weighing station at Harriman Park was jotting information about an eight-point buck that a hunter had killed on November 25, 1981 when the biologist commented, apparently with tongue-in-cheek, "This deer has been starving to death for ten years."

An attempt by C.A.S.H. to stop the 1982 deer hunt in the park proved fruitless. But then something happened that can only be described as a miracle. In late January 1983, the Palisades Interstate Park Commission, after considering additional arguments by opponents of the Harriman Park hunt, voted four to one to suspend the hunts for three years, at which time state biologists would estimate the size of the deer herd and redetermine the feasibility of hunting. Prior to the commission's vote, DEC biologists had been forced to drastically revise their estimates of the size of the Harriman deer herd from 3,350 to 1,600, based upon biological data and the numbers of deer that had been shot by hunters during 1981 and 1982. Even this assessment may have been high. (Dommer estimated only about 600 deer in the park, based upon information that was available.)

The biologists' new estimates were particularly significant since only

122 deer had been killed during the two hunts. Therefore the size of the previously unhunted herd had not been substantially reduced as a direct result of hunting. Even more significant is that state biologists had claimed during the summer of 1982 that deer were destroying the understory of the park (most of which is mature forest containing little natural browse—not the kind of habitat that will support a high deer population). The biologists had recommended hunting throughout the park, and this almost certainly would have occurred had not C.A.S.H. fought the hunt.

According to the *New York Times* (January 30, 1983), Nathaniel R. Dickinson, big game unit leader for the New York State Division of Wildlife, termed the park commission's decision to stop the deer hunts a "cave-in," and said that there are "far too many deer" in the park. But the commission conducted a helicopter survey of deer throughout the previously hunted area. With excellent visibility on snow, only thirty-five deer were counted and very few tracks were seen. Luke Dommer, claiming "a great victory," said afterward that it would probably be "a long time" before hunting is reinstituted at Harriman Park. The two hunts had cost New York State taxpayers more than $30,000. Unfortunately, a large percentage of New York State's parks remain open to hunting, including sizable Allegany State Park in the southwestern part of the state.

Since the late 1960s, wildlife officials in New York have become increasingly concerned about the dramatic increase in the amount of posted private rural land in the southeastern part of the state. Thus, while the numbers of hunters were slowly increasing, the amount of land available for them to hunt had been steadily decreasing. This was no doubt an important reason—or *the* reason—for opening state parks to hunters.

The Hunting Preserve Premise

The starvation argument is brought into clearer perspective when one considers that the wildlife agencies of many states maintain public hunting grounds. In New York State these are called wildlife management areas. On these lands wildlife is maintained for the sole purpose of providing hunters with live targets. According to a brochure published by the New York State DEC, WMAs in that state "are developed and managed primarily for wildlife and as public hunting grounds. Hunters using these units will see the emphasis that is placed on the development of wildlife food and cover." A person could dispute the claim that these areas are being managed "for wildlife," since ecosystems are artificially manipulated to improve hunting opportunities. In view of the net result, it is academic whether it was anyone's intent that WMAs be established for the welfare of wildlife. Animals in these areas are not fed and sheltered for their well-being, as would be true in a private sanctuary. Game managers seek to make conditions in WMAs hospitable for the greatest number of healthy game animals in order to satisfy the greatest number of hunters, a far cry from saving animals from starvation.

Even more revealing is a bulletin that was published by the New York State DEC and distributed on August 17, 1980. It stated in part (author's italics):

> Deer hunters in New York State got some excellent news this week from Robert F. Flacke, Commissioner of Environmental Conservation. There will be larger quotas, smaller group sizes in many DMU's (deer management units). . . . Deer populations *have been allowed to increase* in many DMU's. It is now necessary to harvest a larger number of animals to effect population stability or reduction. Deer numbers must be kept in balance with range carrying capacity and at levels compatible with man's use of the land. . . . In some Catskill units two relatively mild winters have contributed to population increases.

This is an incredible observation, since the report writer first states that deer populations have been allowed to increase and then claims that the expanded herd must be controlled. The inference is that a lack of sufficient "harvests" by hunters has been largely responsible for the population increase, and many people believe this, but *not* the wildlife officials who manipulate deer populations!

According to wildlife officials and game biologists, peak deer populations are a threat to deer habitat, orchards, and farm crops. (And they sometimes are, thanks mainly to wildlife officials and game biologists!) Therefore, according to game management rationale, increased numbers of deer must be "harvested." When deer populations decline, as they will sooner or later (with or without hunting), biologists often point to the numbers of winter-killed "surplus" deer as evidence that hunters did not "harvest" enough of them. Fewer deer may be more difficult for hunters to locate in rugged, forested areas such as the Adirondacks and Catskills. So, rather than reducing the number of big game licenses, effecting closures, or shortening or cancelling hunting seasons, wildlife officials continue their attempts to increase the number of hunters and the sale of hunting licenses. Sometimes the New York State DEC, through promotional literature, the media, and speaking engagements at fish and game clubs, attempts to direct hunters to areas of highest deer concentration or lowest hunter utilization.

The solution that wildlife officials often propose to potential deer starvation may be summarized thusly: 1) entice greater numbers of hunters into the woods through publicity in state publications and press releases; 2) open new public lands to hunting if feasible; 3) try to persuade rural landowners who have posted their property to open their lands to hunting; and 4) if possible, steadily lengthen hunting seasons in order to insure increased "recreation" time and the potential for greater hunting license sales. Heads the hunters win; tails the whitetails lose.

One solution to the deer "population explosion" in New York State during 1980 was to initiate a deer-of-either-sex season during the one-week muzzle-loader hunt in the state's Northern Zone. A DEC pamphlet assures hunters (author's italics):

> Many factors were considered in selecting the open area for this season. First, care was taken to avoid creating an imbalance in the opportunity to take deer. Since the deer and bear population in this area is *underutilized*, it is unlikely that many animals will be taken which would ordinarily be taken during the regular season. Hunting pressure and harvest during this season do not conflict with management designs. There are few conflicts with landowner desires due to the length of season or numbers of hunters.

The DEC publicity writer tells citizens that there are no conflicts between hunters and landowners during the one-week muzzle-loader season. He or she neglects to mention that this preliminary round is followed by six or seven weeks of rifle hunting for deer.* It becomes obvious that the DEC was seeking to increase public interest in hunting by diversifying hunting procedures, in the process gaining increased revenue from hunting licenses and from muzzle-loader stamps, which are required for this type of hunting. There continues to be increasing interest in the Northern Zone muzzle-loader season, since those wishing to shoot deer with primitive weapons have a one-week early advantage over those using high-powered rifles.[11]

Referring to the Southern Zone hunting season for deer and bear, the DEC pamphlet explained (author's italics):

> . . . The number of [deer management] permits has been greatly increased. In fact, for the first time it has become necessary in eight units to drop to a group size of one. *This has been done to achieve an adequate number of applications for available permits.*

---

*The early muzzle-loader deer season is becoming increasingly popular among Adirondack hunters, so much so that by 1983 some hunters in isolated sections of the Adirondacks were shooting deer with high-powered rifles during the time when only muzzle-loaders are legally allowed for deer hunting.

The author of the pamphlet admitted that "[our] policy is to achieve desired harvests and to involve the most number [sic] of hunters."

Optimum Is Insufficient

If there remains any doubt in anyone's mind about the objectives of "starvation"-related deer management, it should be noted that during the 1977 session of the New York State legislature a bill was passed that authorized that state's Division of Fish and Wildlife through the year 1981 to "designate . . . special Northern Zone deer management areas whenever it finds that deer numbers therein are chronically *below* range carrying capacity and it is desirable to increase deer numbers by releasing trapped and transferred deer from areas of over population. . . ." (author's italics)

Fortunately, this plan proved unworkable. According to New York State senior wildlife biologist Gary B. Will: "Besides not being practical, [relocating deer] is extremely expensive. We captured and relocated a couple dozen deer . . . at a cost of approximately $1,000 per deer. To say the least, we are not doing this now!"

Will neglected to mention that during fiscal 1980 the vast majority of the $15.2 million fish and wildlife management allocation to the Division of Fish and Wildlife was channeled into projects that were similar to the trapping and transfer of deer. Examples? They included muskellunge studies, bear tagging and release, fisher trap and transfer from the Adirondacks to the Catskills (to "control" porcupines and then to be trapped by humans), transfer of wild turkeys, transfer of Hungarian partridge, and stocking of trout and salmon in Lake Ontario.[12] (There was also the culmination of a four-year study of waterfowl zoning that produced the noteworthy decision to maintain existing zones!) Naturally, deer are difficult to capture and they are not artificially propagated, as are fish, "game" birds, and small to medium-sized mammals such as marten. Therefore the exhorbitant cost. Even in the absence of deer stocking, the New York State Division of Fish and Wildlife managed to overspend its fiscal 1980 fish and wildlife management appropriation by some $450,000.

Will had the following to say about limited antlerless deer hunting that is designed to maintain high "harvests" while insuring maximum numbers of deer:

In 1960 this technique or tool in wildlife management was considered theoretical. Today it is an accepted and successful prac-

102

tice copied by many states. It has produced tremendous benefits to sportsmen, business people and many others interested in observing deer. Considering the positive economic, recreational and biological advantages this concept seems almost unparalleled in today's management of wildlife.

Will wrote that in cases of a low overall deer population in which some wintering areas had been severely overbrowsed, his suggestion would be to "manage" deer on a unit basis (that is, by geographical location). According to Will, the purpose would be to allow "regeneration of habitat":

Saving these deer will prolong the suffering, increase the habitat destruction, and *maintain the deer at a low population over a longer period of time.* Please remember that winter mortality is a result of too little food for too many animals. [author's italics]

Certainly no one would accuse Will of not attempting to "utilize as many animal resources as possible."[13]

A related subject is worthy of note. The National Shooting Sports Foundation, Inc., publishes a brochure titled *The Hunter and Conservation.* In a section titled "Facts About Wildlife," it is asserted:

Research shows that a healthy deer herd, reasonably sized for good habitat, can be reduced each year by as much as 40 percent with no ill effect on future population. Yet, in most of our states, hunters rarely harvest more than fifteen percent.

Many people would dispute the latter figure. At any rate, either the NSSF writer was unacquainted with New York State game management practices or else DEC officials have not read the "facts" cited by the NSSF. Officials of the New York State Division of Fish and Wildlife have often claimed that the sparsely populated, economically depressed Adirondacks are "underharvested" despite a low deer population and an annual "harvest" rate of about 30 percent of the adult bucks. Average annual "harvests" in the Catskills are about 40 percent of the herd, including does, and in agricultural central and southwestern New York 50 to 60 percent, including does. Since deer populations in the Adirondacks are at consistently low levels, a person might wonder why game managers would consider a greater "harvest" in this region to be necessary. (At least a person who is unfamiliar with wildlife management practices might wonder.)

The Maximum Sustained Yield Syndrome

The *coup de grâce* to deer management in New York State was delivered by regional wildlife manager Terry Moore. The Olean (New York) *Times-Herald* of September 30, 1978 quoted Moore as stating that in order to increase the success rates of big game hunters, "we will attempt to increase the number of deer until we experience high incidences of deer-car collisions, depredation of agricultural crops becomes intolerable and/or the effects on deer habitat begin to result in deterioration."

Two years later, on September 8, 1980, according to a *New York Times* story by Harold Fabor, the chief of the New York State Division of Wildlife, Stuart Free, exclaimed in mock horror, "We've got deer coming out of our ears. The herds have expanded to the point where they can do irreparable damage to farm crops and the winter range that supports them." Free said that the number of party permits would be nearly doubled to more than 110,000. Permits would allow groups to shoot one more deer of either sex than the number of people in the party.[14]

As noted in the August 1980 DEC bulletin, the deer herd had indeed "been allowed to increase." There had been many complaints from farmers and fruit growers in upstate New York that deer had been eating in cornfields, hay fields, and orchards. Warren Smith, of the Cooperative Extension Service in Ulster County, received many reports of excessive damage to fruit trees in Dutchess, Columbia, and Ulster Counties. "It's a very serious problem," he said. Marty Zimmerman, a fruit grower in Clintondale in Ulster County, could not prevent deer from eating almost all the new growth in a sixty-acre apple orchard he had planted a year before. He was forced to purchase a special seven-foot high, slanted electrical fence in an attempt to protect his trees.

More than 150,000 deer were killed during the hunting seasons in New York State in 1980, and the following year, on the heels of another relatively open winter, a record 166,000 died as a result of the bullet or the arrow. After the 1981 deer kill had been tabulated, a spokesperson for the DEC said that the record talley was "good news for conservationists, landowners and hunters" because, as the spokesperson phrased it, "the DEC has been trying to control a rapidly rising state deer population."

Then, in July 1982, the DEC announced that it would issue nearly 250,000 party permits to hunters that autumn. This would virtually assure a third consecutive record deer kill in New York State. Predictably, DEC officials claimed that their intent was to reduce the size of the state's deer herd. (As previously noted, antlerless deer hunting in New

York State, including bow hunting, has usually resulted in the annual deaths of less than one-third of the doe population, since about 20 percent of the antlerless deer that are killed are male fawns.)

According to a report in an August 1982 issue of the Albany *Times-Union*, Clark E. Pell, an official of the Division of Fish and Wildlife, said that without the expanded hunt, thousands of deer would probably starve to death during the winter. Pell admitted that there had been "a deliberate attempt on our part to increase the deer population through management programs. But we didn't think the population would reach these levels."

The DEC could not be accused of shirking its responsibilities. The Division of Fish and Wildlife established a seven-day muzzle-loader season in the state's Southern Zone in 1982, again ostensibly in an attempt to reduce the number of deer in that area. This was an interesting claim because only bucks with antlers at least three inches long would be legal game. Furthermore, by the time the antique weapons hunt was to begin in mid-December, many of the bucks that had not been killed during the preceding three-week rifle hunt would have shed their antlers. (Studies have shown that antler shedding begins in New York State about December 1.) Since about 70 percent of the mature bucks would already have been killed by the end of the rifle season, what was the purpose of establishing a muzzle-loader season? And if it were established, why not schedule it *prior to* the rifle season, as was done in the state's Northern Zone?

One reason for the late muzzle-loader season was apparently to avoid greater posting of land by rural landowners in the Southern Zone, which might result from an influx of early deer hunters. In addition, there would not be the conflicts with large numbers of rifle and shotgun hunters that would result from antique weapons hunters invading the woods a week before *they* were legally allowed to shoot a deer. These factors were probably considered when scheduling the muzzle-loader season. But there were undoubtedly two other important reasons for initiating the muzzle-loader hunt and scheduling it directly after the firearms deer season. For several years, DEC officials, claiming insufficient funds to carry out their programs, had been attempting to convince hunters and state legislators that there was a need to increase the cost of hunting, fishing, and trapping licenses. In 1981 the state legislature voted down a proposal, backed by the DEC, that would have raised license fees and given state taxpayers the option to donate part of their refund to the Division of Fish and Wildlife as a "gift to wildlife."*

*This proposal passed during the 1982 session of the New York State legislature and was signed into law by then-governor Hugh Carey.

Therefore, during the autumn of 1981, the Division of Fish and Wildlife, apparently in an attempt to impress members of the legislature of their dire financial straits and to irritate rural landowners and add their voices to the push for higher license fees, limited the travel of state game wardens to thirty miles. (DEC officials claimed it was to conserve gasoline and vehicle expense.) This policy resulted in reduced policing efficiency and a much greater than normal incidence of jacklighting and shooting deer prior to the opening of legal seasons. The bill that was to increase the cost of existing licenses and create new types of hunting and fishing licenses was signed by then-governor Hugh Carey in mid-1982. The Southern Zone muzzle-loader hunt not only increased the number of muzzle-loader stamps sold (at five dollars a stamp), but added *an extra week* of gun hunting for deer in New York State. During 1982 gun hunting for deer began in the Northern Zone on October 16 with the early muzzle-loader season and ended with the post–rifle season muzzle-loader hunt in the Southern Zone, which concluded on December 21.

Hard Winter and High Harvests

There can be no doubt that there were a greater than average number of deer in New York State during 1982. According to DEC estimates, the size of that state's deer herd had increased from about half a million in 1980, to 600,000 in 1981, to 650,000 in 1982. The "ideal" size of the deer herd for the available habitat was calculated to be 450,000.[15] (You will recall that many farmers in agricultural regions of New York State had complained about excessive crop and orchard damage by deer during the summer of 1980, when the state's deer herd was only 50,000 above the "ideal" population.)

By the summer and early autumn of 1982, deer damage in agricultural New York State had become acute. According to the *Buffalo Evening Tribune* of August 10, 1982, Edwin Crist, chairman of the state Farm Bureau's Eastern Fresh Fruit Committee, said, "This is far and away the worst year we ever had with the deer." C. Clifford Lasher, a Selkirk farmer who had lost an estimated $3,000 in crops to deer during 1981, lamented, "I just don't know where to put my crops to keep them safe." At that time Stuart Free explained, "In the past couple of years, the winters haven't been severe enough or the harvests [by hunters] high enough." The winter of 1981-82 was not severe?* It is true that there is

---

*The winter of 1981–82 was characterized by deep snows that reached depths of three and four feet in some agricultural areas of western New York State. During part of that winter, an icy snow crust prevented deer from pawing through to reach acorns and low-level browse.

The New York State "Deer Population Explosion" and the DEC's Explosive Solution
(New York State DEC Figures)

YEAR	NUMBER OF BIG GAME LICENSEES*	NUMBER OF BUCKS KILLED (REGULAR GUN SEASON)	NUMBER OF DEER MANAGEMENT PERMITS ISSUED (FOR ANTLERED OR ANTLERLESS DEER KILLS)	NUMBER OF ANTLERLESS DEER KILLED (REGULAR GUN SEASON)	TOTAL DEER KILL	PERCENTAGE INCREASE OF TOTAL DEER KILL OVER PREVIOUS YEAR
1977	682,724	55,880	46,791	15,631	83,204	---
1978	692,948	51,872	56,211	19,921	85,559	2.8%
1979	713,855	59,086	61,015	20,685	94,059	9.0%
1980	749,181	75,441	110,013	35,100	136,225	31.0%
1981	770,238	83,667	174,258	46,822	166,027	18.0%
1982	753,541	78,460	247,561	62,338	185,455	10.5%

*Includes the following hunting licenses: Resident and Non-resident Big Game, Resident Hunting and Big Game, Resident Sportsman, and Free Sportsman.

Note that while the buck kill fluctuated, the number of antlerless deer that were killed rose dramatically, as did the number of antlerless deer hunting permits. And while the overall deer kill increased during each year, during no year did the antlerless deer kill exceed, or even approach, the buck kill. Even during 1982, the number of does killed could have been no more than 60–65 percent of the number of bucks killed and a little more than half the number of bucks and male fawns that were killed.

Archery seasons (in which hunters can kill either a buck or doe) resulted in the deaths of between 3,368 and 6,175 deer annually between 1977 and 1982 inclusive. Muzzle-loader kills of bucks and does ranged from a low of 25 to a high of 307.

The New York State deer kill statistics for 1983 were not yet available when the manuscript of *The American Hunting Myth* was sent to the publisher, but the DEC had issued about 205,000 deer-management permits (which allow the holder to shoot one additional deer of either sex) prior to the 1983 hunting seasons.

usually a one-year differential in reproductive rates since deer mate in autumn. If there are two consecutive mild winters followed by a severe winter, reproductive behavior will mirror the former and the number of fawns born the third spring may be high, provided there was sufficient browse and die-off during the severe winter was of a low magnitude. Naturally, if the herd is in good health the vast majority of deer may survive *one* harsh winter. But with two or more consecutive snowy, cold winters, the herd will usually decrease. As to "harvest" rates, 1981 saw a theretofore record issuance of deer-management permits and a theretofore record deer "harvest."

The DEC's deer management policies result in repercussions that may be favorable to the Division of Fish and Wildlife. If deer damage becomes widespread, many uncommitted people and some people who had previously opposed public hunting may change their opinions. Believing the DEC's claims that mild weather and a lack of suitable "harvests" have brought about a high deer population, they may fall into line behind wildlife officials and advocate still greater "harvests," new and longer hunting seasons, opening state parks to hunting, et cetera. Equally important, owners of agricultural acreage who had posted their property may open their lands to hunters after having suffered crop and/or orchard damage by deer.

Few readers will be surprised to learn that the 1982 deer season produced still another "record harvest" in New York State. The deer kill totaled more than 185,000. The herd may expand little beyond its 1982 level, but one recalls the remark that wildlife manager Terry Moore made in September, 1978. In view of the established procedures, it will be interesting to continue to monitor the deer management policies of the New York State DEC.

Clear-cutting in Connecticut

As mentioned earlier, the New York State Division of Fish and Wildlife is not being singled out for its mismanagement of deer and other wildlife. Deer management plans in most other states are similar. Consider the results of deer management in Connecticut and Michigan.

Connnecticut is largely metropolitan, and until the mid1970s it harbored a very small deer herd. The largest concentration of deer was found in the rural northwestern corner of the state. Prior to 1974 there were no *regulated* gunning seasons for deer in Connecticut. Deer were classified as "nuisance wildlife," and the owners and lessees of "agricultural" land and their descendants and employees could receive a free permit to shoot deer at any time of the year. According to Paul G. Herig, director of the Wildlife Unit of the Connecticut Department of Environmental Protection, it was not necessary for any of these people to *prove* deer damage. And since there were relatively few deer there was correspondingly little crop damage by deer. The result was, in Herig's words, that "the program became more of a recreational system rather than a solution to alleviate crop damage." There can be little doubt that this was potentially a biologically and ecologically destructive procedure, since any deer, including young fawns and does about to give birth, could legally be killed. However, since there were few deer and relatively few "agriculturists" to hunt them, the system was, in all likelihood, considerably less harmful than that which followed.

Both hunters and state wildlife officials in Connecticut had long been dissatisfied with the traditional system of *de facto* recreation. Therefore, in 1974, following the usual gentle pressure from hunters' groups and state wildlife officials, the Connecticut General Assembly passed the Deer Management Act, which established regulated hunting seasons on both state and private lands.[16]

Herig, noting the obvious, explained in a letter to the author:

> The main reasons [sic] for this legislation was to give management responsibility of Connecticut's white-tailed deer herd to the Wildlife Unit, enabling the deer resource to be managed as a game species in a biologically sound manner. In addition, by establishing regulated seasons on both private and state land, the recreational opportunity of deer hunting could be extended to many more people.

Hunters seeking recreational opportunity could find little fault with the generosity afforded them by legislators and the DEP Wildlife Unit. Deer hunting seasons included a six-day muzzle-loader season, a fifteen-day shotgun season and a forty-three day archery season, none of which overlapped! Furthermore, deer of either sex were legal game. Since there were estimated at this time to be only about 3,000 deer in the state, the munificence shown to hunters would initially appear to have been an overreaction. But enter the professional wildlife managers with their plans for increasing the deer "resource." As a result of management activities, which included the clearing of areas in state forests, the deer herd by 1979 had increased to 22,000—an astronomical seven-fold rise![17]

The results of the deer management program were predictable. In 1976 the muzzle-loader season was extended from six to nine days. In 1978, archery season was lengthened from forty-three to forty-eight days. In addition, landowners and lineal descendants were allowed a free permit to hunt deer from November 1 through December 31.[18] By

1981 some hunters could obtain as many as five permits. These included Archery, Private Land Shotgun, Private Land Muzzle Loader, Free Land-owner, and either State Land Shotgun *or* State Land Muzzle Loader. The latter two permits were issued to a predetermined number of hunters through a lottery. By 1985 a hunter with the necessary permits could kill as many as *nine* deer in a season

What is wrong with 3,000 relatively healthy deer, existing according to the ability of their habitat to sustain them, as opposed to 22,000 or more healthy or unhealthy deer that have one-seventh as much potential territory per deer and that have reached that population level as a result of "management" activities which create artificial habitat conditions? This question has been answered. Greater consumptive use of wildlife is what the present system of wildlife management is all about.

Mismanagement in Michigan

While Connecticut's deer management program is typical of those in many states where deliberate attempts have been made to increase deer populations for hunters, the activities of wildlife managers in the Constitution State are paled into insignificance by those of the Michigan Department of Natural Resources during the 1970s and early 1980s.

By the close of the 1960s, it was apparent that much of Michigan's 3.7 million acres of state-owned forestlands were attaining maturity. With a decline in low-growth vegetation in the understory, there was less browse for deer, and this had resulted in a decline in the deer population. In 1971 the chief of the Wildlife Division of the Michigan Department of Natural Resources proposed to the state natural resources commission a plan for "habitat improvement" that would be designed to increase the deer population in Michigan from approximately 200,000 to more than 1 million by 1981.

The Deer Range Improvement Program (unofficially dubbed "Project One Million") was approved, and the state was divided into three deer priority zones where different methods of habitat manipulation would be based upon forest types. The most extensive activities would be undertaken in the northeastern part of the state and in the south-eastern section of the Upper Peninsula. In the most intensively managed areas, older or poor quality trees were clear-cut in order to favor aspen, jack pine, or oak. By 1978 the DNR had developed a comprehensive plan that called for habitat manipulation primarily on the winter range of deer. Here herbacious food would be maintained, developed, or "improved." Furthermore, an extensive program of clear-cutting would be undertaken on state lands. Timber cutting would be done mostly by commercial logging firms. (These timber sales would increase revenue for the DNR.) The greatest emphasis on "habitat improvement" would be in winter deer yards, where food and cover would be increased. Grasslands were also to be managed, with emphasis upon developing or improving vegetation. In addition, attempts would be made by the DNR to acquire new lands, which would be used for deer management. By 1982 more than 6,000 acres had been bought for this purpose.

During one year, 1980, a total of 47,107 acres of state forests were clear-cut by loggers. (The Division of Forests had prescribed a clear-cut totaling 84,355 acres, but the market for timber had been weaker than anticipated.) By DNR standards, the project was a huge success. In one nine-square-mile experimental area of the Northern Lower Peninsula that had been 25 percent clear-cut, the winter deer population rose 4½ times between 1972 and 1978! By 1981 there were estimated to be more than 1 million deer in Michigan. That year Michigan's 750,000 resident and nonresident hunters killed more than 175,000 deer. Naturally, there were adverse side effects of the deer management program.

First was the unpublicized destruction of established wildlife habitat and the disruption and dispersal of wildlife that was caused by large-scale commercial logging. Second was the equally unpublicized fact that by changing the habitat from forestland to open or partly open lands and by drastically increasing the number of deer on and near logged areas, the entire biostructure was altered. By opening the forest canopy, more low-growth browse is created for *many* more deer. Deer populations will increase markedly and utilize existing forage. These artificially high deer populations, which are perpetuated by controlled hunting, usually result in temporary decreases of species such as snowshoe hares that would eat the bark and buds of saplings and low-growth vegetation that are overbrowsed by the very large deer herds, herds that have become overpopulated as a result of land mismanagement and inadequate numbers of large predators. Fewer snowshoe hares often mean fewer carnivores that would normally prey on hares, such as owls, foxes, bobcats, fishers, and lynx. (The lynx is rare or threatened throughout most of its southern range, which encompasses most of the northern tier of states.) These carnivores must then find other prey, such as red squirrels, flying squirrels, and mice. But these prey species may also be low in number during a particular year in a certain deer management area, especially if deer have eaten most of the acorns and beechnuts that would normally be available for the two species of squirrels that are native to this region. (In fact, both species of squirrels, being tree-dwellers, may be nonexistent in many clear-cut areas.) As we have seen, habitat manipulation often has disastrous effects for species to whom

111

the altered habitat has become less favorable. But this is a hazard that the habitat manipulators can live with in view of the increases in revenue that result for their departments. Since the mid-1970s, greater numbers of hunters from Ohio and Indiana, presumably lured by reports of fantastic numbers of deer, have bought licenses from the Michigan DNR and have done their deer hunting in the Wolverine State (in which there are now very few wolverines).

The third adverse side effect of Michigan's deer management program was the widely publicized orchard damage caused by deer that were not content to browse in or near logged areas. In 1981 this damage totaled in the millions of dollars. The fourth detrimental effect has been the equally well-publicized annual increase in deer-automobile collisions in Michigan. In 1980 these totaled 19,000.[19]

Instead of saving deer from starvation, habitat manipulation combined with regulated hunting contributes to greater numbers of deer deaths not only from hunting and collisions but from stress, injuries, pursuit by dogs, and winter-kill. Why? Because of the habitat overcrowding that usually exists even *after* the conclusion of each hunting season. The Michigan DNR is now considering longer hunting seasons, in what is officially described as an effort to stabilize that state's deer population. Meanwhile, Professor David Favre has cited a conversation that he had with the assistant director of the Wildlife Division of the Michigan DNR on July 2, 1981, in which it was admitted to Favre that if hunting were discontinued, the state's deer herd would remain at approximately the same size.

Aldo Leopold wrote in *Game Management:*

> After game shortage has been corrected by management, the purpose may extend beyond mere limitation. It may become necessary actually to enlarge the kill in order to bring the game into a desirable relationship to farm and forest crops.

It is obvious that pseudoscientific deer management has progressed very little since the Kaibab disaster.[20]

The Everglades Holocaust

When wildlife populations are in jeopardy, man is usually responsible, either because of wildlife manipulation or habitat mismanagement. But habitat mismanagement does not always mean the manipulation of ecosystems for the purpose of increasing "game" animals. It may also mean habitat destruction. One such case has occurred over a large section of the Florida Everglades, where white-tailed deer are suffering because of human shortsightedness. The story began during the early 1950s, when the Army Corps of Engineers undertook a mammoth flood control project that included large numbers of "holding lakes." By 1972 these artificial ponds, along with their associated canals, had extracted water from parts of the interior Everglades, causing thousands of acres to dry up.

Normally, deer ate the vegetation that grew in wet boglands, but they required dry places for resting. There were limited numbers of these and small numbers of deer until water in parts of the glades began to dry up. Then deer became more numerous. In addition to the water drained from natural areas by the manmade lakes and canals, farmers began pumping large amounts of water from the periphery of the Everglades for irrigation purposes. By the late 1970s, the Everglades deer herd had reached a record level. Then came heavy rains during 1978 and the hurricanes of 1979. Farmers who had previously been pumping water out of the glades now had flooded lands. So they pumped the excess water back into the swamp. The dry land quickly disappeared and large numbers of deer were forced to crowd onto existing shelves, rapidly depleting the vegetation that grew there. Many deer died.

State game officials responded by initiating antlerless deer hunting and extending the length of the deer season. Hunters were allowed to shoot deer from swamp buggies and halftracks! Then, during the summer of 1982, heavy rains combined with a backwash from irrigation pumps isolated many deer on small islands surrounded by thirty-inch floodwaters. This caused the Florida Game and Freshwater Fish Commission to schedule a special four-day "mercy hunt," purportedly to relieve deer suffering. The plan was to kill fawns, small does, and bucks with four or fewer antler points, the reasoning being that younger, smaller deer (which were the most numerous) would be more likely to succumb to starvation than larger, more vigorous animals.

Immediately after the hunt had been called, Michael Hacker, a Miami lawyer, and a small number of other animal protectionists sought a court injunction to bar the hunt. As an alternative, they suggested dropping feed to deer or allowing volunteers to rescue trapped deer and move them to areas that were not affected by high water. Both plans were dismissed as impractical by the Florida Game Commission. Hacker was able to obtain a temporary injunction, but it was dissolved by District Court Judge Eugene Spellman after a hasty series of hearings.

Up to this point, most of the well-known environmental and animal protection groups had stood on the sidelines, prefering not to become embroiled in the controversy. Charles Lee, a lobbyist for the Florida

Audubon Society, said that there would be only two alternatives, to let nature take its course or to allow hunters to kill deer before they died. He told a *New York Times* reporter that deer are by no means an endangered species in Florida. (One wonders what this has to do with saving deer that have become threatened as a result of land mismanagement.)

As media publicity about the impending hunt spread, a few of the larger animal protection groups did become involved. One of them was The Fund for Animals. FFA's court suit failed, but Col. Robert Brantly, executive director of the Florida Game and Fresh Water Fish Commission, told Cleveland Amory, president of FFA, that if Amory's group would not appeal the case, he would call off the hunt in half of the area that had been slated for deer "management" if preservationists could rescue 100 deer by noon on the second day of the scheduled four-day hunt. Since there were only ten hours before the hunt was to begin and there was little chance of having an appeal heard in Atlanta Federal Court, Amory agreed.

On Sunday, July 18, the hunt began and an army of more than 2,000 hunters riding airboats and tracked vehicles fanned out over the Everglades. The first day 507 deer were killed, and the following day about 250 more were shot. On the opening day of the hunt, about fifty animal protectionists protested at an entrance to the swamp. Meanwhile, conservationists transferred about fifteen deer on the first day of the hunt and ten more the second day.

Not all those who participated in the hunt considered it a recreational outing. Some apparently were protecting their interests, saying that they felt compelled to join the hunt because the game officials who had ordered it regulated their "sport." Others claimed that the hunt would lessen the suffering of surviving deer (and not coincidentally insure a supply of healthier deer during the next regularly scheduled hunting season)! But both hunters and deer rescuers may have done more harm than good. The crush of 2,200 hunters with accompanying loud gunshots no doubt greatly increased the stress on the already overtaxed deer in flooded areas. Likewise, the deer that were moved to other locations by well-meaning conservationists were in poor physical condition and their poor health may have been aggravated by contact with humans, which included a lengthy trip by motorized airboat.

The Game and Freshwater Fish Commission, perhaps partly for public relations purposes, ended the hunt after two days. Commission members termed the hunt a failure since hunters had killed only about 40 percent of the deer that had originally been slated for "harvesting." The animal preservationists were disappointed since they had been able to remove only a quarter of their goal of 100 deer. Lani Wigard of the

Fort Lauderdale Humane Society, commenting on the hunt, said, "No matter how you look at it, this is unpleasant. There must be a better way."

Within a month after the hunt, more than 800 stranded deer were estimated to have starved. According to the Associated Press, state wildlife biologist Bob Ellis commented, "We're to the point now where we're just counting dead bodies. We're flagging so many carcasses out here, pretty soon it'll look as though a surveyor came through." John Weiss wrote in *Outdoor Life* that there appears to be no workable solution to the alternate flooding and drying of the Everglades, which results mainly from agricultural irrigation. And he concluded, "Perhaps it would have been better just to leave well enough alone."

Certainly there would have been better ways to solve the problem of deer starvation in the Everglades. An article in the Fund for Animals newsletter expressed the view of some members of that organization that "all that needed to be done in the first place was for a few people to open some flood gates (which would lower the water level in the swamp) and leave the deer alone." Whatever the case, nonintervention by hunters would *not* have been "allowing nature to take its course," because the irrigation system had led to adverse environmental conditions that were anything but natural. Shortly before the hunt and deer rescue efforts, water was being pumped into the Everglades at an incredible rate of between 3 and 5 million gallons *a minute*. Had it not been for existing islands, including manmade islands built by hunters to provide dry refuges for deer and for use as hunting sites during deer season, the entire deer herd in a large section of the Everglades might have drowned.

The ultimate solution to flood-related deer deaths in the Everglades would have been to have prevented this problem before it began by leaving the ecology of the swamp intact. Rather than having provoked an unnatural environmental condition that resulted in an inevitable series of bureaucratic decisions to "harvest" starving deer, there should have been enough foresight never to have arrived at this point; that is, an alternate method of irrigating farmlands should have been explored. This is not merely speculation after the fact. Wise planning could have averted what any experienced ecologist could have predicted: disaster for Everglades deer and the drowning deaths of many small mammals. Once again, the needs of native species of wildlife were never seriously considered. There is a need to balance the perceived benefits of some people against the very real needs of all native animals. At the root of the problem is a lack of responsibility to the land and the life that it supports. This is the same lack of individual and social responsibility that has traditionally placed economic profits above ecological sensitivity.

"Render unto Nature . . ."

Is there a logical—and ecological—method of undoing the damage that has been caused by man's mismanagement of land and wildlife? The solution would be to return ecosystems to a primitive natural state inasmuch as possible and to introduce large predators, such as panthers and timber wolves, and large birds of prey, such as rare species of hawks and endangered eagles, on federal and state wildlands. The latter is being undertaken by wildlife departments in some states, partly with federal money. Most of these funds were cut substantially in April 1982 as a result of the belt-tightening tactics of President Ronald Reagan and then–secretary of the interior James Watt. (Voluntary state tax contributions have taken up some of the slack, although these funds have also been used for much less beneficial purposes.)

There is every indication that there would be fewer and healthier deer and "game" birds if they were allowed to exist within balanced ecosystems that included a proper predator-prey ratio. This, in combination with a gradual scaling down and eventual cessation of public hunting, would be the ideal solution.

But if hunting can result in higher-than-normal wildlife populations due to changes in reproductive behavior, wouldn't this be true in the presence of natural predators? For example, wouldn't the reintroduction of panthers and wolves result in an increase in the number of deer, thus defeating the purpose of reintroduction except to preserve these large predators?

The answer is, in most cases, no; deer would be brought into better balance with their food supplies. There are important reasons for this.

Natural predators contribute to the health of deer herds, since they usually kill a disproportionate number of old deer and those weakened by malnutrition or infirmity. As we have seen, sport hunters kill healthy as well as unhealthy deer. Since most hunters prefer to shoot large bucks, hunting often has the opposite effect of natural predation. Furthermore, when natural predators are in balance with their prey, they will kill *smaller numbers* of deer per year than is true of hunters in most areas of the United States. Thus there is not the severe stress that results from intensive hunting, and consequently there are no dramatic reproductive changes. Heavy hunting pressure and limited natural predation are two entirely different things. Hunting seasons are relatively short, and the net effect of large numbers of deer killed in a two-to-four–week period, as noted earlier, is that of a deer herd undergoing a rapid natural population "crash." Conversely, natural predators kill deer in relatively small numbers during the course of each year, thus helping to maintain comparatively low and comparatively stable deer populations. Finally, when a primary prey species becomes low in number, predators must turn to less desirable prey in order to survive. This usually gives the primary prey species a chance to increase. Likewise, when the population of a primary prey species is high, the numbers of predators increase correspondingly and help to limit prey populations along with self-limiting factors and other decimating factors. Thus the ecological balance that is a part of the normal pattern of Nature.

I cannot emphasize too strongly that I am *not* suggesting predator reintroduction simply for the purpose of limiting herbivore populations. Natural predators are only one of many factors that influence the populations of herbivores. But predators *are* a factor and they have a right to exist. (It is equally true that herbivore populations influence the number of predators. No plants, no herbivores, no predators.) Predators and their prey each have an equal chance for survival. But this is usually not so when a hunter has a powerful weapon at his disposal.

The Angel Island Tragedy

Should predator introduction be regarded as a panacea for establishing a more harmonious ecological balance in natural areas? Usually, but not always. A case in which predator introduction might *not* be appropriate was described in an article by Peter Y. Sussman in *The Christian Science Monitor* of March 27, 1981. Professor Dale McCullough, a wildlife management professor at the University of California at Berkeley, met with generally hostile reaction from animal protection groups when he suggested that coyotes be used to "control" deer on Angel Island. The island, which is in San Francisco Bay, has an annual climatic cycle characterized by a long rainy period followed by a long dry period. During dry periods, vegetation withers, resulting in a scarcity of food for deer. During the drought of 1976–77, more than 100 deer died before the local Society for the Prevention of Cruelty to Animals received permission to transport thirty-eight tons of alfalfa to the island over an extended period as forage for the deer.

At the time the *Monitor* article was written, the deer, which numbered about 150, were in reasonably good health. But concern over the future of the herd led to the McCullough plan to import six neutered coyotes, which had been vaccinated against rabies and outfitted with radio transmitter collars. Fawns as well as older deer would be fitted with "mortality sensors," while "fetal sensors" would be used on pregnant does. The effects of coyote predation would then be monitored by McCullough and his students.

Two facts make the ethics and practicality of the coyote plan questionable. First, Angel Island is small—less than six square miles. Habitat conditions for deer are generally poor, and the total number of mammal species is much less than would be the case in a large national forest on the California mainland. With deer confined to a small area, there would be a measure of truth to the criticism of Virginia Handley, California coordinator for The Fund for Animals, who termed the McCullough proposal "death control," not birth control. Richard Avanzino, president of the San Francisco SPCA, said that "animals should be given *a chance for life*," which the deer would not have had, since they would have been confined on a small island with six hungry coyotes that had no other major food source except small rodents. Coyotes would initially prey on these rodents. But what would happen if rodents were to become scarce?

The second important factor was seemingly lost in the controversy: *the deer do not belong on the island.* They were introduced by army personnel in 1915 for hunting purposes. Thus, in a truly "natural" circumstance, there would be no deer on Angel Island and thus no theoretical need for a solution to periodic deer starvation!

Public opposition to the coyote plan finally forced its abandonment. Predictably, the California Department of Fish and Game suggested a more final solution, a "selective thinning" by a government hunter. This plan also met with strong public protest. Sterilization and adoption were deemed impractical or unworkable by most of those involved in the controversy.

What would be the most humane and ecologically sound solution to deer starvation on Angel Island? Probably the removal of deer to California parks and forests in small numbers of no more than ten or fifteen at a time until most or all of them were gone from the island. Naturally, great care would have to be taken not to cause extreme stress. Deer would have to be removed during the rainy season, when vegetation was plentiful and they were in relatively good physical condition. Care would also have to be taken not to break up herd or family units, particularly in cases of does with dependent fawns. Some California state game officials (including those who favor shooting as the most practical solution) have said that this would be too expensive. But even if deer were removed to state or federal forests on the California mainland they would be "legal game" during hunting seasons.

The irony is that here we have another case in which man's interference with Nature has resulted in the suffering of wildlife. And because our culture bases the value of all things in terms of their "use" by man, both expense and logistics have often been cited as limiting factors in improving conditions for wildlife. Regrettably, many people still do not consider animals to be worthy of their time, effort, and money.

The "Surplus" Fallacy

There are many variations of the "starvation argument," including the "surplus" theory. This is often used as a justification to hunt deer *and* small game such as pheasants. An article by Dwight R. Schuh in *Outdoor Life* titled "Should We Shoot Hen Pheasants?" states that information from studies indicates that "with or without hunting, about 70 percent of pheasants, both hens and roosters, die each year." But the logic that might explain the hunting of pheasants and other "game" birds is lacking. Why hunt them if the same percentage of total birds will die even if they *are* hunted? Hunting does not save a greater percentage of birds from death by other causes.

Questions that must be asked: What are the causes of death of the 70 percent of pheasants that die annually *without* hunting? How much is a result of natural predation? How much is a result of deaths from age or related factors? Few things in nature go to waste; foxes, coyotes, crows, and other animals that sometimes eat carrion will often devour birds that have died as a result of insufficient winter food and cover. But don't try to convince a game manager that animals that are not consumed by hunters are not wasted! According to *Outdoor Life:*

Surplus birds die, whether by shotgun during the season or by natural causes during the winter. Many game managers feel that hunters might as well take the surplus.

The article explained that hunting hen pheasants does not necessarily lead to fewer birds the following season, since studies showed that hens produced larger broods in areas where either-sex shooting has been allowed, another case of reproductive changes compensating for high hunting losses.

But most hunters are still opposed to shooting hen pheasants. Therefore, game biologists in some states are studying the feasibility of limited hen hunting in an effort to convince hunters to change their views. Referring to this, *Outdoor Life* quoted Joe Egan, assistant chief of wildlife in Montana. According to Egan, "You can offer a guy a $5 bill, but you can't make him take it." Whether a living creature can be compared to a five-dollar bill is debatable. But there is no debating the fact that the shooting of wildlife results in a continuous flow of innumerable five-, ten-, and twenty-dollar bills into the coffers of state game bureaus.

An insight into the motives of some of those who use the "starvation argument" to justify pheasant hunting is provided by a quote from Fred Martinsen, small game program manager for the Washington Department of Game. According to *Outdoor Life*, Martinsen theorized: "With carefully controlled shooting of hens we could put an additional 50,000 birds in the bag each year. It's simply a way to give hunters a little more and to use a resource that's now going to waste."

Hunting apologists claim that unless surplus animals are shot they will die prematurely from other causes. But even a highly experienced field biologist would be hard-pressed to plausably define a "harvestable surplus." To effectively remove a surplus, hunters would have to shoot enough animals to minimize starvation rates. However, controlled hunting usually *stabilizes or increases* a game population, and since hunting normally has little effect on the percentages of disease, parasites, malnutrition, and starvation to affect a hunted species, it follows that in order to effectively cull a surplus population, it would be necessary to kill not only those animals that are shot by hunters during a particular season, but *in addition* those survivors that would die prematurely before the following year's hunting season. Within limits there will be non–hunting related premature deaths *regardless of how many animals are shot each autumn.* Therefore it follows that the only way to remove a "surplus" population would be to shoot every individual of each game species. Extinct animals don't starve!

By an ecological standard, a surplus would include only those animals that do *not* die as a result of age or predation and are not consumed by carrion-eaters. And what about carrion-feeding insects? Certainly they contribute to a well-balanced ecosystem. So a "surplus"—those members of a species that die from severe weather, malnutrition, starvation, disease, parasites, or a combination of these factors and are not consumed by other forms of life—would include only a small percentage of the annual die-off. Moreover, habitat and range conditions fluctuate from year to year and die-offs rise and fall with population cycles. Therefore, hunters in a given season may kill more than their share of the theoretical surplus. And each autumn hunters kill many healthy animals that would have survived the winter. Finally, there would usually be no real or imagined surpluses were it not for wildlife-management techniques that are designed to create and maintain them!

The Rabies Rationalization

There is a final argument in the "population control" category that is sometimes used by hunters: This is that hunting certain species helps to reduce animal diseases such as rabies. (This is also a favorite excuse for trapping.) But it is a faulty argument for many reasons.

First is the obvious fact that most hunters would not want to eat or use the fur of a seriously diseased animal.

Second, there is no uncontroversial evidence that the incidence of rabies and many other wildlife diseases is a direct result of high population density. That is, there is no evidence that cases of rabies increase *exponentially* in proportion to the size of an animal population on any type of habitat, as it would if it were related to population density. Naturally if there is a high population of a species combined with low food supplies, animals will be more *susceptible* to certain diseases, particularly during winter in cold climates. But the statistical probability of *individual* animals such as foxes, bats, raccoons, badgers, opossums, gray squirrels, red squirrels, and others that are likely to contact rabies actually becoming infected does not become greater with increases in their populations.

Third, if a hunter is inexperienced in determining wildlife population levels, he may be hunting members of a species during a time of *low* population. Simply because he may notice animals of a particular species near his home, woodland, or farmland does not mean that there is a high population of that species over a broad geographical area. (Most of the animals may inhabit a small area of favorable habitat.) Therefore, at what point do hunters cease "controlling" an animal population to prevent rabies, particularly if there are no closed seasons on that species? Eliminate every member of every potential rabies-carrying species and rabies will be controlled!

Fourth, while there are occasional outbreaks of wildlife-borne rabies in some areas, the disease is *not common* among any species of wild animal. The incidence of a single outbreak of rabies over a wide geographical area is quite rare, and this disease is seldom passed on to a *large* percentage of any species. Outbreaks of rabies are usually spontaneous, restricted to one locality, and of short duration. The Cain report on predator control (produced for the U.S. Department of Interior and the President's Council on Environmental Quality in 1971) stated that by the time a rabies outbreak is noticed, the outbreak is essentially over and control is unnecessary.

Fifth, since most species react to "harvests" with increased reproductive rates, most attempts to permanently control animal populations for whatever reasons are counterproductive—unless there are mass exterminations by many hunters when large numbers of a particular species exist in a limited area. But even this kind of very intensive hunting or trapping may *increase* the incidence of rabies. Dr. H. Charles Laun of Stephens College, Columbia, Missouri, has said, "These methods (i.e., hunting and trapping) are ineffective in practice and unsound in theory. . . . When a population is reduced to a low level by any of the various means of control, the number of new individuals in the population increases, simply because of the increase in birth rate. Population reduction only alleviates the rabies problem for a short time, to be followed by a rapid return to the former level, or an even higher one." Dr. William G. Winkler, Virology Division, U.S. Center for Disease Control in Atlanta, Georgia, has noted that trapping removes many animals that have developed an immunity to rabies by surviving the infection. The larger litters that result from nonselective trapping (or hunting) usually contain no immune individuals. Winkler said, "The reduction of animal numbers through trapping or similar programs might indeed create a vacuum for ingress and increased mortality of susceptible animals. We do not advocate routine trapping programs as being effective for rabies control."[21]

Finally, one of the most common carriers of rabies is the skunk, and I have never known a recreational hunter who has gone on a skunk hunting expedition!

The Demise of the Starvation Argument

There are other factors that discredit the starvation argument.

—From the standpoint of simple logic this argument is invalid because man is applying his subjective standards to Nature's purposeful design. As previously emphasized, when man "manages" Nature mainly out of self-interest, the result will be ecological imbalance. We know that ecosystems need a wide variety of species in order to maintain a reasonable balance. But many species of birds and mammals have become rare, endangered, or extinct.

—There would be *some* starvation of deer and other large herbivores no matter what steps were taken to try to prevent it. There would also be deaths of "game" birds due to malnutrition, exposure, et cetera. Nature is largely harmonious when in proper balance, but Nature is not 100 percent perfect. Nature usually produces more members of each species than will easily survive; it is part of a plan to insure that many *will* survive, reproduce, and contribute to ecological balance.

—There are some areas, such as the Pacific Northwest, where

122

habitat would be more than sufficient to carry larger numbers of deer, yet deer are legal game in these areas. As we have seen, wildlife officials respond to low deer populations with the claim that "the deer resource" is chronically below its range carrying capacity and that it has the potential for much greater recreational utilization by hunters if it can be brought to range carrying capacity as a result of management activities. When wildlife officials make this comment they come much closer to revealing their motives for promoting recreational hunting than they do when they use the starvation argument.

—If the sometimes high mortality rates of deer and "game" birds were a legitimate reason for maintaining their hunted status, then this could be used to justify the hunting of nearly *any* species or wildlife group, including songbirds. According to the Reader's Digest Association book *Birds—Their Life—Their Ways—Their World* (copyright in the U.S. 1979):

The European Robin *(Erithacus rubecula)* is fairly typical of a small temperate possessive in that around 50–60% of the adults die between one year and the next. Hence only a tiny fraction of the birds will survive to reach 10 years of age.

Most songbirds have fairly high reproductive rates, with an average of three or four chicks per brood. Songbirds may have two broods per season and sometimes as many as three in the Mid-Atlantic states. Thus their populations can sustain the high losses. Fortunately no one has yet suggested establishing a hunting season on robins.

—What if hunting were completely selective and the only animals that were killed were those that would suffer and die from starvation, disease, or severe weather at some future point? The starvation argument includes the supposition that it is more merciful to put deer out of their misery than to allow some to slowly starve. (This is assuming that they are dispatched quickly, and this does not always occur.) But is this "humane" argument a sound premise for hunting? Charles Maher, a columnist for the *Los Angeles Times*, made an interesting case for the opposite point of view in his essay "Just Ask the Deer" (copyright 1968 by the *L.A. Times*).

Maher wrote that he had not yet been persuaded that it is more humane to kill deer than to let them risk starvation. He asked readers to imagine that they were lost in winter woods with a friend and asked whether they would rather be shot by their friend or remain alive on the remote chance that they might find food. He noted that even a starving deer would run if it feared for its life, suggesting that the deer would rather risk starvation than die.

Life is the most valuable asset of any creature—human or

nonhuman. Thus, of what significance would it be even if an animal killed by a hunter *would* have suffered a painful death? Is not the life of a highly developed and intelligent creature worth a few months, or weeks, or days? Should animals not be given *a chance to live?*

—The starvation argument is ludicrous when used *as a reason for the act of hunting,* because sport hunters seldom hunt *with the intent* of saving animals from starvation. Can you imagine a hunter sighting on a large buck with the thought flashing through his mind: "Sorry, big fella. I hate to do this, but I'm going to have to save you from possible starvation." Most likely if he has any thoughts at this moment, they are considerably less selfless and less humane.

—Finally, I do not believe that it would be unfair to say that the use of the starvation argument as a supposedly valid defense of sport hunting is extremely hypocritical, since man is the most overpopulated species. Our society has become so deeply immersed in homocentrism that seldom, if ever, does anyone seriously suggest the obvious fact that *human beings* have chronically overpopulated most of the natural habitat of deer, moose, and elk. Having already totally destroyed the natural landscape in many areas, *human* overpopulation and its associated problems far outweigh those that result from real, imagined, or deliberately created wildlife overpopulations. Many game managers consider deer to be above their "range carrying capacity" if there are more than twenty or twenty-five deer per square mile on most types of natural habitat. Yet, it has been asserted that if human beings were spread equally across the earth's land surface, each person would have a "territory" of less than one acre! Somewhere in the world a person dies of malnutrition or starvation *every two seconds.* Unfortunately, we humans are not equipped with the biological population limiting devices that prevent serious overpopulations of unmanaged wild animals. Were it not for a few that feed the many, there would be even greater world hunger.

The starvation argument justifies punishing wildlife for what wildlife officials and commercial biologists consider "overpopulations," when *they themselves* are often guilty of indiscriminate and excessive "resource" use. Likewise, they are sometimes equally guilty of producing three or more children at a time when a sense of responsibility to the earth and to future generations (human and animal) dictates no more than two children per couple.

In summary, the starvation argument, like other defensive hunting justifications, is a rationalization. "Sportsmen" want to hunt, and fish and game bureaucrats have personal, financial, and economic reasons

124

for perpetuating the present system of wildlife management. Therefore, those who profit from this system ferret out the most valid sounding arguments in attempts to convince others that the system is biologically and ecologically sound. The trouble is that *none* of the excuses that are given for game management are sound; nor do any valid reasons for recreational hunting exist.

THE CHECKS AND BALANCES ARGUMENT

Hunters' Argument: ACCORDING TO WILDLIFE BIOLOGISTS —EVEN THOSE THAT ACKNOWLEDGE NATURAL POPULATION LIMITING FACTORS—THE INTRODUCTION OF PREDATORS WOULD NOT BE COMPLETELY EFFECTIVE AS A CHECK ON DEER HERDS AND POPULATIONS OF PROLIFIC SPECIES SUCH AS RABBITS AND SNOWSHOE HARES. THEREFORE, *SOME* HUNTING WOULD BE NEEDED TO INSURE AN ADEQUATE BALANCE EVEN IN A "WELL-BALANCED" ECOSYSTEM.

Analysis: While Nature is not 100 percent perfect, she has spent millions of years evolving and improving ecosystems. A well-balanced natural ecosystem is a relatively harmonious interaction of optimum numbers of all native plant and animal species. It is true that Nature occasionally upsets her own equilibrium by severe weather, volcanos, earthquakes, and lightning-set fires. There has been a great deal written about these aberrations, but they are not common occurrences.

As to the reintroduction of large predators, they would not completely eliminate deer starvation or fluctuating deer populations, since wildlife populations are "checked" principally by a birth-rate response to food, habitat, and territory. But studies have shown that deer populations are lower and more stable in areas where large predators exist.

There are socioeconomic reasons for the inability of ecologists to influence most residents of nonagricultural rural areas about the need for predator reintroduction. In addition to opposition by hunters, there is considerable apprehension by many nonhunters. (Wolves would attack my children and eat all the deer, and I would lose business during the hunting season. Panthers? They're vicious!) State wildlife officials are not anxious to discourage this type of reaction.

Most of the wildlife biologists who openly or secretly favor predator reintroduction (including those biologists who are not employed by the federal government or a state game bureau) accept the view that public hunting is necessary as a final "check" on the numbers of deer, "game" birds, and some small mammals. As we have seen, wildlife biologists have been nurtured on the hunting philosophy and have been taught that ecosystems can be improved by manipulation. Unfortunately, the more man tampers with Nature, the more he must rely upon "management" activities to maintain a semblance of ecological balance; and these activities are harmful to established ecosystems.

Hunting, whether in the presence or absence of large predators, is no guaranteed annual "check" on deer populations. (Unless does are killed at a two to one or three to one ratio, as compared to bucks, and this does not often occur.)

How Many Wolves Are Too Many?

How many predators would be needed to ensure well-balanced ecosystems? The numbers would differ according to environmental factors. Leonard Lee Rue III made some interesting comments on this subject in his book *The Deer of North America*.* He claimed that, based upon studies of the feeding patterns of wolves and cougars, in order to equal the average annual deer kill by hunters in New York State (at that time about 105,000), "a fantastic supply of predators" would be needed—specifically 750 cougars and 3,504 wolves. Assuming that only 15,000 of New York State's 50,000 square miles is suitable wild habitat for both deer and predators (and this is a conservative estimate), this would mean that there would be one cougar per twenty square miles and one wolf per five square miles or a pack of eight wolves every forty square miles on this range. Hardly a fantastic supply! And this is not taking into account that much habitat that is not "wild" and unsuitable for large predators *would* be suitable for white-tailed deer; thus there would be a much smaller deer population on the predators' potential range than would be indicated by the statewide deer population estimate at the time Rue compiled his book. Rue wrote that, while he would like large predators to be restored to wilderness areas such as those in the Adirondacks, predators in agricultural regions of New York State might kill cattle and "dairy and beef cattlemen would surely try to eradicate them." But predators would not be eradicated if they were legally protected. (Nonviolent alternatives for the protection of livestock will be examined more closely in the analysis of the hunters' argument that follows.)[22]

One might ask why it would be necessary for predators to kill as many deer per year as hunters in New York or any other state. Game management maintains deer at artificially high levels in agricultural regions of southern and southwestern New York. If hunting were slowly

---

The Deer of North America, by Leonard Lee Rue III, an Outdoor Life Book published by Book Division, Times Mirror Magazines, Inc., 1978.

phased out, the deer herd in these areas would be no larger than present average prehunt levels and, in all likelihood, would be considerably smaller, due to reproductive changes. As we have seen, hunting results in the deaths of at least twice as many bucks and male fawns as does. It reduces deer populations only temporarily, until the following spring when fawns are born. During late summer and early autumn there are usually high deer populations in agricultural regions of New York State, resulting in crop and orchard damage.

No one would suggest that cougars and wolves should be introduced into parts of Westchester County, fifteen miles north of New York City! Wolves and the large cats normally prefer wild country that is not in close proximity to development and heavy human population. Hunting is practiced *throughout* New York State, not merely in suburban areas where predator introduction would be impractical. A person might use this impracticality as a justification for hunting in areas of human development, but only if individual deer or groups of deer were causing severe garden or orchard damage and nonlethal solutions were ineffective.

The most intelligent method of reintroducing large predators would be to free a small number of them (in the case of wolves, perhaps a dozen of each sex) over a wide area on an extensive tract of wild forestland a considerable distance from human habitation and then monitor the effects on the local deer herd over a period of four or five years.

Naturally, eagles, hawks and small to medium-sized predatory mammals such as lynx, bobcats, coyotes, fishers, marten, and mink also contribute to balanced ecosystems. Unfortunately, all of these mammals are frequently shot or trapped, and these practices are encouraged by state wildlife agencies. But even in the absence of optimum numbers of middle-level carnivores, there are seldom, if ever, serious overpopulations of songbirds and small nonhunted mammals in most areas. (The only exceptions might be occasionally high populations of crows, blackbirds, and starlings in agricultural regions.) A preservationist-oriented zoologist once remarked that nonhunted species such as blue jays and chipmunks do a good job of keeping their populations in check while frequently hunted species such as deer and grouse always seem to be in danger of serious overpopulation, according to game managers and commercial biologists. (Naturally, the land can support much larger numbers of songbirds and small mammals as compared to birds of prey and larger mammals since small animals require much less food and territory.)

Ecologists should not expect the reintroduction of large predators in isolated areas of most states in the near future. A bit of thought will suggest that there may be at least one factor other than economics, the placation of hunters, and uninformed public opinion that causes state wildlife officials to shun this practice. If Nature were allowed to "manage" itself (except in cases of serious natural disasters or destruction of habitat that threatened one or more species of animal), there would be no demand for harvest-oriented wildlife biologists and no contrived need for fish and game bureaus as they are presently structured. Self-perpetuation is a basic biological trait, and humans, like other animals, usually follow the path of least resistance.

French philosopher Michel de Montaigne wrote: "Let us give Nature a chance. She knows her business better than we do." He might have concluded: *much* better than we do.

IV./"NUISANCE WILDLIFE" AND PSEUDOECOLOGICAL ARGUMENTS

WITH THE EXCEPTION OF THE FIRST ARGUMENT IN THIS SECTION, BY WHICH HUNTERS SEEK TO JUSTIFY THE KILLING OF WILDLIFE THAT CONFLICT WITH HUMAN INTERESTS, THESE ARE ARGUMENTS THAT HUNTERS USE IN AN ATTEMPT TO PROVE THAT RECREATIONAL HUNTING IS ECOLOGICALLY SOUND BECAUSE OF THE ABUNDANCE OF "GAME" ANIMALS AND BECAUSE OF THE RELATIVELY FEW SPECIES OF ANIMALS THAT ARE LEGAL GAME. OTHER PSEUDOECOLOGICAL ASSERTIONS ARE BASED UPON HUNTING REGULATIONS AND THE FACT THAT IN MANY LARGE WILDERNESS AREAS HUNTING PRESSURE IS COMPARATIVELY LIGHT.

In Allegany State Park, Paul Bozard, head of the park police, feels an overall lack of mast crops from the fall is resulting in a loss of fawns, particularly those whose mothers were killed during deer season.
—News item in the Olean (N.Y.) *Times-Herald* (February 20, 1982)

THE NUISANCE WILDLIFE ARGUMENT

Hunters' Argument: KILLING WILDLIFE BECOMES NECESSARY WHEN MAN'S ECONOMIC OR PERSONAL INTERESTS ARE THREATENED. DEER EAT FARMER'S CROPS. COONS RAID CORN. WOODCHUCKS BURROW THROUGH HAY FIELDS. FOXES RAID HEN HOUSES. COYOTES KILL SHEEP. THUS, EVEN IN THE ABSENCE OF SPORT HUNTING, THERE WOULD BE TIMES WHEN KILLING WILD ANIMALS WOULD BE UNAVOIDABLE.

Analysis: "Varmint" is the term most often used to describe these miscreants. I have lived in the woods for more than a decade, but I have never seen a winged or four-legged varmint. I have seen a sharp-quilled devil that insisted on chewing the latticework around my cabin foundation. (The damage was minimal.) I have seen a sassy red troublemaker that delighted in chasing birds from my feeders. (I discouraged this by constructing squirrel-proof feeders and establishing a separate feeding

129

place for him.) I have seen the work of a masked character that, under cover of darkness, partook of a cherry pie that I had left to cool on my porch. I have even experienced the depredation of a large, black marauder that once consumed most of the edible contents of my garbage pail. But these minor problems have been infrequent.

There are people whose life-styles make them more vulnerable to occasional animal damage. I can sympathize with a livestock farmer who shoots a coyote that has developed an uncontrollable appetite for lamb. I can understand the exasperated last-ditch "management" of a fox that has repeatedly carried away a farmer's prize pullets. But frustrated people can easily overreact and use the slightest provocation to exterminate every coyote, fox, or other so-called varmint within shotgun range. Worse yet, poison is sometimes substituted for guns or traps. A coyote-poisoning program using the notorious "Compound 1080" was undertaken in western states until 1972 and proved to be an ecological disaster. The poison killed not only coyotes but bears, foxes, wolves, mountain lions, bobcats, badgers, eagles, hawks, and many other species of animals that took the cyanide-laced bait that was either injected into the bodies of dead sheep or calves or placed in special collars on the dead animals. In 1981 Secretary of the Interior James Watt began to press for the reintroduction of Compound 1080, and by late 1982, the way had been cleared for its reauthorization by the Environmental Protection Agency. After almost a year of hearings, during which animal protection organizations presented evidence and witnesses, Administrative Law Judge Spencer Nissen approved the use of the compound in collars and single lethal doses. This was done despite the presentation of evidence that indicated that the rate of predation losses had not increased since 1972 when the compound had been banned by executive order.

The only way to rid the world of all the animals that someone, somewhere would consider to be "nuisances" would be to exterminate every member of every native species of bird and mammal. Beavers flood roads. Moles tunnel through lawns. Rabbits eat garden greens. Chipmunks steal grain. For that matter, bats nest in attics and dogs and cats void on suburban flowerbeds. In the case of wildlife, the quickest and easiest solution to most of these problems is the most inhumane. That is to resort to traps or a rifle and, if these fail, to give the regional wildlife manager an irate telephone call.

These actions are usually unnecessary, or *would be* if proper preventive measures had been taken. As a frustrated final resort, one may have little choice but to use violent methods of wildlife "control." But there are nonlethal solutions, and these should be examined at the onset of difficulties. Farmers with less than ten to twenty acres that are used either for crops or as pastureland for free-roaming livestock can construct sturdier and higher fences. They can inspect hen houses more frequently and keep them securely locked from dusk to dawn, with openings sealed and wire mesh on open windows during warm weather. Farmers who cultivate large areas can usually absorb minor losses. Wild animals must eat, and they usually take what is most readily available.

Unfortunately, animals cannot voice *their* side of a controversy but ranchers and agri-business people can. Animals have no representation except from protection organizations, which have few members living in rural areas. The result is predictable. Those who loudly voice displeasure about wildlife damage, whether or not it is of a serious nature, usually receive the conscientious support of professional wildlife managers.

"Alleviating" Crows and Blackbirds

The object of many complaints by farmers is the common crow. The crow is a highly successful bird throughout North America—often too successful for its own good! According to an article by Jack Denton Scott that appeared in *Outdoor Life* and was later reprinted in *Bird Watcher's Digest*, there are now more than 3 billion crows on the North American continent.

Scott wrote that the crow will probably "continue to prosper":

> Regulated hunting for the common crow has been established under federal regulations for migratory species. Rules permit sport hunting for crows in the 48 contiguous states only during a season not to exceed 124 days each year.

Apparently this is quite a concession for the U.S. Fish and Wildlife Service. Scott further states:

> Hunting from an airplane or during peak nesting seasons will not be allowed, and crows may be taken only by firearms, archery, or falconry. The big slaughter is finished, except, of course, in rare cases of extreme crop depredation.

Thus, in theory at least, if a crow-hating agri-businessman can convince fish and game officials that his problem is a rare case of extreme crop depredation he may be able to dispatch the offending birds by methods other than firearms, archery, or falconry—as if any were needed! Also, he may be able to circumvent his state's established crow-hunting seasons and bag limits.*

*In some states, such as New Hampshire, there are no bag limits for crows during the hunting season (in the Granite State August 1–November 30).

A recent annual report by the U.S. Fish and Wildlife Service states that one of the major goals of its Animal Damage Control Program is to "develop safe and selective methods for alleviating damage caused by wild vertebrates." Unfortunately, the method that is often used is to alleviate the wild vertebrates that appear to be doing the damage. The Fish and Wildlife Service emphasizes that it shall "provide operational and extension animal damage control services when and where [they are] needed."

The report writer claimed that during the previous year blackbirds, particularly red-winged blackbirds, had caused a loss of more than 1 million bushels of corn in the state of Ohio. (While blackbirds are more numerous in some parts of that state than in others, the total loss represented only four-tenths of 1 percent of Ohio's corn crop.) Blackbirds eat the inner portion of the kernel. While in the early "milk stage," an ear of corn may be lost to molding and sprouting if more than one-quarter of the ear has been damaged.

Why are there large flocks of blackbirds in many agricultural areas? Mainly because the human population is rapidly increasing and suitable wild habitat is declining. (Red-winged blackbirds normally nest in open marshes.) Many wintering and/or nesting birds are now found in thickly populated suburban areas, a fact to which any suburbanite with a bird feeder can attest. Areas of human habitation do not provide red-winged blackbirds or other songbirds with an ideal habitat, but a tolerable habitat does exist in these areas. Many red-wings have been crowded by human development from the natural marshes that they would normally favor. If food is available, especially in large quantities in a relatively small area, the birds will congregate and feed there.[1]

The Fish and Wildlife Service report states:

> Based on preliminary data gathered by the Service, the Environmental Protection Agency granted experimental registrations to private companies that allowed the Service to conduct field evaluations of Avitrol (a toxic substance). The compound shows promise in protecting small grain crops.

This type of nonecological overreaction is usually self-defeating. Lorus J. Milne, a professor of zoology at the University of New Hampshire, and Margery Milne condemned the destruction of blackbirds in Canada in their book *Ecology Out of Joint: New Environments and Why They Happen* (Charles Scribners and Sons, 1977):

> What changes due to burgeoning insects near sites of blackbirds would ensue if few came to nest and pursue insects as food

for nestlings? Grackles hold down the number of caterpillars in the spruce forests of Ontario. . . . Blackbirds work unintentionally and unpaid for the newsprint industry. Redwings similarly suppress the insects of the North Country. This protects the plant cover that ducks and geese need while reproducing their various kinds.

Since we live in one world, the benefits created by blackbirds in the ecosystems of Canada and the northern United States exert a positive influence upon the ecosystems of other regions. Furthermore, in agricultural areas of Ohio and other states, red-winged blackbirds eat millions of insects that would otherwise destroy crops.

Assassins versus Health Police

Much of the Fish and Wildlife Service report concerns coyote predation on livestock and methods of coyote "control." According to the report writer, coyote depredations are acute in seventeen western states, where as many as 500,000 sheep per year may be lost to coyotes. (This may be an overstatement gathered from reports of ranchers who exaggerate their losses, and even if it is an accurate figure, much sheep loss is a result of inadequate safety precautions.) The report writer asserts that part of the coyote predation problem is a result of the large open areas that are characteristic of sheep-grazing country in western states. Two-thirds of the more than 1,000 counties in a seventeen-state area have fewer than six sheep grazing per square mile. With this few sheep, it would seem that protective fencing of limited grazing areas would be an effective solution to coyote predation. A study by Defenders of Wildlife indicated that better livestock husbandry could reduce coyote predation to 1 or 2 percent a year. Defenders cited the use of protected lambing sheds, electric fences, or coyote-proof barriers and greater use of trained guard dogs.

Naturally all of these cost money. When a rancher is trying to make a profit on his investment, the easiest and least expensive solution to the coyote question is the use of poison and/or traps and/or bullets. The Fish and Wildlife Service report informs us:

> The increased use of aircraft (helicopters and fixed-wing) has been a significant factor in enabling the Service to keep coyote predations on domestic livestock at a tolerable minimum in most areas. Aerial hunting accounted for approximately 30 percent of the coyotes taken. . . .
>
> Safety and effectiveness . . . was enhanced by using a ground crew with radio capability to maintain ground-to-air contact.

Interestingly, the report writer stated that coyotes are adaptable partly because they are able to eat many different types of food, including rabbits, snakes, insects, fruits, and vegetables, even cacti. According to the bulletin, "if the rabbit population experiences a die-off, coyote numbers the next year will be less, but never low enough to endanger their survival. . . ." The report writer could have added "more's the pity."

Coyotes are not as great a danger to livestock as many ranchers believe. According to a feature news article by columnist Bayard Webster, one Charles Smith, a hunter from Putnam County, New York, has seen coyotes in the woods and fields that surround his home and sometimes has been able to observe them at fairly close range. Smith said that on one occasion, "I stood and watched [a] coyote on the lower end of the field hunting mice while sheep were on the other end of the field. They just ignored each other."

Dieter Radtke of Fort Myers, Florida wrote in a letter to *Defenders* that while working as a farmer and rancher in Oklahoma, Kansas, and Colorado, he had been disgusted with the wholesale slaughter of coyotes. He wrote that "coyotes can be the friends and helpers of farmers and ranchers. . . . Coyotes keep jackrabbits from overpopulating, eat damaging rodents, keep ponds clean by eating sick fish and frogs. Coyotes are just four-legged health police which do not cost the taxpayers one dime." The same cannot be said of the U.S. Fish and Wildlife Service.

Some critics complain that coyotes and foxes, and some other natural predators, will sometimes kill more chickens than they can eat. When this occurs the culprit is often a domestic dog that has gone semiwild. But marauding predators have been known to wreak havoc in poultry yards. The reason? People have created an artificial environment by confining dozens of chickens in a relatively small area. This is something that a coyote, fox, bobcat, or other predator would not normally encounter if it were hunting in fields or forests. Since these animals are hunters, they do what nature has equipped them to do: kill for food. When mass-killing occurs, it may be that the predator has become confused, since it is in an unnatural and unfamiliar situation. Or the predator may be sick or emaciated. Or it may believe that the large concentration of fowl poses a threat to its welfare.[2] For every effect there is a cause, and human beings are usually responsible, either directly or indirectly, for the biological aberrations of some wild animals.

A Trumped-up Case against the Cougar?

If there is one predator that is considered the Devil incarnate by sheep and cattle ranchers in western states, it is the cougar, otherwise known as the mountain lion. The cougar population is much lower than that of coyotes in this region, due in part to the cat's large size and the amount of territory it requires and in part to a systematic campaign of cougar extermination by the use of guns, traps, and poison prior to its protection or partial protection in some states under the Endangered Species Act of 1974. (This protection, where it exists, is periodically reviewed.) Partly as a result of this protection, the cougar population increased in some parts of its range during the 1970s and as of 1982 was estimated at several thousand.[3]

Complaints about cougar predation by stockmen—particularly sheep ranchers—increased during the late 1970s and early 1980s. In the spring of 1982, in response to complaints from ranchers, the assistant secretary of the interior for fish, wildlife, and parks, G. Ray Arnett, reversed a government policy of fifty years and allowed the superintendent of Carlsbad Caverns National Park in New Mexico to assist Fish and Wildlife Department employees in capturing and removing from the park a cougar that had been tentatively identified as a killer of sheep. It was decided that the lion would either be transferred to another area or killed by a federal game manager or government hunter. (We may safely assume the latter.) The decision was apparently prompted in part by the fact that in the fall of 1981 two ranchers had filed damage suits totaling more than $40,000 against the federal government, claiming that cougars had come out of parks in which they were protected and had killed a total of more than 800 sheep. (Neither of the ranchers employed herdsmen, but one wonders how this many sheep could have been killed without some kind of preventive action being taken.) One of the spreads borders Carlsbad Caverns National Park in New Mexico, while the other is adjacent to Guadalupe Mountains National Park in western Texas. The ranchers' suits were both denied since they could not substantiate their losses, but officials at the U.S. Department of the Interior and the New Mexico Natural Resources Department, possibly fearing future suits, began to question the protected status of the cougar in national parks.

To make things more difficult for mountain lions, ranchers in New Mexico and west Texas have enlisted the aid of federal and state predator control personnel, who have shot cougars and provided ranchers with lion traps. According to George Laycock, a field editor for *Audubon* magazine, a study of the stomach contents of eighty-four mountain lions revealed sheep wool in the stomach of only one animal. Sport hunters have done their share to "manage the cougar resource" in New Mexico, killing ninety during 1981. That same year, ranchers killed about twenty-five outside park territory. Mountain lions have a large range, and a Park Service study during 1980 concluded that there were at that time fewer than half a dozen resident cougars in Guadalupe Park.

But ranchers in that area continue to press for greater cougar "control" measures. Transfer of cougars to other areas has proven impractical due to the cats' large range, the difficulty of locating a sufficient number of animals, and the usual monetary considerations. There may also have been concern about improving public relations. According to Bill Dunmire, a twenty-five–year veteran of the National Park Service, there has been a long history of antagonism between Park Service personnel and New Mexico ranchers. In the late spring of 1982, the National Park Service announced that it would study the feasibility of selective cougar control. If the plan were implemented, cougars suspected of killing livestock could be tracked into the parks and killed. (This would be left to the discretion of Park Service personnel.)

In July 1982, the Sierra Club and Defenders of Wildlife filed a joint suit in U.S. District Court in Albuquerque, New Mexico, to prevent the killing of mountain lions in national parks by asking for a review under the National Environmental Policy Act. The suit is pending at the time of this writing. The suit claimed that, under the National Park Organic Act of 1916, the law that established the park system, the National Park Service is required to protect and preserve all wildlife within park boundaries. The plaintiffs feared a dangerous precedent if Park Service officials allowed cougars to be killed.

The National Park Service has asked for a two-year study that would monitor sheep losses, which could prove to be much lower than those that have been claimed by ranchers. The study would also determine whether, in the opinion of Park Service officials, there should be a shift away from the traditional policy of cougar protection in national parks. If the killing of mountain lions were allowed in parks, it might result in lessened protection for *all* species of wildlife in these "inviolable sanctuaries." This would be particularly likely to occur in view of the reduced protection for wildlife sought by G. Ray Arnett, and James Watt's successor, Interior Secretary William Clark.

A Reign of Terror against the Prairie Dog

If the mountain lion and coyote are numbers one and two (in either order) on the "nuisance wildlife lists" of most ranchers, then the prairie dog rates a close third. During the late summer of 1980, several South Dakota livestock ranchers lodged protests with the U.S. Fish and Wildlife Service and the South Dakota Department of Game when an "overpopulation" of prairie dogs began to deplete grass on their rangelands. For many years, prairie dogs had been competing with cattle for forage in this region, which has poor grazing conditions during much of the year.

There are two important facts to consider: 1) coyotes prey extensively on prairie dogs, but they have been severely reduced in the Dakotas by "control" practices; 2) open country is the natural habitat of the prairie dog, which was a native of the South Dakota countryside long before the first cattle ranchers arrived.

Nonetheless, federal animal "control" officials, with the help of South Dakota ranchers, are now engaging in mass exterminations of prairie dogs. In an article titled "War on the Dog Towns," in the October 1982 issue of *Defenders,* Hank Fischer wrote that badgers and bobcats as well as coyotes depend on the prairie dog as a source of food. These and many other animals are adversely affected by a decrease in the numbers of prairie dogs and the destruction of "dog towns," which consist of dozens of burrows in a limited area of grassland. The rare burrowing owl, several species of jackrabbits, and snakes live in unoccupied burrows that have been dug by prairie dogs. This type of habitat also provides nesting grounds for mountain plovers and sharp-tailed grouse and dusting areas for bison.

Fischer wrote that prairie dogs are usually the *result* rather than the cause of overgrazed ranges. He quoted Dr. Tim Clark who wrote his doctoral dissertation on the ecological role of the prairie dog. According to Clark, "since prairie dogs have existed in the grassland community for at least a million years, probably in large numbers, prairie dogs must be an integral part of that community, or else they would have destroyed it long ago."

Since the late 1970s, state wildlife managers in South Dakota have been poisoning prairie dogs in Custer State Park. Now the National Park Service, once again forsaking its "inviolable sanctuary" mandate, has begun using zinc phosphide as a poison in baited oats and phostoxin gas–producing tablets in burrows to reduce the number of prairie dogs at Wind Cave National Park, which borders on Custer State Park.

Since cattle are still an important element in the human economy, the naturally occurring prairie dog (along with the animals that are dependent upon it) can be expected to suffer more in the future as a result of "management" activities.

Dwarf Apples and Deer "Harvests"

The "economic connection" to the nuisance wildlife argument was exemplified in an article by Daniel J. Decker and James W. Caslick that appeared in *The Conservationist.* Titled "Deer Damage to Orchards in New York," the article described various methods that are employed to discourage deer from eating apples. These range from erecting wire mesh fences and electrified fences to hanging bags of tankage and kerosene-soaked rags. Predictably, Decker and Caslick (who are a wildlife research support specialist and wildlife science instructor, respectively, at Cornell University) concluded that all of the commonly used methods of nonlethal dispersion are either too expensive or ineffective. Therefore, the solution they proposed was "control through innovative deer harvest." This means that special hunting seasons would be initiated during periods of "most severe deer depredation." According to their plan, these hunts would be conducted in localized areas. But localized areas may become larger and larger areas when wildlife managers implement their innovative harvests, and wildlife respond with increased reproductive rates. Decker and Caslick claimed that, "from a management standpoint, the recreational aspects of these hunts would be secondary to the need for controlling the deer herd," which in all likelihood would have no real or imagined need to be controlled if it had not been "managed" for hunting in the first place!

But since deer feed only on the lower branches of apple trees, why do large numbers of deer cause excessive damage? One reason is that there is an innovative breed of apple tree—a dwarf variety—that is being planted in increasing numbers by apple growers in the northeastern states. These smaller trees produce a greater yield per acre and have lower pruning, harvesting, and *spraying* costs. The dwarf trees can be planted in higher densities—from 100 up to 800 per acre—thus providing "maximum sustained yield" deer with an abundant supply of food, another case of man's unnatural life-style resulting in demands for animal "control."

More Geese for the Gun

There are times when "nuisance animals" are conveniently used for sport hunting and even transported to new locations for this purpose. From the late summer of 1981 through the late spring of 1982, thousands of Canada geese congregated on reservoirs, ponds, beaches, and golf courses in metropolitan areas of Westchester County, New York, suburban Connecticut, Long Island, and northeastern New Jersey. Geese usually migrate each autumn to the southeastern United States, the Caribbean, and Central America. But these flocks of geese wintered on the outskirts of New York City and the surrounding area. Finally, municipal officials, claiming that the geese were becoming nuisances, asked the federal government for help. Jon Rosenberg, of the Morris County, New Jersey, Parks Commission, described the geese as "aggressive," and he said that "they move in and take over." (Apparently it did not occur to Rosenberg that, for three centuries, human beings have been engaging in essentially the same activities on and near Canada goose habitat in North America.) In mid-June, employees of the U.S. Fish and Wildlife Service descended upon the geese, capturing more than 1,200 in a series of raids. (Geese can be collected in late spring and early summer because their primary feathers are molting and most are unable to fly.)

The Fish and Wildlife Service relocated many of the geese in South Carolina and Georgia. Most were taken by the South Carolina Wildlife and Marine Resources Department and the Georgia Department of Natural Resources and released on private lands were waterfowl hunting is encouraged. In addition, about half a dozen Georgia farmers requested that state resource officials provide them with flocks of the captured geese, so that they could charge as much as $100 a day to hunt on their properties.

Why didn't the geese migrate farther south during the previous autumn? Perhaps because of habitat destruction in their normal wintering areas, although natural habitat has been mostly destroyed in the metropolitan district where they chose to establish themselves. Another possibility is that they may have found it easier to spend the winter in their places of summer residency. They had good grazing on open water and golf courses. And some of the reservoirs in metropolitan Connecticut, New York, and New Jersey do not freeze completely during some winters. A third possibility was suggested by Al Godin of the U.S. Fish and Wildlife Service, who coordinated the capture of the geese. Large numbers of Canada geese are killed each autumn on their southward migrations and Godin told William E. Geist of the *New York Times* (June 22, 1982): ". . . They seem to know that there are laws against hunting them in the metropolitan area. They are very, very smart."

Thus we see once again that hunting and game management may be a *cause*, rather than a solution, to the conflicts that sometimes occur between humans and wild creatures that are pursuing their natural inclination to live in a reasonable degree of comfort.

When Is Killing Justified?

Are there any instances in which the nonselective killing of "nuisance" animals would be justified? Yes, but only in extremely rare cases. For example, I do not doubt that the extermination of lampreys from the Great Lakes was the only way to deal with this parasitic eel. Apparently this was one of the very rare cases in which an animal has no apparent beneficial function in the ecology. Lampreys migrated through the Great Lakes during the 1950s and were destroying fish populations

139

by attaching themselves to fish and draining their fluids. Today, the lamprey is almost nonexistent in the Great Lakes chain.

In the summer of 1982, someone introduced piranhas into an Arizona lake, apparently as a prank. The piranha is a native of rivers in Equatorial regions of South America, principally the upper Amazon and its tributaries. This narrow fish, which averages about a foot in length, has razor-sharp teeth and will eat almost anything, including human bathers and swimmers, quickly stripping away their flesh. As of this writing, federal and state agencies are planning to eradicate the piranhas. I believe that it is a sound decision, as long as the eradication efforts do not adversely affect other forms of aquatic life. The piranhas are out of their normal range and habitat and pose a threat to aquatic life in the lake and possibly to life in other lakes and streams if they were to migrate. But aside from exceptionally rare cases such as these, there is little or no justification for the elimination of so-called nuisance animals, or, for that matter, for labeling animals as nuisances.

If more people had used the nonlethal approach in dealing with animals that they considered bothersome, there would be more varied species of wildlife and far fewer endangered species. One reason some people demand the elimination of many members of certain species is that these people are ignorant of the habits of these animals and do not know that animals of these species are usually much less of a problem than they believe. This lack of knowledge could be corrected by objective study, including field investigation.

For example, how many people know that weasals eat nuts and seeds, that fishers eat fruits and berries, that the otter's main diet does not consist of trout and other "game" fish, that wolves will usually give areas of human habitation a wide berth? Or, for that matter, how many are aware that coyotes are not strictly carnivorous?

Every species of native animal has a purpose in a balanced ecosystem. The sooner people realize this, the sooner the natural environment will be returned to a state of comparative harmony.

THE HUMAN PREDATOR ARGUMENT

Hunters' Argument: MAN, AS A PART OF NATURE, IS SIMPLY ANOTHER PREDATOR. BY TAKING THE PLACE OF THREATENED NATURAL PREDATORS, HE IS FILLING AN ECOLOGICAL NICHE AND HELPING TO KEEP NATURE IN BALANCE.

Analysis: One might ask why take the place of natural predators when these predators would do a much more efficient job of contributing

140

to ecological balance than hunters, who simply help to create an ecological *imbalance*? The fact is that a human being is *not* just another predator for many reasons:

1) Nonhuman predators hunt and kill because it is necessary for their survival. (They are biologically and physiologically adapted for predation.) This cannot be said of human beings who hunt because of personal choice, mainly for pleasure or recreation.

2) Since man is the most overpopulated species, this general overcrowding has resulted in the endangerment and extinction of many other species. Even if everyone wished to pursue a more primitive life-style in a natural environment, it would be impossible due to sheer weight of numbers. The result would be a rather sparsely populated suburbia. From this perspective, among others, humans have little justification to further disrupt ecosystems by unnecessary hunting.

3) Nonhuman predators usually live within the framework of a natural ecosystem that is as well balanced as could be expected considering game management and other environmental disruptions for which people are responsible. Natural predators contribute to the well-being of Nature and seldom, if ever, have an adverse impact upon their physical surroundings—the natural forest, grassland, desert, or tundra of which they are normally an integral part. Man, by contrast, lives in a largely artificial environment that is not within the framework of natural ecosystems. As a species, we humans are not a part of the natural environment, because we do little or nothing to contribute to ecological balance.

4) The system by which humans hunt is unnatural. We have seen how game management results in abnormally large numbers of deer and "game" birds in many areas and how natural predators would help to bring Nature into better balance. Likewise, while natural predators such as wolves and coyotes often hunt in packs, groups seldom consist of more than eight or ten individuals. These social groups, at least in wilderness country, are sparsely scattered throughout wide geographical areas. This is in contrast to the groups of a dozen or more hunters who often utilize limited areas of woodlands during deer seasons. Even when people hunt alone or in very small groups, hunter density in many areas is so great that at a given time there are often more hunters than deer.[4]

5) It is a commonly accepted myth that people must eat some meat in order to stay healthy. But many vegetarians have proven that they can remain in excellent health (and actually achieve much *better* health) by excluding meat from their diets.

6) It may surprise some people, but humans are not biologically equipped to be meat-eaters. This has been explained in many books

about vegetarianism. One of the more interesting is a concise sixty-five–page handbook by Barbara Parham titled *What's Wrong With Eating Meat?* (Ananda Marga Publications, Denver, Colorado, 1979). Parham notes that many anthropologists believe that our early ancestors were vegetarians and that during the Ice Age, when the changing climate reduced the amount of plant food, those living in northern latitudes were forced to become flesh-eaters.[5] The human species developed in warm climates where there were many wild fruits and vegetables. Parham compares human physiology with that of animals that are primarily leaf-grass eaters, animals that are primarily fruit-eaters, and animals that are primarily carnivorous. Humans match the first two groups in all respects and differ from the carnivores in all respects. Meat-eaters have claws, perspire through their tongues, have sharp, pointed front teeth, secrete acid saliva, have no flat back molar teeth, have strong hydrochloric stomach acid, and have an intestinal tract only three times their body length in order to quickly eliminate decaying meat. Humans and other noncarnivores have no claws, perspire through pores in their skins, have no sharp, pointed front teeth, have well-developed salivary glands that secrete alkaline saliva, have flat back molars, have stomach acid twenty times less strong than that of meat-eaters, and have an intestinal tract that is twelve times their body length.

The Omnivore Misconception

But don't human beings have canine teeth that resemble those of carnivores? And what about animals that eat both flesh food and plant food? Isn't man an omnivore? It is true that the canines, which are commonly, though incorrectly, called eyeteeth, resemble the teeth of natural predators in their basic shape. But in human beings these are rounded, helping us to chew leafy vegetables, such as lettuce, into fine pieces. The teeth of predatory mammals, particularly those at the front of their mouths, are bluntly pointed in order to tear apart the flesh of prey. Most "omnivores" living in the wild have evolved essentially as predators (for example, coyotes, fishers, martens, weasels, and also the two species of bears native to the lower forty-eight states, whose seasonal diets when living in areas of abundant free-flowing streams often include fish). In the northeastern United States, the raccoon most closely fits the definition of a true omnivore. But the coon's pointed front teeth and tapering claws suggest that its evolutionary forebears may have been carnivorous.

Presumably, during the evolutionary process, today's "omnivores" and their predecessors learned during times of low prey populations to supplement their meat diets with fruits, nuts, berries, and other plant foods that were sometimes abundant during late summer and early autumn. By eating plant food that did not have to be pursued and subdued, these predators conserved physical energy. But more important, the ability to digest a variety of foods enhanced their chances of survival. Most so-called omnivores could live on a diet of flesh food if necessary, but would have difficulty obtaining necessary levels of nutrition from a diet that consisted solely of plant foods.

Simply because a substance can be digested by a certain species does not mean that that substance is an ideal food for that species. Meat is not an ideal food for human beings even as a supplement and even if obtained from animals in the wild that lack the cancer-causing hormones, growth stimulants, chemical feed residues, et cetera that are commonly used on today's "factory farms." In most cases, people will acquire *better* physical health by pursuing vegetarian diets and by eating a minimum of fat- and chloresterol-rich animal products such as milk, eggs, and butter. Many vegans have reported feeling much better mentally, physically, and emotionally after having excluded all animal products from their diets. (It is true that protein is necessary in the human diet, but sufficient amounts can be obtained by eating soybeans, lentils, and some *combinations* of vegetables.)

Sometimes the most effective way to deal with a problem is through an indirect, rather than a direct, solution. While it is not the primary purpose of this book to convert people to vegetarianism, a vegetarian diet, if pursued by everyone in our society, would be the ultimate solution to man's mismanagement of wildlife. British animal rights activist Phillip Windeatt (author of *The Hunt and the Anti-Hunt,* available in the U.S. from Flatiron Books, New York, N.Y., copyright 1982) has commented on this. "The consumption of animals," he said, "is at the base of animal liberation. If you can break that relationship then people [will] regard animals in a far different intellectual and ethical light." If our society were to adopt vegetarianism as a way of life and substitute synthetic furs for those of animals, then except in very rare cases of self-defense and persistantly destructive animals where no nonviolent means of "control" sufficed, the only reason for killing any wild creature would be cold-blooded sadism.

Human "predators" who wish to live in harmony with Nature might investigate organic food sources and/or gardening. And they might petition their state fish and game department to help create a more harmonious natural balance by the reintroduction of large *natural* predators.

THE NUMBERS ARGUMENT

Hunters' Argument: SPORT HUNTING HAS A MINIMAL ENVIRONMENTAL IMPACT BECAUSE OF THE RELATIVELY SMALL PERCENTAGES OF MOST GAME SPECIES THAT ARE HARVESTED EACH YEAR AND BECAUSE OF THE COMPARATIVELY FEW SPECIES THAT ARE HUNTED. OF 796 SPECIES OF BIRDS IN NORTH AMERICA, ONLY 74 ARE HUNTED. OF 914 SPECIES OF MAMMALS IN NORTH AMERICA, 35 ARE HUNTED IN THE UNITED STATES, ONLY 16 IN CANADA. THERE ARE NO ENDANGERED SPECIES THAT ARE HUNTED. FURTHERMORE, THOSE WHO ARE EMPLOYED BY STATE FISH AND WILDLIFE DEPARTMENTS ARE CONCERNED ABOUT THE WELFARE OF WILDLIFE POPULATIONS: MOST WILDLIFE BUREAUS HAVE NONGAME AND ENDANGERED SPECIES UNITS.

Analysis: As of summer 1984, the wildlife agencies of forty states had nongame programs and about two dozen had state income tax checkoffs whereby a taxpayer could donate a specific amount (in some cases *any* amount) of his or her tax refund to the nongame wildlife programs of his/her state. In Missouri a constitutional amendment was passed in 1976 that increased the state sales tax by one-eighth of one percent, the funds from which were channeled into "comprehensive" wildlife programs and nongame management. As a result, Missouri has purchased 90,000 acres (almost exclusively hunted) of wildlife habitat. However, some of these "nongame" funds have been used for more devious purposes. According to the *New York Times* of March 16, 1980, Larry R. Gale, director of the Missouri Department of Conservation, said that some of the money obtained from state sales taxes would be used to expand the department's public school educational program—meaning among other things teaching children about wildlife from a game management perspective. (More will be written about these programs later. Many state wildlife agencies have incorporated hunter training into secondary schools, sometimes with the aid of public funds.)*

Most states that have a voluntary state income tax checkoff for nongame management use some of these funds to perpetuate hunting. This has been true in Colorado, as explained by the editor of *Colorado Outdoors*, the publication of the Colorado Division of Wildlife. In re-

---

*The Missouri Department of Conservation has also used sales tax revenue to reinstitute quail hunting and plant prairie grass for use as cover by ring-necked pheasants.

sponse to a letter from a reader in the May-June 1981 issue he made the following comment:

> Money from the non-game income tax checkoff program is currently helping to [buy habitat]. Utilizing $190,000 from the *non-game* cash fund, the Division is in the process of purchasing 633 acres to add to the Russell Lakes State Wildlife Area. (Added was $361,000 from the *game* cash fund.) This $551,000 addition is pond and marsh habitat and will provide waterfowl hunting for game bird enthusiasts. It will also benefit many species of nesting shore-birds, including the snowy egret, great blue heron, white-faced ibis, and avocet.

Hunters and Colorado wildlife officials would argue that since almost twice as much money was allocated from the state's game fund as from the nongame fund, hunters are aiding nongame birds to a greater degree than nonhunters are supporting "game" birds. But this skirts the issue. Protected birds and nonhunted mammals *must* share habitat with "game" birds and hunted mammals. They have no choice, any more than "game" species have a choice whether they prefer to live on non-hunted lands! Furthermore, as was pointed out earlier, a variety of nongame species is necessary in order to maintain a semblance of ecological balance on hunted lands. Meanwhile, habitat manipulators often increase "game" species at the expense of nongame wildlife that would normally coexist over the same type of habitat but that must compete with the larger than normal numbers of "managed" game birds and mammals for available food and cover.

It is from the root of "shared habitat" that springs the hunters' myth that money from hunting licenses and Pittman-Robertson funds benefits nongame species. These monies benefit nongame species only insofar as these species must share habitat with "game" animals and only as long as one or more nongame species are not declared "game" species or individual nongame animals are not illegally shot or caught in traps. In fact, "nongame" animals are often reintroduced or restocked into an area or are "favored" by habitat manipulation with the intent that future generations will produce theoretical harvestable surpluses. Most notably this has been true of martens and fishers, which have been restocked in the northeastern states, and also of moose, a small number of which have been relocated. Most of the financial support that nongame animals receive from hunters is coincidental, resulting from a small percentage of their license fees combined with some P-R revenues. Conversely, most ecologically oriented citizens who donate part of their tax refund do so because they believe that they are supporting unadulterated *nongame* management. But they are not. Taxpayers should not have their

145

money misspent to help support a commercial enterprise that is biologically and ecologically destructive.[6]

The Catch-22s of Nongame Management

Federal nongame funds that are allocated to states may also help to perpetuate hunting. The Forsythe-Chaffee Act, signed by former president Carter on September 29, 1980, allocated $20 million of federal funds (to be used from 1982 to 1992) to state fish and wildlife agencies, supposedly for nongame conservation. The F-C Act, or the Fish and Wildlife Conservation Act of 1980, appropriates these monies for so-called comprehensive management programs and for the management of "nongame" wildlife. Significantly, there is nothing written into the F-C Act or the laws of any state that stipulates that nongame species aided with these funds, or with state tax contributions, shall *under no future circumstances* be hunted or trapped. Consequently, many of these "nongame" programs may prove to be a bane, rather than a boon, to nonhunted wildlife. While there are exceptions, nongame birds and mammals are usually managed within the larger framework of game management—that is, their ecological relationship to hunted species. For example, if improving habitat for ground-nesting songbirds will also improve conditions for cottontail rabbits and provide cover for pheasants or ruffed grouse, then "nongame" management is undertaken. If nongame management would conflict with habitat manipulation for a popular hunted species, then it is usually not undertaken. The most obvious exception is in the case of endangered species, which are very few in number and usually have less than favorable range conditions. Often they are found in limited geographical areas.

In official management terminology, comprehensive management programs are designed to improve conditions for a variety of species, supposedly a more ecological approach than single or limited multiple species management. Again, if a habitat management plan did not result in increases in a certain game species (or a number of game species), then it would not be undertaken. Some of the common methods of habitat "improvement" have already been described. These activities are anything but ecologically sound.

What about predatory birds such as peregrine falcons, eagles, and large hawks? Aren't they often reintroduced and restocked despite their nonhunted status and despite the fact that they feed on game animals such as rabbits and squirrels? And don't large predatory birds often feed on "game" birds such as pheasants and partridge? Yes, but these birds of prey are stocked only when they are very low in number or nonexistent in a particular region. If, by some unforeseen circumstance, one or more species of large pred-

146

atory bird should increase dramatically, it is my belief, based upon past management decisions, that these species would be reclassified as nuisances and treated accordingly. As we have seen, the predator-prey ratio in most wild areas and wilderness areas is abnormally low in comparison to what it would be in a well-balanced natural ecosystem. Most commercial wildlife biologists consider ideal predator populations, whether hunted or nonhunted, to be in the range somewhere between a low level of "endangered" and an upper level that poses little or no threat to maximum sustained "harvests" of game animals.

For example, a certain area may offer excellent opportunities for the hunting of ruffed grouse. Nongame biologists may release Eastern goshawks into vacant goshawk territories or place captive goshawk eggs in the nest of another species of hawk in order to increase the number of goshawks in that area. But this will usually be done only if biologists feel that there are more than enough grouse for both goshawks and hunters and if they believe that by increasing the number of goshawks, the grouse population will not decline substantially. The goshawk population would, in all likelihood, continue to be maintained at a level below that which it would be in a well-balanced ecosystem that is characterized by optimum predator-prey ratios. This is virtually assured by the fact that pheasants, partridges, and some other "game" birds are often stocked in heavily hunted areas just before hunting seasons. Since most of these birds are killed by hunters, there will be few "game" birds for the restocked goshawks to feed on—particularly during late autumn and winter in those areas where goshawks do not migrate farther south. Thus they will be forced to prey on resident songbirds or small mammals such as squirrels and rabbits (which are also hunted but which are relatively high in number in many areas). With a partial reduction in prey as a result of hunting, there will be fewer large hawks than would otherwise be the case. Furthermore, we have seen that wildlife managers have suggested the removal of perch trees for predatory birds in prime "game" bird habitat, thereby helping to insure that these predators do not conflict with game management.

As to the nature of nongame animals, they are usually those that are low in number in a particular state or geographical area, those that pose a minimal threat to hunted species, those that cause little or no crop damage, or those that are small in size, thus arousing little interest among hunters. Or, as noted, they may be *game* animals that are too low in number to allow hunting or trapping. In Colorado nongame funds have been used to reestablish the river otter (a would-be trapped species), the greenback cutthroat trout (normally a "sport" fish), and the greater prairie chicken (under other circumstances a "game" bird).

147

One of Wisconsin's nongame programs is a trade of Wisconsin otters for Colorado pine martens (both of which are trapped in many states). Nongame biologists in Wisconsin are trying to determine the reasons for a decline in the population of frogs in that state. Frogs are an important food for mink (which are trapped) and raccoons (which are hunted *and* trapped). Frogs are also eaten by several species of large game fish.

Other states are also using nongame funds in ways that may benefit future game species. Idaho is studying caribou with nongame funds. South Carolina is conducting an alligator survey. Michigan is reintroducing the gray wolf. This might appear to be a commendable nongame project. But in nearby Minnesota the Department of Natural Resources has authorized the trapping of eastern timber wolves despite their classification as a "threatened" species.* As of this writing, the Minnesota DNR is considering a plan that would: 1) establish a sport hunting season on wolves, 2) permit interstate and international commerce in wolves and wolf pelts, and 3) allow state officials broad latitude in killing wolves at any time of the year.

It is impossible for an outside observer to predict how many species presently "aided" by nongame funds will someday be hunted and/or trapped. But, given sufficient populations, it is likely that members of *some* nongame species in a number of states *will* someday be killed and maimed by bullets, arrows, and traps.

A Matter of Ethics

Manipulation is the key even when the management of nongame species is not directly associated with the management of game species. And some of the methodology of commercial nongame biologists is both ecologically and ethically questionable. Consider a plan by the U.S. Fish and Wildlife Service in Montana that would place trumpeter swan eggs under wing-clipped, flightless mute swans. The mute swans are more numerous, and since mutes do not allow their progeny to occupy their territory after the young have become self-sufficient in the autumn, this is viewed as a method of increasing the number of trumpeter swans while decreasing the mute swan population.

This might be an unobjectionable procedure if a species were seriously threatened or endangered. But nongame biologists often develop

---

*Wolves believed to be preying on livestock in Minnesota are trapped by federal game managers, but trapping is restricted to within a quarter of a mile of a farm where predation has occurred and is limited to ten days (or twenty-one days if further depredation occurs).

a preference for a species and experiment in such a way as to favor a single species or a very few species at the expense of many other nongame species that have become established through natural succession. Once again, this is largely a result of homocentric educational conditioning, which fosters the supposition that animals are things to be used rather than sentient beings that should be left alone unless it becomes apparent that a species is in danger of extinction. And in some cases it might be better to allow the extinction of a species if this would not seriously disrupt ecosystems and if the procedures that would be used for saving the species would result in adverse conditions *for many members of nonendangered species.*[7]

Hunting is often used as an adjunct to nongame management. The theoretical well-being of one or a very few nongame or endangered species may be used as a justification to hunt *many* competing species. Albert W. Heggen, the chief of nongame management for the Utah Division of Wildlife Resources, wrote in a letter to the author that he did not understand the rationale of equating nongame lands with non-hunted lands.

> From the standpoint of a total wildlife management program, acquisition of a parcel of mountain brushland, for example, to protect the nesting habitat of a passerine species shouldn't preclude the use of that land from the harvest of deer, elk, or upland game bird species. In fact, control of browsing animal numbers might be necessary to protect the shrub species the nesting passerines need.

Thus even when nongame management is not undertaken in direct conjunction with game management, the management of nongame species often pits members of a few favored species against *many more members* of hunted species in an attempt to increase the populations of the favored species while creating a greater theoretical justification for recreational hunting. This is done despite the fact that controlled annual hunting usually does not result in long-term population reductions of established hunted species. But members of hunted species often suffer because of nongame manipulation.

Hunted and trapped animals also suffer as a result of scapegoating. A typical case is now occurring in the Adirondacks, where a few nongame biologists working with members of the High Peaks Audubon Society for the preservation of loons have created artificial islands on a lake. These islands are expected to be used as loon feeding and nesting sites. At face value, this would appear to be an altruistic procedure that has no relationship to the management of one or more game species. But this is not true. Loons have declined in recent years, partly because

149

of acid rains, which have reduced the numbers of fish (the loon's primary food) in many central and western Adirondack lakes and ponds. At the same time, it has been noted that deer, which have been drinking at the marshy edges of the lake, have destroyed loons' eggs by inadvertently stepping on their nests. Therefore biologists would consider deer hunting in this area to be one method of helping to increase the loon population. But deer are not responsible for acid rains or the commercial development and pollution of many lakes and ponds that would otherwise harbor loons.

Otters eat fish. Budget cuts are forcing a reduction of stocking operations in many states, including those that are affected by acid rains. Fishing license fees are a major source of revenue for state fish and wildlife agencies. Therefore, expect lengthened otter trapping seasons in many northeastern states. But otters are not responsible for environmental contamination! Intentionally or unintentionally, wildlife officials and commercial biologists are using wildlife as scapegoats for environmental problems that *they* have helped to create.

Degradation and Retrogression

But what about activities such as the New York State breeding bird survey, which is conducted by citizen volunteers and is supported and partially funded by the state Division of Fish and Wildlife? Certainly programs such as this have nothing to do with the management of game animals?

An item in the 1980-81 Program Report of the New York State Division of Fish and Wildlife may answer this question. According to the report:

> In the long term, comparative studies of breeding bird distribution may provide important clues to the general welfare of wildlife in the state and early monitors for possible problems involving environmental degradation.

Such as the degradation of habitat for "game" birds and hunted mammals. Healthy and abundant birdlife is a reliable indicator of game habitat quality. In the words of the report writer, even the study of acid rains is designed to "steer fishermen to better waters, schedule netting operations more effectively, avoid wasteful stocking in unsuitable waters, and become alert to potential losses of high priority fisheries."

There *are* progressive nongame projects in some states that are aiding true *nongame* species, but some of these species provide food for hunted and trapped wildlife. (Moreover, hunting opportunities may sometimes be increased by the establishment of a greater ecological balance.) Louisiana is reintroducing the brown pelican. Indiana is conducting a colonial nesting bird survey. New Mexico is surveying endangered fish and crustaceans. Ohio is reintroducing the eastern plains garter snake. New Jersey is reestablishing the eastern tiger salamander. New York State, in addition to half a dozen programs that directly aid hunters and trappers, other programs designed to increase "sport" fish populations, and still others of questionable ecological value, is conducting about a dozen beneficial programs with the use of state tax donations. Among them are the publication of a brochure on the bluebird (a species in decline) and the acceptance *as a gift* of 200 acres to be used as a state-run wildlife sanctuary. (Other projects undertaken in New York State during fiscal 1984-85 with the use of voluntary income tax contributions will be described in a later chapter.)

Unfortunately, as long as public hunting, trapping, and fishing exist and as long as hunters, trappers and fishermen are paying most of the operating expenses of state wildlife agencies, wildlife management, either directly or indirectly, will continue to be mainly a system by which maximum populations of game animals and sport fish are maintained. Furthermore, for every step forward in the establishment of nongame programs and endangered species restoration in most states, there have been at least *two steps backwards*, because hunting and trapping opportunities have been greatly expanded in recent years. The net effect has been retrogression and wildlife and habitat destruction.

The Endangered Endangered Species

Endangered species sometimes vary from geographical area to geographical area, and a species that is listed as endangered in one state may be listed as "rare" or "threatened" (lesser classifications) in an adjacent state.[8] We have seen that there is often pressure from hunters and livestock farmers to have large predators removed from endangered lists in those areas where they are protected by law. We have also seen that there is usually pressure to eliminate "nuisance wildlife," whose populations may be comparatively high in one area but rare or threatened in another area.

There are many examples of species that many people erroneously believe are classified either as endangered or nongame in every state but that are legal game in some states—not during limited seasons but at any time during the year. Examples: In Arizona, javelina and coatimundi; in Alaska, the wolf, bison and Arctic fox; in Montana, the lynx; in Massachusetts, (incredibly) chipmunks, flying squirrels, and skunks! The badger and oppossum are also legal game in some states. Some of these animals may have been reclassified in these states by the time you read this, because species classifications undergo periodic reviews. But in most states, the number of hunted and trapped species continues to increase as reintroduced species and those that are extending their range (such as the coyote, marten, otter, fisher, and wild turkey) become established and state game bureaus seek increased funding. Naturally, a nongame or endangered animal that is unable to avoid bullets, arrows, traps, or poison becomes *truly* endangered!

In Massachusetts the Division of Fisheries and Wildlife as of this writing has refused to place a limit on the number of bear hunting licenses it issues despite the fact that there are fewer than 100 bears in the state. Incredibly (or perhaps predictably) the Massachusetts Fish and Game Board increased the length of the state's bear hunting season by one week in 1982. Claiming that its purpose is to "create recreation for those who can go hunting," the board also voted to authorize the use of .357 magnum handguns in addition to shotguns, rifles, and longbows, all of which were legal weapons for bear hunts. The hunting and trapping of bobcats continues in Massachusetts despite an annual statewide "harvest" of only ten to twenty from 1976 through 1980. In 1978 the division suggested that the bobcat trapping season be cut in half while the hunting season remained the same, also that the eastern half of the state be closed to bobcat hunting. But the bobcat is virtually extinct in heavily developed eastern Massachusetts; no one has seen a bobcat in this region for many years. In Connecticut and Pennsylvania, there continues to be legal bear hunting despite protests from environmental groups that bears are at or near an endangered level in these two states.

As this is being written, a controversy is brewing along the Atlantic coast over the possible hunting of *whistling swans*. During the period 1961–81, the number of whistling swans in the Atlantic Flyway increased from 28,000 to 78,000. Despite this increase, the latter figure is a mere 23,000 birds above the minimum established by the U.S. Fish and Wildlife Service. Yet some wildlife biologists, citing crop damage by swans, want to establish swan hunting. Other reasons given are a reduction of natural mortality, easier swan management, and an increase in hunting opportunities for "sportsmen." Human nature being what it is, one would expect the latter two factors to influence the biologists' recommendations. As to a reduction in mortality, limited hunting would normally result in a stable or slightly increased swan population, due to larger broods and more abundant food and nesting territory for survivors.

The biologists no doubt took this into consideration. They sought a thirty-day swan season with a one-swan–per–day bag limit. This meant that a hunter could have legally killed as many as *thirty* swans per season! This would have been reminiscent of the market hunting of a century ago. The irony is that the biologists estimated that a "harvest" of this proportion would result in an annual kill of only 5,000 birds, thus *not significantly reducing the swan population*!

If you are struck by the illogic of this logic, you are not alone. Either the swan hunting advocates grossly underestimated the projected annual swan "harvest," in which case the total number of Atlantic Flyway swans would very likely have fallen well below the established minimum, or else a mere 6.5 percent of the swan population along the flyway would have been killed annually by hunters. And if this small a "harvest" satisfied game biologists, then a person might question the validity of their complaints about crop damage, natural mortality, and the difficulties of swan management.

Officials of the U.S. Fish and Wildlife Service, fearing a public uproar if swans were hunted, have let it be known that the states would be required to establish swan hunting regulations.

The swan management rationale is not uncommon. Consider the case of the black duck. During the 1950s, the population of this species along the Atlantic and Mississippi Flyways was approximately 700,000. A decade later, the black duck population had declined to about 450,000, and the winter count during 1982–83 was only 300,000. Yet the Fish and Wildlife Service still permits hunters to shoot two black ducks per day during waterfowl seasons. Some states, including upstate New York, have dropped the "bag limit" to one per day, but still allow a total season "harvest" of *five ducks per hunter*![9]

Meanwhile, in the Willamette Valley of western Oregon the dusky Canada goose is threatened. During 1982–83, there was a wintering population of only about 20,000, indiciating a continued decline from previous years. The "solution" proposed by Fish and Wildlife Service biologists? Any goose over six pounds (a number of large species of ducks and geese resemble the dusky) would have a "bag limit" of *one per day by each hunter* during the hunting season! In all likelihood, continued hunting of black ducks and dusky Canada geese will *reduce* their populations because of the magnitude of "harvests" and also because there are many competing species of ducks and geese that would move in to fill the vacuum created by their decline. The hunting of black ducks and dusky Canada geese is symptomatic of the continuing mismanagement of American wildlife by wildlife officials, game managers, and commercial biologists on both the federal and state levels.

The Turkey Hunting Syndrome

Some forms of legal hunting are so reprehensible that they are criticized even by a small number of hunters. An example is the spring turkey hunts that are held in many states, including Pennsylvania. They are conducted at a time when the young of many species are being born and when most female turkeys (hens) are sitting on their nests incubating eggs. According to wildlife officials, this has been taken into consideration. Since only the male turkeys (toms) may be legally shot, the reasoning is that the females, most of whom are glued to their nests, will not be mistaken for the bearded toms, many of whom are still courting. But there have been many cases of mistaken identity. According to sanctuary owner Norman Ives,* some hunters have expressed outrage over the shooting by their colleagues of hens on their nests.[10] Ives, who owns Wildlife Acres sanctuary on the New York State border in western Pennsylvania, says that it is not uncommon for spring turkey hunters to flush incubating hens from their nests. Alerted by a hunter, Ives periodically checked an abandoned nest. Eight days later, the hen had not returned to the dissheveled nest. (Hens often do not return to their nests if they have been flushed a great distance.)

According to Dr. Willard Stanley, a biology instructor at Fredonia State University College in Fredonia, New York, a hen turkey usually will not lay another clutch of eggs when her nest has been destroyed or seriously disturbed. This is particularly true, says Stanley, if the hen has been incubating for several days or more.

R. H. Hesselbart, noted ornithologist, columnist, and lecturer, wrote that most naturalists agree that there should be no hunting or disturbances in the woods during nesting time. Said Hesselbart: "This stands to reason for the simple reason that it is not only the turkeys that are disturbed but all ground and many tree nesting birds that are disturbed or the nest destroyed completely."

Ives has seen crippled hens that he says were shot during spring hunts. He claims that a biologist for the Pennsylvania Game Commission once told him that one reason for the spring gobbler hunts is to crop the large toms because when they breed they can injure a hen's back.[11]

The Pennsylvania turkey hunts have resulted in a substantial number of hunting accidents. According to an article in *The Potter Enterprise* (Coudersport, Pennsylvania), a total of ninety-nine hunters were accidentally shot during fourteen spring and fall hunts from 1975–81. This included twelve fatalities. Most of the accidents occurred at close range.

---

*Ives is president of the Allegany County (N.Y.) Bird Club. He often lectures about wildlife at schools and community gatherings.

The average distance was about 110 feet. It is not easy to mistake a human being for a turkey at this range. But shooting can legally commence one-half hour before sunrise, when visibility can be restricted, especially on cloudy or misty mornings. Pennsylvania Game Commission officials have suggested better safety training, increased proficiency at turkey calling, and mandatory blaze orange clothing during turkey hunts. Naturally, wildlife officials have not suggested abolishing the spring hunts.[12]

Two Hundred and Fifty Million and Rising

In New York State, some hunters' groups have expressed interest in hunting mourning doves. Therefore wildlife biologists are studying the feasibility of dove hunting (which already exists in some states). Doves are uncommon in the interior Adirondacks, but more numerous in south-central New York, where they sometimes feed on agricultural grain. Normally, the dove's diet consists of seeds, berries, and small fruit. Doves eat wheat and corn, but they will usually eat only what they find on the ground after harvesting has taken place. The mourning dove is scarcely larger than a blue jay. It is migratory throughout most of New York State except in the extreme Southern Tier, where it is found throughout the year.

Barney Fowler, an outdoor writer for the Albany (New York) *Times-Union*, is by no means an "antihunter." But Fowler termed the mourning dove "a pleasant, inoffensive bird . . . familiar at feeders." And he added, "Open season on mourning doves? What next, chickadees?"

Fowler's hypothetical question is not as absurd as it may sound. A written comment by an official of the Washington State Department of Game shows the lengths to which some wildlife managers are prepared to venture in order to satisfy hunters and insure a generous flow of revenue into the coffers of their respective game bureaus. In response to an inquiry about the hunting ban that was enacted in part of Washington following the 1980 eruption of Mount Saint Helens, J. K. Patterson, research program manager, wrote in a letter to the author dated February 9, 1981, that a large area surrounding Mount Saint Helens had been closed to public access, including hunting and fishing, because of the potential danger of continued eruptions. But he was quick to point out: "If it weren't for this ban, we would permit hunting because the area that is still vegetated needs a harvest to prevent animal overpopulation and damage to the existing vegetation."

Since wildlife populations were completely wiped out in the most severely devastated area around Mount Saint Helens, one might ask how wildlife from fringe areas of the devastated terrain could be expected to overpopulate in the absence of a sufficient food supply or, for that matter, to populate to a level where they would seriously threaten existing vegetation. And if large animals such as deer, elk, and bears had migrated away from the fringe areas of devastation into areas that were not seriously affected by the eruption, they would be out of the territory affected by the ban and could be legally hunted!

Should sport hunting be vindicated because a minority of bird and mammal species are legally hunted in the United States? Don Atyeo (*Blood and Guts,* published in Great Britain by Paddington Press) revealed the number of animals that were killed in the United States during a single year (autumn 1975 to autumn 1976). The totals? In round figures, 24,000 bears; 55,000 caribou; 67,000 moose; 84,000 antelope; 102,000 elk; 2,600,000 deer; 21,000,000 waterfowl; 27,000,000 rabbits; 32,000,000 squirrels; 94,000,000 upland game birds. This is more than 175 million animals. Atyeo's figures do not include the "harvests" of minor hunted species or the large number of animals that were trapped, poisoned, shot illegally, or killed as "nuisances" by private individuals, state wildlife managers, and the U.S. Fish and Wildlife Service. Taking these into consideration, Atyeo estimated that more than 250 million wild animals were deliberately killed by people in the United States during this one-year period. This is more than one animal for every American man, woman, and child, an incredible death rate of eight animals per *second*!

When viewed as *one aspect* of man's mistreatment of his nonhuman brethren, sport hunting assumes a new and grotesque dimension. (How many animals are killed each year in American vivisection laboratories and on factory farms? How many seals are killed along the coast of Alaska? How many dolphins are killed by tuna fishermen? And on and on.) In the final analysis, it is not of such great importance *how many* species of wildlife are hunted as how and why they are hunted, how many people hunt them, the nature of the species that are legal game, the role of these animals in a healthy ecosystem, the environmental effects of the loss of a certain number of individuals of these species, the ecological results of intensive public hunting, the effects that hunting has upon family units and social structures of hunted species, and the fact that *all* recreational hunting is nonessential and exploitive.

THE SPECIES ARGUMENT

Hunters' Argument: MODERN HUNTING POSES NO THREAT TO WILDLIFE POPULATIONS, AND THIS CAN BE PROVEN BY THE FACT THAT THERE ARE MORE DEER, GROUSE, PHEASANTS, RED SQUIRRELS, GRAY SQUIRRELS, RABBITS, AND MANY OTHER

GAME SPECIES NOW INHABITING MOST WILD AREAS THAN THERE WERE 50 OR 100 YEARS AGO. IN FACT, IT WAS BECAUSE OF THE EFFORTS OF HUNTERS THAT MANY SPECIES THAT WERE NEARLY EXTINCT AT THE TURN OF THE CENTURY HAVE RE-POPULATED AND ARE NOW WELL ESTABLISHED THROUGHOUT MOST OF THEIR NATURAL RANGES.

Analysis: There are also greater numbers of elk, pronghorn antelope, and wild turkeys than there were at the turn of the century. There are more ducks and geese as a result of water containment projects in Canada and the United States supported by Ducks Unlimited, a waterfowl hunters' organization. But there are fewer wolves, foxes, mountain lions, lynx, bobcats, eagles, and large hawks in most wild areas than in 1900. Coyotes are making a comeback, but they are suffering as a result. As might be expected, greater numbers of certain species often indicate a poorly balanced ecosystem. There are several reasons for this:

1) The relatively high populations of some species were deliberately created by game management so that these species could be hunted, either immediately or in the future. As we have seen, most wild areas are managed as huge hunting preserves, where hunted species that are high in number exist (according to game management theory) to be hunted and trapped.

2) In the case of large ungulates such as white-tailed deer, elk, and caribou, there is much less territory per animal in most areas than there was at the turn of the century—partly as a result of game management practices that created high populations. Without sufficient land there will usually be insufficient browse for large herds during winters in cold climates—*except where habitat has been manipulated*. Greater numbers of large herbivores result in stress and related die-offs, particularly in winter deer yards, where competition for food is most intense (for example, small woodlots in agricultural areas). The potential for this problem faces some species of "game" birds in certain areas. In one state (South Dakota), there are such a large number of ring-necked pheasants that an average of ten per season are killed by *each hunter*! As previously noted, a large percentage of the pheasants that are stocked in areas of less than favorable habitat and that survive hunting seasons die during winter from a lack of adequate food and cover. This is a dangerous situation both biologically and ecologically.

3) Since regulated hunting is often accompanied by unnatural reproductive changes (i.e., in the case of deer, a greater percentage of mating does, a greater percentage of does that bear two and occasionally three fawns, earlier ovulation of does, greater sex dif-

ferentials among fawns, and greater numbers of does mating with fewer and younger bucks; and in the case of "game" birds, larger broods and a greater ratio of females to males among chicks), the populations of these and some other hunted species will not adjust to more ideal ecological levels in areas where food would be sufficient and habitat conditions would be favorable for *smaller* numbers of animals. Thus, as long as these species are "managed" for hunting, there will continue to be more "game" birds and mammals in many areas than the land and the sources of food can easily support even after the conclusion of hunting seasons.

4) With the exception of the "game" animals that exist in a limited number of wild or wilderness areas, the high numbers of hunted species in the United States are confined to rather compact tracts of remaining natural habitat. It is true that some deer have adapted to conditions on the outskirts of suburban districts, but these are not ideal or natural habitats. Since there are large numbers of game birds and deer in some compact natural compartments, mainly as a result of changes in land use and game management, impetus is given to the "harvestable surplus" theory.

Disaster for Land and Wildlife

Game management has proven to be an ecological nightmare. During the Nineteenth Century, man caused the near-extinction of many species by land development and overhunting. Animals of many species were then reintroduced in some areas by wildlife managers, and the numbers of these animals increased. In areas where there were the greatest populations of deer and "game" birds (usually agricultural regions interspersed with woodlands), crop damage sometimes resulted. Therefore there was a convenient excuse to declare more species either "nuisances" or legal game and to kill more members of existing "game" species. The reproductive patterns of hunted wildlife changed, and large populations more than compensated for controlled hunting. Meanwhile, state wildlife bureaus continue to lengthen hunting seasons and attempt to increase the numbers of hunters, since "game" species in many areas will be able to sustain gradually increasing "harvests." This problem could have been averted if natural ecosytems had either been maintained or established and if many species had not been overhunted to the brink of extinction during the last century. But hunters and wildlife officials do not consider longer hunting seasons, increased "harvests," and greater numbers of hunted species to be a problem—far from it!

We have seen that the artificially high populations of some hunted species are detrimental to competing species that are rare, threatened, or endangered and that consume the same foods and normally share the same habitat. Man has completely altered the balance of nature by creating an overabundance of a small number of commonly hunted species.

Since the mid-1960s, increasing winter incursions into northern wild areas by snowmobilers have added an additional element of stress on wintering deer. Deer require natural silence to an even greater degree when they are in a weakened condition because of cold, snow, and/or an absence of high-quality browse. Many snowmobilers hunt during autumn.

There is virtually *no* wilderness area in the United States that may be classified as a truly *natural* ecosystem in normal balance—*normal* meaning, among other things, ecologically compatible populations of *all* species that existed when the European settlers first arrived. Hunter-dominated wildlife management, from its inception through the most pseudoscientific methodology, has done more to disrupt than to balance Nature. Those who use the "numbers argument" should reconsider their views in the light of ecological consequences.[13]

THE ECOLOGY ARGUMENT

Hunters' Argument: HUNTERS AREN'T RESPONSIBLE FOR UP-SETTING NATURE'S BALANCE. MODERN HUNTING HAS NOT RE-SULTED IN THE EXTINCTION OR ENDANGERMENT OF A SINGLE SPECIES. IN FACT, IT WAS HUNTERS, AS EARLY CONSERVATION-ISTS, WHO STOPPED THE SLAUGHTER OF WILDLIFE AND ESTAB-LISHED SEASONS AND BAG LIMITS. TODAY IT IS NOT HUNTING, BUT HUMAN OVERPOPULATION THAT CAUSES THE DRAIN ON NONRENEWABLE RESOURCES. IT IS INDISCRIMINATE PROGRESS-AT-ALL-COSTS THAT DESTROYS HABITAT AND WILDLIFE.

Analysis: This is an extension of the previous two arguments. But since hunters frequently make this assertion, it deserves a close examination.

When people speak in absolutes (i.e., "not a single species"), their statements are automatically suspect. The U.S. Fish and Wildlife Service is doing very little to discourage the worldwide extinction of species, as evidenced by their CR-150 "Hardship Permit" and Import-Export License, which allows holders to bring into the United States sport-hunting trophies of endangered wildlife such as the snow leopard (which is still found in parts of the Himalayas). Safari Club International is one organization that has applied for a license to import parts of endangered trophy wildlife into the United States.

In general, modern hunting is not as damaging to *already imbalanced* wild ecosystems as the indiscriminate slaughter of passenger pigeons, herons, moose, wolves, buffalo, et cetera proved to be a century ago. This is simply because game management is designed to maintain high numbers of commonly hunted species. But those who say that "game" populations are not seriously depleted by hunting neglect to mention that the habits and reproductive behavior of *individual* animals *are* adversely affected.

We have seen that there are times when some "game" species may be hunted in some areas despite being at low population levels. If members of a popular "game" species such as the pheasant, ruffed grouse, quail, or raccoon, or a commonly trapped species such as the marten, mink, or fisher should become very low in number in an intensively hunted area, biologists may restock that area. But when there is a low population of a "game" species in a large wilderness that receives relatively light hunting pressure, game managers usually will not stock, reasoning that fewer animals will be more difficult for hunters to locate. Therefore, few members of the species will be killed until natural factors such as increased food, reproductive changes, and greater survival rates begin to increase the population.

Regulating the Destruction

It is true that the first "conservationists" were hunters, but they called for regulated hunting seasons and legal "bag limits" only when it became obvious that if they did *not* do this most species of wild animals would become either extinct or endangered in many wild areas. This could be compared to a person who shoots every animal in sight and then decides that unless he slows his rate of destruction he will soon deplete his supply of live targets. We may safely assume that these turn-of-the-century "reformers" were motivated not so much by a concern for Nature as by self-interest and a concern about the preservation of recreational hunting. Today there are national parks and some national wildlife refuges where hunting is still prohibited, but this has been due largely to the foresight of environmental protectionists. It is not a result of action initiated by hunters' groups or state fish and game bureaus!

President Theodore Roosevelt and Gifford Pinchot were the first well-known American conservationists. They accomplished a great deal, establishing the first areas of semiprotected wilderness in America. But both men were notorious trophy hunters. Roosevelt's study was lined with the stuffed heads of many species of animals he had shot on his foreign and domestic big game expeditions. (In hindsight, we should not be overly critical of either of these men. They lived in an age of environmental ignorance and were thoughtlessly pursuing a popular pastime.)

The framers of the Endangered Species Act of 1973 listed both habitat destruction and hunting as reasons for the decline of many species of wild animals in America.[14] But the wording of the ESA was changed in 1982 to eliminate the reference to hunting having contributed to the endangerment of species.[15] This was a result of heavy lobbying by hunters' groups, led by the Wildlife Legislative Fund.

Humanitarianism versus Self-interest

Dr. C. H. D. Clarke, himself a hunter, wrote in the *Technical Report on Wildlife* of the Temporary Study Commission on the Future of the Adirondacks (the predecessor of the Adirondack Park Agency, which now regulates land use within the park):

> Do hunters, I wonder realize that the strongest argument in favor of "no hunting" areas is the apparent fact that rare species and new introductions—moose (if they come), lynx, panthers, marten—cannot survive in the presence of hunting? A substantial number of people want intact or restored environments and if hunting is an obstacle and hunters will not cooperate, then the social value of hunting must be considered on trial. It need not be.

I would agree with all but the final statement. Hunting should be a social, ecological, and ethical issue. It is an important humanitarian issue because a person's love of nonhuman life is an accurate gauge of his or her compassion and concern for the earth. A person who believes in the protection of wildlife for the animals' sake is also likely to believe in the preservation of wilderness for the sake of wilderness rather than wanting to preserve it simply because it offers "recreational" opportunities of one sort or another. Once again it is a matter of self-interest versus the welfare of the earth, of what one can do to benefit the environment as opposed to how the earth's "resources" can benefit the individual.

Like most prohunting arguments, the one now being considered is illogical. Hunters who use this argument realize that habitat is rapidly being destroyed and that there are endangered species. There is human overpopulation and hunter overpopulation. If a hunter realizes this, then why should he not be willing to give up hunting? It is irrelevant whether development, overpopulation, air and water pollution, chemical contamination, hunting, or a combination of these factors has resulted in the endangerment of species, loss of habitat, and deteriorating

161

ecosystems. A problem exists, and if a person realizes this, he or she should be willing to help solve it by constructive means. This would include the replacement of game management with a system whose goal would be to restore optimum numbers of all nonextinct species normally found in each type of natural habitat throughout the United States.

The decline and deterioration of habitat that is rampant throughout the United States and elsewhere has resulted from a wide variety of activities that do not encompass a sense of individual and social responsibility to the earth and the life that it supports. It is true that nonhunting factors such as human overpopulation, habitat destruction, and pesticide contamination are more significant factors than sport hunting in the disappearance of wildlife. But habitat for many species is often destroyed in the process of manipulation for game management, and toxic chemicals are sometimes used for "managing" wildlife. Moreover, the existence of these practices is due in very large part to the excessive number of American hunters. There are many more hunters in the United States today than during the late 1800s, when many species were hunted to extinction or near-extinction. The present system of wildlife management, which creates high populations of game species, is the only way to provide enough target animals to satisfy 30 million American hunters.

We should not lose sight of the fact that insensitivity is a state of mind. It is the same utilitarian philosophy that spawned indiscriminate progress-at-all-costs that is also responsible for the present system of wildlife management and the nonessential killing of wildlife! Many people still hold the archaic view that the earth and its plant and animal life exist for the benefit of mankind. Therefore, rather than making changes in their life-styles to compliment the normal patterns of Nature, most people try to mold Nature to fit their false and elusive concept of Utopia, characterized by ease, comfort, and self-gratification. This has been a major factor in the destruction of the natural environment as well as another important reason for the establishment of today's wildlife mismanagement practices.

A final point to consider: It has been established that the worldwide extinction rate of all species from all causes has increased from one species per year during the 1950s to one species per day in 1984. It is estimated that by the year 2000 the rate of disappearance of species will be one per *hour*. Will present methods of managing wildlife be adequate to stem the tide of extinction, and, moreover, will they be able to prevent now abundant species such as the white-tailed deer, ruffed grouse, and pheasant from being added to the endangered lists in many parts of the United States?

World-renowned oceanographer Jacques Cousteau said in testimony before Congress, "The real cure for our environmental problems is to understand that our job is to salvage Mother Nature. . . . We are facing a formidable enemy in this field. It is the hunters . . . the hunters who feel compelled to carry on the courageous struggle against nature that was true for a million years, and to convince them that they have to leave their guns on the walls is going to be very difficult, very difficult."

THE WILDERNESS HUNTING ARGUMENT

Hunters' Argument: PERHAPS HUNTING *IS* BIOLOGICALLY HARMFUL TO SOME HUNTED SPECIES IN THOSE PARTS OF THE COUNTRY THAT ARE HEAVILY HUNTED. BUT MANY WILDERNESS AREAS IN THE UNITED STATES AND CANADA RECEIVE VERY LIGHT HUNTING PRESSURE. CERTAINLY NO BIOLOGICAL HARM RESULTS TO HUNTED SPECIES IN THESE WILDERNESS AREAS, WHERE VERY SMALL NUMBERS OF ANIMALS ARE KILLED ANNUALLY BY HUNTERS.

Analysis: Like many other prohunting arguments, this one reflects a gross shortsightedness. There *are* remote wilderness areas in Canada and the United States that are utilized by very small numbers of hunters. These include large sections of Alaska, parts of the Rocky Mountains, and, in the east, interior portions of the Adirondacks and the White Mountains of New Hampshire. But those who use this argument overlook several important factors.

First, as the human population increases so does public use of wildlands and wilderness areas. If hunting remains legal in these remote areas, within thirty or forty years hunting pressure will increase substantially, as will the harmful biological and ecological effects of hunting in these regions.

Second, state wildlife agencies do not operate in order to maintain light hunting pressure. The goal of wildlife officials is to *increase* the number of hunters and consequently increase hunting pressure to a level as high as wildlife populations in various geographical regions can withstand. And this is what may occur in *all* areas that are now characterized by light hunting pressure unless efforts are made to curtail hunting in these regions or, at the very least, to establish limits on the number of hunters that are allowed to utilize them.

Third, while very light hunting pressure may cause little biological harm to hunted species, there are other factors that exaggerate the effects of *any* hunting. These include imported tree diseases and, in the northeastern states, acid rains and snows. These and other adverse environmental factors contribute to decreases in the populations of some species of fish and wildlife and result in an interspecies imbalance. When hunting is added to these degrading influences, it may magnify the ecological consequences.

Fourth, while light hunting in some wilderness areas may cause relatively little biological harm to hunted species, neither does hunting have any *positive* biological or ecological value. The only way in which very limited hunting would benefit a species would be if hunters were completely selective, shooting only those animals that were old, diseased, crippled, or malnourished, and this is not the case.

Fifth, this argument overlooks the adverse effects of light hunting (or *any* hunting) on families and societies of social animals such as deer, elk, and caribou and on *every* animal that is killed. The death of any animal in its prime is a misfortune, much more so when it results from a nonessential activity such as recreational hunting.

V./CONSERVATION ARGUMENTS AND HUNTERS' PRACTICES

THESE ARE ARGUMENTS BY WHICH HUNTERS PORTRAY THEMSELVES AS LEADERS IN CONSERVATION. AMONG THE COMMON THEMES ARE THAT HUNTERS' GROUPS FIGHT FOR THE ESTABLISHMENT OF PUBLIC WILDERNESS AREAS AND THAT MONEY FROM HUNTING LICENSES AND FEDERAL TAXES ON FIREARMS AND AMMUNITION PROVIDE THE BULK OF THE MONEY THAT IS SPENT FOR HABITAT ACQUISITION AND THE WELFARE OF WILDLIFE. I HAVE ALSO INCLUDED AN ANALYSIS OF THE ASSERTION THAT MOST HUNTERS SCRUPULOUSLY OBSERVE GAME REGULATIONS, RESPECT LANDOWNERS' RIGHTS, AND POLICE THEIR RANKS IN AN ATTEMPT TO FERRET OUT THE "SLOBS."

Hunters are almost the only effective protectors of wildlife. Without their interest, without their strong organization and overwhelming conviction that they have a stake in the natural order of things, game and wildlife would disappear before the advance of civilization far more rapidly than it does.
—The late Roderick Haig-Brown, quoted by John Power, outdoor columnist for the Toronto (Ont.) *Star* (July 24, 1982)

THE WILDERNESS PROTECTION ARGUMENT

Hunters' Argument: HUNTERS ARE AMONG THE MOST VOCAL PROPONENTS OF WILDERNESS PRESERVATION. THEY HAVE BEEN AT THE FOREFRONT OF THE CONSERVATION MOVEMENT. SPORTSMEN'S GROUPS HAVE FOUGHT HARD FOR THE ESTABLISHMENT OF NEW AREAS OF PROTECTED WILDERNESS.

Analysis: Ted Trueblood, the well-known hunting writer, is among those who have used this argument. An article by Trueblood in the January 1981 issue of *Field and Stream* titled "How They're Won" described his struggles to help establish Idaho's River of No Return Wilderness and preserve that state's Upper Snake River area from inundation by a flood control project.

In his fight to save the RNR Wilderness, now a 2.2 million acre

165

federal preserve, Trueblood helped to form the River of No Return Council, a coalition of environmentalists, preservationists, and "sportsmen." Wrote Trueblood:

> We were opposed by logging and mining interests, the Farm Bureau, cattlemen's and sheepmen's associations, ORV organizations, and developer types. . . .

Trueblood wrote that it is important for "sportsmen" who are seeking the extension of the wilderness system to enlist the support of established conservation organizations. He cited the Sierra Club, the National Wildlife Federation, The Wilderness Society, and the Izaak Walton League. He contended that overwhelming public support is necessary if "sportsmen" are to win any conservation struggle:

> The other side—the loggers, miners, developers, or whatever—will always have more money for propaganda and lobbying. Lacking money, the only way we can sway the public to our side is through sustained effort.

Trueblood did not state specifically that most hunters support wilderness protection, but his article implied that hunters' groups are often active in seeking the public and political support that is necessary if wild areas are to be preserved. While most preservationists would not quarrel with the results of Trueblood's environmental activism, they might question his motives. (Would he be as zealous in his battles for wilderness if fish and wildlife in the area that he was fighting to save were to be protected?)

I doubt that anyone knows the exact percentage of American hunters who either support or oppose increased protection for wilderness. I have been unable to find any such statistics. But even if a poll or polls *have* been taken, there are such a large number of variables that must be considered, including types and amounts of protection of which a hunter would approve or disapprove, that the poll(s) would probably be unreliable. In view of this, it will be necessary to draw upon my personal experience as well as my research.

First, it is important to distinguish between the opinions of *organized* hunters (those belonging to hunters' groups) and the opinions of *a majority* of hunters (or hunters *taken as a group*). While it is true that there are many hunters who belong to well-established conservation organizations (or to hunters' organizations), it would be safe to say that of the 30 million hunters in the United States, the overwhelming majority do not belong to any group that openly advocates and attempts to legislate the preservation of wilderness.[1]

Perhaps the largest and most well-known group that seeks its membership mainly from the ranks of hunters is the National Rifle Association. But one would be hard-pressed to find a single example in which the NRA *as an organization* has actively fought for the preservation of a specific wilderness area. The National Shooting Sports Foundation booklet *What They Say About Hunting* lists the official policy statements of nineteen organizations, including conservation, hunting, and wildlife protection groups. Official goals are not necessarily a flawless gauge of organizational policies, but it is significant to note than *none* of the groups whose memberships include the largest percentages of hunters list wilderness protection as an objective. These include the National Wildlife Federation, North American Wildlife Foundation, Wildlife Management Institute, The Wildlife Society, Wetlands for Wildlife, the National Rifle Association, and the National Shooting Sports Foundation. The closest allusion to wilderness protection appears in the charter of Wetlands for Wildlife, which (author's italics)

> . . . advocates and participates in the acquisition of wetlands and wildlife habitat in the U.S. which will be transferred to federal or state agencies exclusively for public purposes to be *managed and maintained.*

One official goal of the National Wildlife Federation is,(author's italics) "the wise use and proper management of those resources of the earth upon which the lives and welfare *of men* depend, the soils, plant life, and the wildlife." The Izaak Walton League, which was originally founded as a fishermen's organization but which now boasts within its ranks a small number of environmental activists, is committed to "protect and restore the soil, forest, water, and other natural resources of the U.S. and promote the enjoyment and wholesome utilization of these resources."

According to the IWL policy statement, hunting is one means of wholesome utilization of resources, provided that it is "characterized by the highest order of humaneness, sportsmanship and respect for the species hunted."

Naturally, not every member of these organizations supports official policy, but we are dealing with *groups* of people and not with individuals who are exceptions to the rule. As a general rule, a person will not join a group unless he or she is in general agreement with the official objectives set forth by its administrators. It is true that prohunting conservation organizations have, at various times, actively campaigned for the "preservation" of America's wildlands. But here we are faced with conflicting definitions. If one accepts a very loose definition of *preser-*

vation, then any group that at one time or another has set aside natural acreage or has sought some form of wilderness legislation for any purpose whatever could be termed a "wilderness protection organization." By this definition even the Boone and Crockett Club would have to be considered a preservationist group!

The primary purpose of the major hunting organizations is to preserve wildlife and other "resources" strictly for human use, meaning hunting, trapping, and fishing. Thus, even if the concept of "resource preservation" may be applied to the goals of hunting organizations, it exists for reasons of individual and collective self-interest and not for the protection of wilderness as an end in itself.

Stagnation versus Progress

While it is true that most ecological organizations have not officially expressed opposition to sport hunting, it is equally true that the character of activist groups such as the Sierra Club, the National Audubon Society, The Wilderness Society, and the World Wildlife Fund has been changing since the early 1970s. There is every indication that these and similar organizations that are dedicated to wilderness and wildlife conservation now consist of a much larger percentage of nonhunting backpackers, nature photographers, and bird-watchers and a much smaller percentage of hunters. Aside from the 1980 Kellert survey, which included only a minute sampling of opinions, there are no statistics that would give an indication of the attitudes about wildlife exploitation (including hunting) that exist within most of these groups. The reason is that the majority of these organizations do not include attitudes about recreational hunting on the questionnaires that they sometimes send to their members. But emphasis is definitely shifting away from "saving" the wilderness and its wildlife for hunting and trapping to preserving wildlife and its habitat for intrinsic values. Increasingly, the administrators of these groups and writers for their publications are emphasizing the ways in which balanced wildlife populations benefit the earth's ecosystems.

There are many environmental and animal protection groups, such as Greenpeace, Friends of the Earth, The Environmental Defense Fund, the Natural Resources Defense Council, the North American Wildlife Park Foundation, the Animal Protection Institute, and the Fund for Animals, that have been formed since the mid-1960s that are gaining members at steadily increasing rates. (For example, membership in the Fund for Animals increased from about 80,000 in 1974 to more than 200,000 in 1982.) Gradually, the old-line conservation groups that were dominated by consumptive "recreationists" (such as the Boone and Crockett Club, the Izaac Walton League, Ducks Unlimited, and, more recently, Wetlands for Wildlife) have become essentially lobbying groups for hunting, fishing, and trapping. Meanwhile, the newer and more progressive environmental organizations have become the *avant-garde* of the ecology movement.

It is true that many conservation organizations are operating on tight budgets and some of these groups, such as Defenders of Wildlife, are deeply in debt. Likewise, groups such as Friends of Animals, which are attempting to establish protection for many hunted and trapped species, often find that necessary expenses nearly outstrip their income. On the other hand, the National Rifle Association (about 60 percent of whose members are hunters) and organizations that consist almost entirely of hunters are not greatly hindered in this respect. Part of the reason is that they usually are not trying to *change* laws, but are merely attempting to maintain the status quo or prevent laws from being changed in such a way as to adversely affect their special interests. The organizations whose major goal is to perpetuate the hunting-trapping-fishing ethic are comparatively well funded. This is especially true of the NRA. As of 1984, annual NRA membership dues were fifteen dollars.* Multiply that by 2.3 million members and the resulting figure is a hefty sum! Yet, for lobbying purposes, the NRA remains officially a "non-profit organization."[2]

The more familiar one becomes with hunters' organizations, the more apparent it becomes that these groups are not comprised primarily of altruistic Nature-lovers. What about the opinions of hunters who do not belong to any organization, and what is the overview of conservation that is most typical of hunters taken as a group? First, we should remember that a hunter is simply someone who hunts. This is the only requisite that is needed for a person to be considered a hunter. He or she does not have to hunt deer or ducks or grouse or pheasants. He or she may be anyone from a "varmint" shooter on a Wyoming ranch to a lion-stalker in the African jungle. Thus there are many loggers, miners, cattlemen, sheepmen, ORV operators, and "developer-types" who hunt. On this basis alone, one can determine that many hunters are opposed to wilderness preservation.

---

*Ten dollars is designated for a subscription to one of the NRA's two magazines, *The American Hunter* or *The American Rifleman*. Assuming that the full amount is used for publication expenses, this would leave more than $11 million per year for other activities. The NRA employs a staff of 350.

The Opponents of Wilderness

By all indications a significant percentage of American hunters—particularly those who live in rural areas—are opposed to the establishment of protected wilderness, even when that protection does *not* cover fish and wildlife. Likewise, many hunters are strongly opposed to federal or state regulations that would curb development or commercial exploitation on existing wildlands. This has been illustrated in case after case.

A few typical examples:

—In Vermont a coalition of loggers, snowmobilers, and hunters have fought attempts by environmentalists to designate some of the 55,000 acres in six roadless areas around that state as wilderness areas. The environmentalists favor an end to logging on these state lands and a ban on the use of off-road vehicles such as snowmobiles. But there is no antihunting stipulation in their proposal. So why would hunters lobby against it? 1) While this plan would guarantee the protection of wildlife habitat, and thus enhance hunting opportunities, hunters would not be allowed easy motorized access into these areas. 2) Many trappers use snowmobiles during late winter to transport themselves and their traps to secluded beaver ponds. 3) Most hunters believe that logging is beneficial to wildlife since it creates additional browse for deer—despite the fact that commercial logging kills and displaces many small animals and destroys their natural habitat as well as drastically altering the environment.

—In the early 1970s, rural Vermonters, most of them hunters, strongly opposed the establishment of the Silver Lake Wild Area located in the Green Mountains northeast of Brandon. The proposed wild area was less than fifty square miles, hardly more than a pocket wilderness. The only major restriction was that motor vehicles *other than snowmobiles* would be disallowed. The Silver Lake Wild Area was eventually legislated into existence in a somewhat weakened form after vocal opposition from hunters who disliked restrictive laws and apparently did not entertain the prospect of a time-consuming hike into their favorite hunting territory.

—In the Adirondacks, most resident hunters vociferously oppose the Adirondack Park Agency. Their motives are partly economic. They fear that protected wilderness will result in the curtailment of business opportunities and encourage economic stagnation. In addition, many rural Adirondackers are employed by forest industries. Neither the management nor the laborers in these businesses have established reputations as wilderness preservationists! Yet a large percentage of loggers, logging truck drivers, lumber company employees, and paper mill workers are hunters. Bumper stickers run the gamut from "Adirondack Park Agency—Another Word [sic] for Tyranny," to "Out of Work and Hungry? Eat an Environmentalist!," to the familiar "God, Guns and Guts. . . ."

—Most resident hunters in the Adirondacks either favor or have shown no concern about the ecological hazards posed by the black fly and mosquito spraying programs, which, until they were halted on state lands by court action in 1982, were administered under the auspices of the New York State Department of Health and the Department of Environmental Conservation. The opposition to this ecologically destructive undertaking has come mainly from the environmentally oriented Adirondack Council, the High Peaks Audubon Society, and other members of the Federation of New York State Bird Clubs. The vast majority of those who belong to these groups are nonhunters. The Adirondack Conservation Council (a coalition of hunters' groups) has never actively opposed the aerial or mobile application of pesticides. In fact, the ACC has never officially gone on record as opposing these programs. Most resident hunters in the Adirondacks consider environmentalists to be outsiders or "tourist-types."

—In the autumn of 1983, the Adirondack Conservation Council opposed the classification of the 10,000-acre Perkins Clearing Forest Preserve in the Adirondack Park's West Canada Lake Wilderness as a "wilderness area." The ACC and most other resident hunters favored either a "primitive" or "wild forest" designation (lesser classifications). The Perkins Clearing, which had originally belonged to International Paper Company, had been acquired by the State in a land swap that had been approved by New York State's voters in 1979. The tract, which had been logged, consists mainly of immature trees. Why did hunters prefer a nonwilderness designation? 1) Adirondack lands that are classified as wilderness cannot contain roads or vehicle trails; therefore, hunters would have to *walk* greater distances to reach the best hunting grounds. 2) Most Adirondack tracts that have been classified as "primitive" or "wild forest" have no prohibitions on the authorized use of off-road vehicles and float planes in designated areas. 3) Most resident hunters in the Adirondacks oppose the classification of Adirondack parklands as wilderness because this would preclude habitat manipulation on these lands for the purpose of deer management if a state constitutional amendment were to permit logging in the park. A compromise classification of the Perkins Clearing finally passed, whereby interior areas were designated as wilderness, with a buffer zone of wild forest near roads.

—In Minnesota, hunters vocally criticized the establishment of the Boundary Waters Canoe Area, which has been declared a haven from motor boats and ORVs. Many hunters are equally adament in their opposition to the Voyageurs National Park. The park has not been formally opened as of this writing, but visitors are permitted to use parklands provided they respect the rights of those who still own private property. In the late 1970s, the federal government allowed the owners of camps and resorts twenty-five years to sell their land to the park or dismantle their buildings and leave the land as Nature created it. The park is small, about thirty miles in diagonal length and only twelve miles wide at its broadest point. It hugs the Canadian border. It is actually an extension of the huge Superior National Forest, which spans most of northeastern Minnesota. Hunting is allowed in the national forest. But many residents, including a large percentage of those who hunt, consider the formation of the park to be a communist-style land grab.

—During the winter and spring of 1980, many residents of the village of Haines, Alaska, including a substantial number of hunters, actively opposed efforts by environmentalists to prevent a local contractor from logging an environmentally sensitive area that serves as a wintering ground for about 3,500 bald eagles, the largest concentration of this species in North America. Some residents (presumably hunters) threatened to shoot the eagles if a coalition of environmental groups led by the Sierra Club won a suit filed in a district court that would prevent the logging of 54,000 acres of an 84,000-acre tract of *state land* classified as commercial forest. The operation would employ fewer than 100 workers, many of them not from the Haines area. Meanwhile, the state of Alaska had guaranteed the contractor a 17.5 percent profit on the gross worth of the logs—which, according to the U.S. Forest Service, are 70 percent rot!

—Alaskan hunters reacted angrily to an amendment to the Alaska Lands Bill,* sponsored by Sen. Paul Tsongas (D-Mass.) in 1980, which would have established protection for wildlife on sensitive interior tracts. Many hunters reacted with anger and suspicion when the California legislature, in the mid-1970s, passed a resolution recognizing in principle that animals have the right to humane treatment. Some hunters were incensed when HR 4805 was introduced by Congress in 1981. This bill, which has been reproposed (Spring 1984) in a weakened form, would have prohibited public funding of medical and behavioral experiments on animals where alternative procedures have been perfected and

*This bill established the Alaska National Interest Lands Conservation Act (ANILCA), which designated about 100 million acres of federal lands in that state as protected wilderness.

where there would be duplication. This bill was viewed as a potentially dangerous precedent toward the establishment of legal rights for animals.

Conservatism versus Conservation

Those who protest the extension of the wilderness system and increased protection for existing wildlands usually do so as private citizens and not as hunters. This is one reason it would be difficult to confirm specific numbers or percentages of hunters who might be classified as "antiwilderness." But considering my research, experience, and acquaintences with many hunters in the northeastern states, I believe that the percentage is substantial—in all likelihood a majority. It is doubtful whether Ted Trueblood would have won many new friends among *Field and Stream* faithful if his January 1981 article had not detailed his activities on behalf of the 1938 Idaho referendum that established a game commission in that state. His article was published at a time when hunters, having gained access to many national wildlife refuges, were (and still are) attempting to have hunting restrictions removed in national parks in Alaska and the other states. These are among the last remaining inviolable sanctuaries in America.

It should be remembered that the hunter lobby strongly supported Ronald Reagan in his successful 1980 presidential campaign. Reagan, a lifetime NRA member, opposes any form of gun control. Another reason for his support by many hunters may be that he opposes the "forever wild" concept, preferring convenient public access into national forests, resource exploitation where opportunities exist, and limited development.

Why do many hunters oppose a wilderness ethic? One reason is that most American hunters are politically conservative (as opposed to "conservationist"). Most hunters resist social change and resent government paternalism. And, in the traditional view, Nature is man's domain and animals exist for his consumptive use. The irony is that the unrestricted use of natural lands threatens the habitat of the animals that hunters pursue!

Hunters who are actively involved in the fight to preserve wilderness would probably contend that whether a person hunts has no relationship to his or her opinions about conservation. They would undoubtedly express the view that hunters who are active conservationists should persuade those who oppose wilderness protection to change their opinions (assuming that this were possible.)

But what about hunters who seem to favor wilderness preservation? Are they true conservationists? An example might help to place this into

173

perspective. In 1980, many employees at an International Paper Company plant near Ticonderoga, New York, signed a petition designed to thwart the planned rerouting of state Route 74 along a dirt road that traversed a large area of wild forest. Most of those who signed the petition were hunters. Does this mean that they favor wilderness preservation? No, because the argument that prompted them to sign the petition was that if the road were rerouted, a considerable amount of valuable hunting territory would be lost and a large percentage of those who signed the petition hunted in the area that would have been affected by the proposed highway. The irony is that most of those who are employed at the mill strongly oppose the Adirondack Park Agency, whose purpose is to protect the wild character of the park!

I once had a conversation with a hunter who was a middle-level executive at a tool manufacturing company in a town in Massachusetts. The plant piped its wastes into a river that flowed between the company's two main buildings. The state had served notice that the manufacturer, along with others who were dumping effluents into the river, would have five years to seek alternate methods of waste disposal. I asked the hunter-executive whether he thought that it was a sound conservation practice to allow his company's wastes to pollute a river. His rather indignant reply: "We don't run this business according to a conservation principle. We run it according to the principle of profit and loss!" Perhaps nothing could better describe modern hunting and the current system of wildlife management.

In summary, it is true that some hunters support some forms of conservation. But to claim that a majority of hunters support the concept of protected wilderness is to ignore convincing evidence to the contrary.

THE CONSERVATION ARGUMENT

Hunters' Argument: HUNTERS UNDOUBTEDLY DO MORE TO BENEFIT CONSERVATION IN AMERICA THAN THE REST OF THE POPULATION COMBINED. IT IS MAINLY HUNTERS' MONEY THAT SUPPORTS WILDLIFE RESTORATION, WHICH INCLUDES NON-GAME AND ENDANGERED SPECIES PROGRAMS.

Analysis: With the exception of the "starvation argument," this is probably the most frequent defense used by hunters. A typical example is found in the policy declaration of the North American Wildlife Foundation, which is closely allied with the Wildlife Management Institute:

The majority of the funds that support [wildlife conservation] come from the so-called consumptive users of wildlife—the hunters and anglers. For the most part, the non-hunting taxpayer who enjoys bird watching or other nonconsumptive uses of wildlife gets essentially a free ride in the pursuit of his hobby.

Considering the facts, this statement could be compared to that of an ex-convict who attempts to convince a potential employer that if it were not for thieves, burglars, and embezzlers the employer would not have a thriving business! The statement makes no mention of those who subsidize public lands where hunting is encouraged. Nor does it mention those who purchase land for private wildlife sanctuaries where hunting and trapping are to be prohibited and thereafter pay maintenance costs and taxes on these lands.

It is true that hunting, fishing, and trapping license fees and P-R funds account for about 70 percent of the revenue that is collected by the fish and wildlife agencies of most states specifically for the management of fish and wildlife.[3] But this is part of the *problem* that is inherent in the current system of wildlife management. It is not a method of funding that would lead to an environmentally sound *solution* to unsound methods of managing wildlife.

The overwhelming percentage of money that is received by state fish and wildlife agencies from license fees and P-R funds is used either directly or indirectly to maintain populations of game animals and sport fish. The funds specifically earmarked from these sources for endangered species and nongame wildlife are negligible or nonexistent. As we have seen, nongame management is often undertaken for the purpose of insuring future "harvestable surpluses." But even taking into account the fact that many nongame species are managed as potential game species and that hunting is often used as an adjunct to nongame management, fish and wildlife bureaus in the forty-eight contiguous states spent an average of only 3 percent of their funds on nongame animals during 1978, despite the fact that these animals comprise 90 percent of domestic species. (This figure does not include the money that was spent on "comprehensive" management programs.) Between 1978 and 1981, there was some progress in expanding nongame and endangered species programs in some states. But the Reagan-Watt budget cuts of 1981 put an abrupt halt to this trend. For example, as of April 1, 1982, $400,000 per year in federal endangered species funds was cut from the allocation to the New York State Division of Fish and Wildlife. This is the entire amount that this agency had been receiving annually from the federal government since 1975. There is no logical reason why other sources of revenue could not compensate for this loss, including revenue from hunting and fishing licenses, combined with cuts in game—particularly big game—programs. But since the activities of state wildlife agencies are determined by economic logic rather than ecological considerations, this option will not be considered in the foreseeable future.*

A few typical examples of the disparity in the amount of funds spent for game management versus those allocated for true *nongame* management:

—During fiscal 1980, the New York State Division of Wildlife spent a relatively meager $588,000 to restore endangered species† and $302,000 for "habitat protection," which included the maintenance of wildlife management areas. All other funds, with the exception of a grant for the New York State Breeding Bird Atlasing Project, were directly or indirectly allocated for the management of game animals and sport fish. This means that only about *7 percent* of the $15.7 million spent by this department for fish and wildlife management during fiscal 1980 *directly* aided nongame wildlife, endangered species, and environmental protection programs. (Hunting, fishing, and trapping license fees funded about 85 percent of the Wildlife Division's wildlife management activities. The remainder came from federal aid,‡ interest, fines, deer management permits, and "miscellaneous"—the latter totaling $160,000.) Meanwhile, the wildlife pathology staff, which investigates wildlife diseases and illegal poisoning of nontarget birds and animals, has an annual budget of only about $60,000. Only two of the three staff members are full-time employees.[4] (The chief pathologist, Ward Stone, is a vocal defender of hunting and trapping.) Many states have no wildlife pathology facilities.

The wildlife departments of other states operate in essentially the same fashion.

—In one recent year, the New Jersey Fish and Game department spent approximately $1 million on game habitat manipulation, $700,000 on pheasant and quail propagation, and only $25,000 on endangered species, of which there is no shortage in the Garden State.

—The Montana Wildlife Department includes a nongame branch that receives $40,000 per year and is staffed by a single biologist. By contrast, Montana's seventy game species receive $13 million annually. Montana has more than 700 species that are officially classified as nongame, including eagles, falcons, badgers, and marmots.

*During fiscal 1984–85, a meager $174,000 of an estimated $2 million in voluntary state income tax contributions was used by the New York State Division of Fish and Wildlife for endangered species restoration. An additional $143,000 from this source was used to fund three new endangered species enforcement positions.
†This included only $188,000 in state funds.
‡This included $800,000 in Pittman-Robertson funds.

What the Hunters Want

What about hunters' claims that money from hunting licenses and federal excise taxes on guns and ammunition aids nongame and endangered species? Part of the reason for the minimal funding of nongame programs (particularly from these sources) and endangered species is that many hunters *do not want* their money spent for nongame management and endangered species restoration and make their views known to their legislators and state wildlife bureau or game commission.[5]

The situation that exists in New York State is emblematic. The New York State Conservation Council (a coalition of hunters' groups) has consistently refused to endorse any increases in state funding for nongame wildlife, even though nongame animals are often managed within the larger framework of game management. This funding might enhance hunting opportunities in some locations by contributing to a greater variety of non-hunted species that would not seriously compete with major hunted species for food and territory. Therefore a semblance of ecological balance would be created. But like hunters elsewhere, most of those in the Conservation Council support more effective game management—and *only* game management. Meanwhile, the Conservation Council has for many years advocated the creation of a New York State Wildlife Department separate from the DEC and controlled by a game commission (i.e., members of the Conservation Council).[6]

Topping the list of priorities of most hunters are the perpetuation of high "game" populations, new and longer hunting and trapping seasons, and new lands where hunting and trapping are permitted.[7] This was exemplified during the late summer of 1982, when a measure supported by the New York State Conservation Council that would have set up prohunting committees to consider expanding hunting into *all* public parks in that state passed both houses of the state legislature before being vetoed by then-governor Hugh Carey. Carey's decision came after members of environmental and animal protection groups beseiged the governor's office with telephone calls and telegrams protesting the proposal.

In 1983, a bill supported by hunters' groups and the New York State DEC that would have given the Division of Wildlife the authority to establish hunting in all New York State parks (including, presumably, Harriman Park) passed the legislature but was vetoed by Governor Mario Cuomo—after the governor's office had received many letters from environmentalists asking him not to sign the bill.

Then, in February 1984, members of fish and game clubs from across New York State met in Syracuse to further weaken the nongame programs that had been proposed or were already funded by state income tax contributions to the Division of Fish and Wildlife.

Among their recommendations were:

—Cut the cost of endangered species program from $174,000 to $100,000.

—Approve $17,000 for training wildlife rehabilitators *for one year only.*

—Eliminate $20,000 for a status survey of the common loon.

—Eliminate $8,000 for a brochure on how to build bluebird houses and establish bluebird trails.

—Eliminate a cooperative $50,000 contract with Nature Conservancy (for the collection, processing, and storage of data on rare plants, animals, and ecosystems).

—Eliminate $137,000 for a waterbird sanctuary on Shooter's Island in New York City.

—Reject a gift of 200 acres of land near Cheektowaga in Erie County that would be administered as a wildlife sanctuary. (Twenty-five thousand dollars had been proposed by the DEC for a ranger to help administer programs on the sanctuary.)

Meanwhile, the "Gift to Wildlife" tax donations that benefited hunters (including proposals for pheasant management, management of state game lands, prohunting manuals for use in public schools, and a "fish and wildlife exhibit" of stuffed animals that had been shot or trapped were vigorously endorsed.

The reader should remember that funds for these programs do not come from hunting licenses, Pittman-Robertson funds, or even general tax revenues. They are *public donations,* a considerable percentage of which come from nonhunting environmentalists (who are helping to pay for hunter's programs!). The hunters' proposals were submitted to the Conservation Fund Advisory Council* for its consideration.†

Tilting the Scales of Injustice

Such large percentages of state and federal wildlife funds are funneled into management programs that favor popular "game" species that there are often not enough funds to aid less frequently hunted species. A tragic example is the plight of the woodcock. Along the At-

---

*See Notes—"Conservation Arguments," footnote 6.

†Apparently these hunters were not acting in an official capacity as members of their fish and game clubs because they requested anonymity and their names were never published in the media. However, the meeting was well planned and well attended, evidence that these hunters were influential members of the New York State Federation of Fish and Game Clubs.

lantic Flyway, the woodcock population is decreasing at a rate of 10 percent a year. Many of these birds have deformed eyes; some have a single eye. Biologists suspect pesticide poisoning, possibly as a result of the aerial spraying of coniferous forests in Maine and New Brunswick for the "control" of spruce budworms. (There is evidence that toxic components of this insecticide may be responsible for Reye's [pronounced "Rise"] syndrome, a deadly degenerative disease of young people.)

Woodcocks are not covered by federal duck stamp revenue, and due to the "shortage" of money that is available for research, commercial biologists are not studying this problem. Predictably, federal and state game biologists assume that hunting does no additional biological harm so there has been no shortening or cancelling of woodcock seasons. (One wonders what harm may result from eating parts of a diseased woodcock!)

A small number of hunters now favor the replacement of waterfowl stamps with migratory bird stamps that would fund the "management" of all hunted migratory birds. But Congress and the U.S. Fish and Wildlife Service (not to mention Secretaries Clark and Arnett) believe that there are higher priorities than funding research that might help to prevent the extinction of an infrequently hunted species. Furthermore, influential executives within the lumbering industry favor budworm spraying, and spraying operations have been conducted under the supervision of a federal agency, the U.S. Forest Service.

It is doubtful whether the issuance of mandatory federal stamps for migratory bird hunting would be of much help to the beleagured woodcock population. The revenue obtained from the sale of federal waterfowl stamps helps to pay for natural and artificially created marshlands that harbor ducks and geese, but it does very little to fund health care for waterfowl. This revenue *does* contribute to the demise of large numbers of ducks and geese as a result of shotgun pellets and lead poisoning.

Subsidizing Recreational Hunting

Do nonhunters pay for wildlife management? During one recent year, the funds allocated to the U.S. Fish and Wildlife Service from the Department of the Interior amounted to $235 million. Of this, $13 million resulted from the sale of duck stamps, $18 million from taxes on fishing gear, and $56 million from the 11 percent (Pittman-Robertson) excise tax on firearms and ammunition. The remaining $148 million (63 percent) came from general tax revenues. During some years the figure has been as high as 90 percent!

Both hunters and nonhunters pay federal income taxes. But since

179

only about 15 percent of the employed U.S. population are hunters, the remaining 85 percent of the tax funds allocated to the Fish and Wildlife Service come from the pockets of nonhunting taxpayers. (This is assuming that average percapita wages earned by nonhunters are approximately the same as those of hunters.) If 75 percent of the funding for federal "wildlife conservation" is a result of taxpayers' money—and this is an average annual figure—this would mean that about *two-thirds* of federal game management programs are directly financed by nonhunters! This includes the infamous coyote control program that consumed more than $9 million of nonhunters' tax money during 1978.

In addition, the 15 million nonhunters who own firearms (which are used for target or skeet shooting or gun collections) are paying about $20 million a year in Pittman-Robertson funds. This money helps to provide land and target animals for hunters and, as we have seen, helps to destroy natural ecosystems.

National Wildlife Refuges: Refuges from What?

As of the spring of 1984 the National Wildlife Refuge System totaled 89.7 million acres, including 53.7 million acres added in Alaska in 1981. It is comprised of 410 individual units. A full 85 percent of the money for the system's maintenance is taxpayer funded, the remainder coming from the sale of duck stamps. As of 1983, some form or forms of hunting were permitted on 214 refuges (52 percent of the total).* This percentage is not affected by Alaskan refuges; more than half of the refuges in the lower forty-eight states allow the hunting of some species. In fact, the number of National Wildlife Refuges where hunting is permitted has been steadily increasing since 1958.

The National Wildlife Refuge System was formed during the 1930s, using duck stamp revenue. (These stamps were originally authorized under the provisions of the Migratory Bird Hunting Stamp Act of 1934.) In 1958 the "inviolable sanctuary" concept was breached by an amendment to the 1934 act that permitted part of any National Wildlife Refuge to be classified as a "wildlife management area" for the hunting of migratory birds and resident species. The Refuge Recreation Act of 1962 opened more national wildlife refuges to hunting. And in 1966 the National Wildlife Refuge Administration Act instituted the hunting of resident "game" birds on a greater number of refuges. (Some environmentalists believe that the NWRAA was a congressional trade-off to hunters who opposed the Endangered Species Act of 1966.) The

*In addition, the trapping of certain species is permitted on eighty-six refuges (21 percent of the total).

Fish and Wildlife Service continues to open an average of ten to fifteen refuges to hunting each year.

"Shortstopping" is undertaken on some of the refuges along the Atlantic and Mississippi Flyways where waterfowl hunting is permitted. This is the planting and/or placing of copious amounts of corn and/or grain in feeding areas to encourage migrating ducks and geese to remain on and near refuges for longer periods of time during autumn hunting seasons.

The death toll from hunting on National Wildlife Refuges has been significant. In 1982, more than 750,000 animals were killed on these lands. The annual budget of the NWRS is about $40 million. Calculated in terms of nonhunter revenue and the amount of land where hunting is practiced, this means that nonhunters are paying approximately $17.5 million annually to support lands that are not refuges, but hunting preserves!

Hunters argue that National Wildlife Refuges support many non-hunted species and realtively few hunted species. This variation of the "shared habitat" argument is academic. First, because the number of hunted species on NWRs are increasing, not declining. Second, because hunting seasons are usually lengthened, seldom shortened. Third, because non-game species are often disturbed and dispersed if there are a large number of hunters in a given location (or if habitat is manipulated for hunting).[8] Fourth, is the matter of definition. According to Webster's Dictionary, a *refuge* is "a place where one is safe or protected, a shelter, a sanctuary." But according to wildlife management terminology *conservation* is not conservation, it is controlled killing. Likewise, "refuges" are often not refuges. Even if the system of managing wildlife is not reformed in the near future, it would seem that wildlife officials on both the federal and state levels should use more precise terminology to describe their activities and the lands where hunting is encouraged.

Legalized Vandalism on NWRs

As long as there are no massive public protests, an increasing number of National Wildlife Refuges will be opened to some form or forms of hunting in the future, resulting in a further dilution of the sanctuary principle. The Great Swamp National Wildlife Refuge edition of *The Refuge Planner,* a publication of the U.S. Fish and Wildlife Service, leaves little doubt about official policy on NWRs. According to this publication:

> The conventional meaning of "refuge" has probably changed little since the turn of the century, but definite changes in legal direction and permitted public uses have occurred within the Na-

tional Wildlife Refuge System. . . . The dichotomy between what the dictionary says a refuge should be and the kinds of activities occurring on National Wildlife Refuges probably will never be resolved to everyone's satisfaction. The important point is that this nationwide network of lands and waters is managed and maintained to safeguard species and populations and their habitats.

With the exception of the final sentence, which in many cases is utter nonsense, there is little in this paragraph that anyone could criticize on factual grounds. But the *most* important point is that National Wildlife Refuges are, in many cases, federal game lands. In recent years, officials of the Fish and Wildlife Service have reinforced the "game habitat" concept on refuge lands. According to Lyn Greenwalt, former chief of the Fish and Wildlife Service: "While we agree that [National Wildlife] Refuges should not be managed primarily to provide harvestable game species for hunting, the result of good management often is a harvestable surplus of game species. A harvestable surplus is often a biological fact and we will not manage the system to change that."

Supposedly, National Wildlife Refuges, in addition to harboring wildlife, exist for the benefit of all Americans. But once again we are faced with conflicting definitions. Ideally, the word *all* would not be used to denote "almost any." Refuge officials would no doubt arrest anyone they found vandalizing public or private property within refuge boundaries. But hunting and destructive habitat manipulation on wildlife refuges are among the most serious forms of vandalism since they result in the unnecessary and premature deaths of many animals that live on these lands. In addition, one would assume that "all Americans" would include those who would like to hike, ski, observe wildlife, or simply experience solitude amidst the flying lead of repeatedly extended and newly initiated hunting seasons. Those who seek peaceful communion with Nature pose no danger to hunters. But the reverse is not true.

Assistant Interior Secretary G. Ray Arnett summed up official NWR management policy in his defense of his April 1983 "Guidelines for Implementing . . . Economic Use Expansion on Wildlife Refuges." Arnett allegedly stated, "There's nothing in the law that says you run the refuges to be better for wildlife."

More Abuse of Tax Money

Nonhunters' tax money helps to support hunting in other ways. State conservation departments aid their federal counterparts in wildlife administration on 187 million acres of national forests, 28 million acres of natural lands under the jurisdiction of the Bureau of Sport Fisheries and Wildlife, and 473 million acres of other public lands. Hunting is encouraged on most of these lands. Almost without exception these natural areas were purchased with federal tax revenue. And nonhunters' tax money supports these lands at a present rate of more than $25 million per year.

Taxpayers' money is helping to destroy natural ecosystems. The 1978 Draft Environmental Impact Statement (DEIS), published by the Department of the Interior, estimated that $180 million would be spent for habitat manipulation between then and 1985. This included bulldozing on parts of two million acres and half a million acres poisoned with pesticides and herbicides. In addition, 260,000 acres would be logged, 41,000 miles of roads and trails developed and 8,400 hunting blinds constructed. According to the DEIS, these "alterations" would benefit deer, make hunting more accessible, and increase the success rates of big game hunters.

But aren't hunters, by their purchases of licenses, guns, and ammunition helping to support nonhunting recreation on public lands? This is true to a relatively small degree. But not to the extent that many hunters believe—and want nonhunters to believe. After the passage of the Wilderness Act by Congress during the Johnson administration, the federal government allocated $2.3 billion of federal tax money for land acquisition for national parks and National Wildlife Refuges. The total amount collected from purchases of U.S. hunting licenses *since the year 1923* has been only $2.4 billion. Using the 85 percent nonhunter conversion factor, this means that the approximately $1.95 billion of nonhunters' money used in this single instance almost equalled the revenue gained from the sale of American hunting licenses during the sixty years prior to 1983! Even taking into account the high rate of recent inflation, these figures place into perspective the relative unimportance of the hunting license as compared to the nonhunter tax dollar for the acquisition of wildlands and for federal wildlife management programs.

The Great Land Takeover

There are many more supporting statistics that could be quoted, but detractors will be quick to point out that identical figures can often be used effectively to prove either of two opposing points of view. Indeed, they sometimes can. But facts are facts. And the fact is that nonhunters are financing hunted lands and federal game management programs in considerably greater amounts than hunters.

While American hunters have been increasing only in approximate proportion to the total population, this increase results in additional pressure on state forests, national forests, and private lands where hunting is encouraged. State legislators in Vermont and Wisconsin were among the first to recognize the effect that this could have on the future of sport hunting. In the early 1960s, they authorized their respective fish and game boards to acquire hunting and fishing rights and privileges on any lands or waters in their states with necessary rights of ingress and egress.

The wildlife agencies of many states are now engaging in public relations campaigns to encourage the owners of large posted tracts to open their lands to hunters. In Ohio the Division of Wildlife of the Department of Natural Resources allows farmers several options to enhance pheasant habitat on their lands by letting mammoth red clover, sweet clover, timothy, or broome grass remain undisturbed. Landowners may receive ten birds for every ten uncultivated acres up to a maximum of fifty birds per landowner. Wildlife managers aid farmers by establishing additional cover or placing food at intervals for the pheasants. There is also a plan being considered by which the Division of Wildlife would pay farmers for leasing part of their acreage to the state for three to five years to restore pheasants. This would compliment the cooperative hunting system by which farmers who allow hunting on their restocked lands receive "Hunting with Permission Only" signs from the Wildlife Department and greater protection of their property by local game wardens who make regular patrols during hunting seasons.

In New Jersey, a state with a high percentage of posted private woodlands, the "Green Acres Bond Issue" raised over $800 million for the acquisition of wildlands. Almost without exception, these are hunted lands. The Garden State has fewer than 200,000 hunters (only about 3 percent of the population). But despite its large population, New Jersey is a small state with relatively little wild acreage. Since state forests and state game lands continue to receive heavy hunting pressure, the Department of Environmental Protection is attempting to persuade the owners of posted property in rural and undeveloped areas to open their lands to hunters.

This is also being done in New York State. In February 1977, the DEC, in collaboration with the Cornell University Department of Natural Resources, conducted a study of 6,500 New York State resident hunters to determine the effects of increased posting of private rural lands, particularly in southern New York. Fifty-four percent of the hunters who responded favored private land for hunting, compared to only 46 percent who favored all other types of land. These included state forests and parks, wildlife management areas, other types of public land, Fish and Wildlife Management Act Areas, commercial shooting preserves, and sportsmen's clubs. Approximately 60 percent of the hunters said that *if all types of land were available* they would prefer to hunt on private property. (The adverse results of this preference to hunt on private lands will be thoroughly examined in the analysis of the next prohunting argument.)

Predictably, about 65 percent of the hunters who were surveyed stated that they would hunt more if they could find more land open to hunting. Equally predictable is the fact that about the same percentage said that they would hunt more if they had the time. This information was included in an article titled "Land Access for Hunting," by Tommy L. Brown and Daniel J. Decker, in the November-December 1978 issue of the *Conservationist.* According to the article,

. . . The potential percentage increase in hunting days for big game would be 34 percent; for small game 59 percent; and for waterfowl 92 percent.

This was assuming that 65 percent of hunters in New York State received their collective wish and were able to hunt more often, presumably on private lands. Brown and Decker foresaw a potential for 5 million extra hunting days annually if more lands could be opened to hunters.

Brown and Decker wrote that hunting days could be increased by expanding New York State's Fish and Wildlife Management Act Program. This program, which has been in effect in New York State since the late 1950s, establishes, with a landowner's permission, state-regulated hunting areas on private lands. In return, the DEC posts safety areas, regulates access, and patrols the lands. Naturally, a landowner must do all of these himself if he wishes to establish private protection for wildlife. (Soon after the Brown-Decker article was published, the DEC stepped up its campaign to open New York State parks to hunting.)

Officials of the New York State DEC claim that they try to minimize conflicts of land use between recreationists. But their typical solution is to place economic considerations above responsible land use. Non-hunting, nonfishing, nontrapping hikers, backpackers, bird-watchers, nature photographers, et cetera pay relatively little money to the Division of Fish and Wildlife (except for a small per capita amount of state tax funds and those who innocently donate part of their tax refund to help support hunting programs as well as nongame projects). And during particularly heavy hunter influxes (such as peak periods during "big game" seasons), most hikers and animal-watchers do not venture into the woods. With only *one* group of recreationists utilizing natural lands, there will automatically be no conflicts with any of the others. Simple, but from the official point of view, sound dollar diplomacy.

State wildlife agencies are not alone in their attempts to open more private lands to hunting. The U.S. Department of Agriculture has a "Public Access Program" on which more than $1.5 million is spent annually.

A Modest Proposal

The landowner who wishes to protect wildlife on his property and fails to take the proper precautions may be placing himself and the wildlife on his land in jeopardy. According to outdoor columnist Floyd King, in the Rochester (New York) *Democrat and Chronicle* (November 1, 1981), Regional Wildlife Manager Terry Moore (mentioned earlier in connection with the DEC's program to increase the size of New York State's deer herd) recommended Keeney Swamp in Allegany County as an excellent place to hunt deer. According to King:

> Moore said that the state owns 600 acres of the swamp that is open to public hunting and most of the surrounding areas are unposted and available for hunting.

One of the readers of King's column was Bina Robinson, a wildlife preservationist who is the New York State representative of the International Ecology Society. She wondered, *Simply because rural land is unposted, does this mean that hunters have a legal right to trespass unless ordered not to do so by the landowner?* She wrote to King, who informed her by return mail that the courts have repeatedly held that unposted land that has the appearance of harboring sufficient wildlife habitat can be presumed to be available for hunting. According to Robinson, Moore confirmed that this was the case but denied having said so to King.

The wildlife protectionist who posts his or her acreage against hunting must do so at his or her expense, knowing that he or she will be incurring the disfavor—perhaps the wrath—of neighbors who hunt. In view of this, the system would be much more equitable if those who wished to allow hunting on their property were required to post their land for this purpose, while unposted lands would be "off limits" to hunting and trapping. The boundaries of properties that border public lands could be clearly defined by state or federal forestry or wildlife personnel using paint and steel markers at frequent intervals. These markers would contain the printed message that beyond them is public land open to hunting and other "recreational" activities.* Where it is necessary to use private property to gain access to state or federal lands, the determination of access rights would be left to the discretion of the landowner, as is now the case—at least in legal theory. But hunting would not be allowed without the required hunting posters. At the very least, state wildlife bureaus would issue metal posters marked "No Hunting, Fishing, or Trapping" and similar posters lettered "Wildlife Sanctuary—All Animals and Plants on These Lands Are Protected" et cetera. These would be imprinted with the official state insignia or the emblem of the state wildlife agency. Wildlife bureaus might offer them free in numbers up to fifty, with nominal payment thereafter. Or signs might be given free on request to the owners of large parcels with the number of free signs based upon the amount of acreage.

The owners of wildlife sanctuaries (i.e., rural lands over forty acres not used entirely for agricultural crops) might register with their state wildlife bureau. The names of sanctuary owners and the location of sanctuaries in each area of the state would then be pinpointed on maps at each of the wildlife department's regional offices. When possible, conservation officers would make daily inspections of sanctuaries by automobile during hunting seasons and make regular patrols if notified of recent violations of hunters. Wherever possible, wardens would maintain regular contact with sanctuary owners—either by telephone or in person.

Unfortunately, like many other inequities of the hunting-wildlife management system, the posting procedure will not be modified without persistent pressure from nonhunting landowners, including those who wish to establish havens for wildlife.

Hard Feelings and Wasted Money

Hunters point out that they are paying more *per capita* for wildlife management than nonhunters since they are not only paying income taxes but are also supporting *their* brand of conservation through purchases of hunting licenses, guns and ammunition, and duck stamps. It is understandable that most waterfowl hunters favor duck stamps and that many hunters support the Pittman-Robertson tax since both serve their interests. As for hunting licenses, most hunters purchase them for one reason: *it's the law!* An insight into this was provided by Charles Alsheimer, an outdoor columnist for the *Hornell Evening Tribune*. Refer-

*Ideally there would be 400- or 500-foot "no hunting" buffer zones around posted wildlife sanctuaries where they were bordered by state or federal lands.

ring to the issuance of deer management permits by the New York State DEC, he wrote (October 27, 1981):

> About 75,000 deer management applications will be rejected because there were about 260,000 applications submitted for the 177,575 available permits. This will no doubt cause some very hard feelings among area residents.

If a hunter's application is rejected, his fee is returned and his name is placed on a preference list for permit applicants the following year. (In 1982, during the New York State deer "population explosion," more than 247,000 deer management permits were issued—resulting, we may safely assume, in relatively few hard feelings.)

No doubt there are a certain percentage of nonhunting taxpayers who do not support the acquisition and preservation of wilderness. But they do not boast about how they benefit the environment! We should not be as concerned about how most hunters spend their money as whether their actions benefit Nature and human society. Are they active in organizations dedicated to the restoration of endangered species? Do they support wilderness legislation? Do they willingly do anything to offset the negative environmental effects of public hunting? Would they aid a sick or injured bird or wild mammal and notify a qualified wildlife rehabilitator if necessary, or would they simply let the animal suffer? Are they otherwise good citizens? Does their life-style reflect an ecological awareness and a concern for Nature?

If you are a hunter who feels motivated by a conservationist's altruism, you might ask yourself the following question: how much money would you voluntarily donate to support forests, parklands, and wildlife refuges if sport hunting were eliminated throughout North America and all species of fish and wildlife were protected? You might also consider the tremendous benefits to wildlife that would have resulted if even a sizeable percentage of the $2–3 billion that has been spent to create high *game* populations had been used to restore ecosystems to a more natural state, to help reestablish rare predators and other threatened or endangered species, and to aid the species that are succumbing daily to vanishing habitat, to air, water, and pesticide pollution, and to land mismanagement.

THE SLOB HUNTER ARGUMENT

Hunters' Argument: MOST SPORTSMEN ARE CONCERNED ABOUT THEIR PUBLIC IMAGE AND RESENT BEING STEREOTYPED AS "SLOBS." ONLY A VERY SMALL PERCENTAGE OF HUNTERS DE-

LIBERATELY BREAK GAME LAWS OR DISRESPECT LANDOWNERS' RIGHTS. LOCAL FISH AND GAME CLUBS TEACH YOUNG HUNTERS TO ACT RESPONSIBLY AND WARN ALL VIOLATORS TO BEHAVE ACCORDINGLY. FURTHERMORE, NEW HUNTERS IN MOST STATES MUST PASS STRINGENT HUNTER TRAINING AND SAFETY COURSES BEFORE THEY WILL BE ISSUED A LICENSE.

Analysis: Until now I have directed my criticisms at the prevailing system of wildlife management and *the practice of hunting*. With a few exceptions I have not dealt with the ways in which hunters often practice their activity. In my analyses of the preceding hunting justifications and my descriptions of the biological and ecological consequences of public hunting, I have assumed that all hunting is done in strict compliance with game regulations and according to what is sometimes referred to as "hunter etiquette"—requesting permission to hunt on private lands, carrying one's refuse out of the woods, et cetera. Naturally, this does not always happen.

The term "slob hunter" may convey a different image to different people. I have never been given a detailed definition of it. So it might be helpful if I explained my personal feelings. To me, a "slob hunter" is a hunter who exhibits one or a combination of the following traits: 1) A callous contempt for the intrinsic value of wildlife in a natural environment (i.e., animals are thought of as nothing more than rifle targets); 2) a disrespect of the sanctity of the natural environment (careless disposal of trash, et cetera); 3) a contempt for the rights of landowners who post their land or establish nature sanctuaries where hunting is illegal; 4) a violation (or violations) of game regulations; 5) a deliberate breach of the peace that is designed to disturb, harass, or physically abuse one or more people. Before documenting some cases in which hunters have conspicuously demonstrated these characteristics, there are some important things to consider.

First is the questionable suitability of the term "sportsman." There is much room for debate about whether hunting can be considered a sport. Syndicated columnist Bob Green wrote:

> Unlike other sports, hunting takes little agility, no physical conditioning, no speed. Any slob with a gut full of booze can go into the woods and—if his weapon is powerful enough, if his telescopic sight is strong enough—stand a good chance of making a kill.

While Green is basically correct, I would agree with hunters that he made an overstatement. A hunter must know how to use his weapon, how to track, and how and when to aim and pull the trigger in order

189

to insure the greatest possibility of a "kill." He must have enough physical stamina to hike through woods or fields and locate an animal of the species he is hunting. He must also know something about the animal's habits and the type of habitat in which it is most often found. And hunter success rates are relatively low. During most deer seasons in most states, only one of every ten to twenty legal hunters shoots a deer. The kill rate of upland birds and small mammals is greater, while waterfowl-hunting success rates are sometimes even higher, depending upon the geographical area and the number of duck and goose hunters that utilize it. But does this mean that hunting is a sport? Hardly!

By definition, a *sportsman* is one who plays fair. The term also implies that one's opponent has consented to a contest. Are animals willing rifle targets? How fair a matchup is a man with a high-powered weapon against a defenseless bird or mammal, which must rely upon its speed, agility, or quickness of flight if it is to escape death? Is it fair for four or six or eight men to pursue one deer? In one section of the Adirondacks, outdoor writer Hugh Fosburgh once saw two charter busloads of deer hunters—about thirty-five to a bus—deploy in two parallel lines and sweep toward each other. According to a friend of mine, this tactic is sometimes used in southern New Jersey. Busloads of hunters from the Philadelphia and Atlantic City areas sometimes attempt to drive nonexistent deer through five-to-twenty-acre blocks of undeveloped woods that are divided by a network of gravel roads. "You have to see it to fully comprehend its barbarity," she says.

Is this the exception? Do most hunters rely on their individual skills? Perhaps, but they seldom criticize those who use gang warfare to kill an animal. Seldom is this method of hunting condemned by outdoor columnists and the editors of hunting periodicals. Neither do the wildlife officials of most states denounce this practice. In fact, they encourage it by the issuance of party permits. (And this is an accurate description of the process that sometimes results.) Within the bounds of game regulations, greater "harvests" result in greater revenue for wildlife agencies. So why should wildlife officials criticize frequently employed, if unfair, methods of hunting?

According to Webster, the word *sport*, in addition to its more common definitions, may also mean "mockery or derision." Certainly sport hunting is a mockery of subsistence hunting. Someone once suggested that stalking mountain lions with a bowie knife or hunting grizzly bears with a softball bat could be considered a sport. At least the contestants would be evenly matched. But recreational hunting is a one-sided mismatch. The only consolation for the hunted animal is that if it escapes it continues to live.

Overanxious or Overly Aggressive?

A related subject is hunting accidents. Accidents can happen to anyone, but most hunting accidents are caused by undue carelessness. During the 1979 deer season, a neighbor of mine, carrying his rifle with his finger curled around the trigger-guard, misjudged the distance to the trigger and wounded his companion in the foot. My neighbor had earned a reputation as a safe hunter. The 1980–81 *Hunting Regulations Summary,* published by the Maine Department of Inland Fisheries and Wildlife, issues a warning about hunting accidents. It reads: (Author's italics)

> Fatal accidents frequently involve experienced hunters, who may be overanxious to bag their deer or other game. These accidents are classified under the heading Mistaken Identity. There isn't any need for them to occur if every hunter will wait until he is sure of his target. Experienced hunters usually hit what they aim at, and when human lives are at stake, they should be absolutely certain they are shooting *only at game.*

On the other hand, if hunters had a greater respect for *all* life and were not anxious to kill wildlife there would be no hunting accidents. In fact, there would be no sport hunting!

Anyone who doubts this might consider the results of the deer hunt that was held in late December 1981 on Clemson Island in Pennsylvania. The twenty-acre island is located in the Susquehanna River near Duncannon, about ten miles north of Harrisburg. Until 1981, hunting had been banned on all Susquehanna islands. However, a large number of deer had swum to Clemson Island from the mainland. This was partly because of encroaching development; by contrast, the island offered a relatively natural habitat. In addition, the deer may have realized that the island was a sanctuary from hunters who combed the nearby mainland during the two-week firearms deer season held each year in early December. Consequently, the Pennsylvania Game Commission decided to end the hunting ban on the island, predictably using as its justification the possibility of deer starvation. The game commission made no attempt to limit the number of hunters that would be invading the island during the deer hunt.

Before dawn on December 26 (ironically the day after Christmas!), carloads of hunters armed with muzzle-loaders and crossbows began to arrive on the shore of the river, pushing boats into the water and ferrying themselves and their hunting equipment to the island. Shortly after daylight, an estimated 400 hunters had arrived there. (Incredibly, this is a density of twenty hunters per *acre!*) What happened next was described to an Associated Press reporter by William Bissett, the father of a seventeen-year-old hunter who was wounded in the leg during the ensuing shootout: "There were crossfires—I could hear slugs coming through the trees from both directions. . . . I could see at least 50 yards in all directions and every direction I looked I could see two dozen hunters."

Shortly after daylight, Bissett's son, Scott, killed a deer with his muzzle-loader. But he and his father did not move from their position for fear of being shot. After about half an hour, the younger Bissett stood up so that he could clean the deer. Immediately, the upper part of one of his legs was shattered by a slug. Bissett's father lifted him from the ground, preparing to carry him to the boat they had taken from the mainland. According to the teenager, "When Dad picked me up and put me over his shoulder to try to get me out of there, guys were running right past us, trying to shoot deer." Finally a small group of hunters helped to evacuate the wounded youth on a state police helicopter. One of them said that the scene reminded him of television news films of the mid- and late 1960s that showed U.S. Marines, under fire by Vietcong troops, evacuating their wounded by helicopter. According to William Bissett: "It was a hunter's nightmare. I didn't know people could get that excited about shooting deer."

Apparently the specter of hunters making the woods as unsafe for other hunters as for wildlife was too great an outrage for hunting groups in Pennsylvania. One of many criticisms of the Clemson Island hunt came from Dennis Ricker, president of the Pennsylvania Deer Association, who wrote in the Association's newsletter:

> This incident, and others where lack of control of hunter entry and pressure results in embarrassing hunting conditions, points to the need to adopt new methods of deer management that encompass consideration of special demographical, biological, and geographical conditions.

Ricker admitted that a lack of control *by hunters* had been as great a problem as the failure of the game commission to limit the number of hunters on the island.

The Casualties Multiply

While overanxious experienced hunters may accidently shoot a human being, inexperienced hunters pose a worse hazard. Many states now require hunter training, but when a young hunter enters the woods with a rifle or shotgun, lectures about firearms safety may quickly be forgotten. In many states the legal hunting age is sixteen, although sixteen- and seventeen-year-olds usually must be accompanied by a licensed hunter eighteen or older. But in some states, such as Ohio and Maine, a youngster of ten can obtain a license (or "junior license") to hunt small game. The stipulation is that hunters between ten and sixteen must be accompanied by a parent or guardian or by an adult approved by a parent or guardian. There is no question that some young hunters can be "overanxious." This was epitomized by an Associated Press news story of November 1980 concerning the annual one-day bear hunt in Pennsylvania.* Describing a sixteen-year-old hunter, the release said:

> A permanent grin seemed plastered to Kelly's excited face as he said: "I don't know how far away he was. I don't know which of my shots hit him. All I know is I heard a noise, saw him running for the swamp and fired."

Wildlife officials realize that practices that are developed at an early age often become established habits that are difficult to break even after one becomes an adult. Convince almost any youngster that hunting is fun, and except where unforseen circumstances intervene or where he later develops a greater sensitivity, game officials can be certain that the youth will continue to hunt throughout much of his active life. And the lower the minimum hunting age, the greater the number of hunters and the greater the cash receipts for fish and game bureaus.[9]

The 1980 Pennsylvania bear hunt particularly rankled preservationist groups such as Defenders of Wildlife. For the first time in the history of the hunt, bear *cubs* were legal game. There are estimated to be only about 4,000 black bears in Pennsylvania. In 1980 hunters killed 919, nearly one-quarter of the bear population in that state. Of these 219, or 23 percent, were cubs. No doubt members of the Pennsylvania Game Commission reasoned that since many cubs had lost their mothers during previous hunts, it would be expedient for hunters to end the cub's potential misery during 1980 and subsequent bear hunts. (Some bears become independent by their first autumn. Others are dependent, or partially dependent upon their mothers throughout most of their second year.)

Hunting accidents are not confined to young, inexperienced hunters. In November 1981, a thirty–four–year–old Michigan hunter was

---

*In 1982, the Pennsylvania bear hunt was lengthened to two days.

critically injured as a result of carelessness. He was holding a dead rabbit he had shot over his two young beagles to train them for hunting. He had propped his shotgun, barrel-up, against his leg. One of the dogs leaped up and caught the trigger with a paw, discharging the gun. Although the hunter was hit by pellets in the lower stomach and lung, he eventually recovered.

Many hunting accidents occur when the victim is out of sight of the shooter. In November 1982, a forty-nine–year–old hunter from Henrietta, New York, was shot in the upper right arm while standing beside a hedgerow. He had fired his rifle when some deer were driven past him from adjacent woods and was hit when others in his nine-member party fired at the deer from the opposite direction. The victim told sheriff's deputies that he did not see the other hunters, and they said that they had not seen him. (This was an interesting defense, since all nine men were members of the same hunting party and should have known each other's whereabouts.)

While hunting accidents are always tragic, they are sometimes tinged with an aura of poetic justice. Early in 1982, a twenty-seven–year–old man was hunting with a companion in the desert north of Phoenix, Arizona. He made the mistake of choosing a huge saguaro cactus with six-inch spikes for target practice. When he hit the twenty-seven–foot–high plant with a blast of pellets from his shotgun, it began to topple. According to his hunting partner, he started to yell, "Timber," but his call was cut short when a twenty-three–foot section of cactus landed on him, crushing him to death. (It was later revealed that the hunter was a convicted felon on parole from New York State and was not legally permitted to use a firearm.)

A Gambler's Odds

How frequent are hunting accidents? Very infrequent, according to the National Rifle Association, which compiles annual statistics. In fact, the NRA calculates that hunting is a safer activity than swimming, canoeing, or mountain climbing. Naturally, the NRA has every reason to understate the impact of hunting accidents. Many state game bureaus compile hunting accident statistics, but they include only the mishaps that are *reported*. Minor hunting accidents, which have the potential to be much more serious, often go unreported.

According to an article in the Fall 1982 issue of *Family Safety*, the magazine of the National Safety Council, between the years 1977 and 1981 there were a total of 5,784 *reported* hunting accidents in the United

States, including 723 fatalities.* This is an average of 1,265 injuries and 180 deaths per year. Based upon the total number of American hunters, assuming that annual statistics were to remain at this rate, this would mean that if a person hunted each year for forty years, he would risk 1 chance in 4,000 of being killed and 1 chance in 600 of being wounded in a hunting accident. Any gambler would be anxious to bet on 600 to 1 odds in his favor. But in terms of the numbers of people killed or disabled, in terms of hospital bills, convalescing, lost income, bereaved widows, funeral expenses, fatherless children, and other elements of personal tragedy, it is safe to say that 1,445 casualties per year is substantial!

The most frequent causes of accidents, as listed by *Family Safety* (in descending order), were "victim out of sight of shooter," "shooter swinging on game hits victim," "victim mistaken for game," "shooter stumbled and fell," and "trigger caught on object." The accident rates quoted by *Family Safety* do not include mishaps that resulted from carelessness with guns when a hunter was not in the act of hunting or in transit to or from a hunt. For example, the day before Thanksgiving 1982, a seventeen-year-old Saratoga County, New York, youth fatally shot and killed his fifteen-year-old sister when a loaded rifle he had been inspecting discharged as he was placing it back into its case. The youth and his family were to leave on a hunting trip the following day.

Cleveland Amory, in his book *Man Kind? Our Incredible War on Wildlife* (Harper & Row, 1975), quotes Donald Foltz, former director of the Indiana Department of Conservation, from an article by Foltz that appeared in *The Saturday Evening Post*. According to Foltz, laws governing hunting accidents are extremely lax throughout the United States. He noted that in Minnesota a "mistaken for game" killing is a felony punishable by five to twenty years in prison. But no one had been convicted under this statute in fifty-seven years. (His article was published in the early 1970s. Regrettably, things have changed very little in the intervening decade.) Meanwhile, in New Jersey, no one had been prosecuted for hunting under the influence of liquor or a drug in fifteen years. In Colorado, seventeen hunters were killed during a two-week preseason hunt, yet not one hunter who had caused a death was prosecuted. Foltz concluded with the following:

> Indiana is one of the states that do not forbid people to hunt while intoxicated. When I asked one of our conservation officers

---

*These figures were based upon statistics obtained from the North American Association of Hunter Safety Coordinators.

195

what he would do if he came across a drunken hunter, he replied, "I'd run like hell!"

Hunting accidents prove that there are unsafe hunters roaming the woods during hunting seasons. But employees of state wildlife agencies and members of state agencies that work in conjunction with them usually favor hunters over hikers and nature-enthusiasts at this time of year—sometimes to the point of insult. In the fall of 1981, a group leader trying to arrange an outing for young people at Letchworth State Park in western New York was told by a park official that he had better not come to the park during hunting season if safety was one of his concerns. (Meanwhile, in Livingston County, New York, hunting is permitted in Stony Brook State Park, which is so small that nonhunters are virtually excluded from the park during hunting seasons.)

How to Get Away with Murder

Lewis Regenstein wrote in *The Case Against Hunting* that hunter revenue is so important to state game agencies that seldom if ever are hunting licenses revoked. He cited the case of a New Jersey hunter who had illegally shot an endangered peregrine falcon, mistaking it for a pigeon. The falcon had been outfitted with a radio transmitter and was being reintroduced into New Jersey by scientists from Cornell University. The hunter was fined $2,000, but his hunting license was not revoked; thus he was able to purchase a license the following year. Regenstein remarked:

> Illegally shooting humans is taken a little more seriously—but not much more. In a typical instance, the *Pennsylvania Game Law Book* says in Section 825, in a subdivision titled "Killing Human Beings by Mistake," that "for the first offense" you will be fined "not less than $500 nor more than $1,000," the sum to be paid to "the personal representative of the deceased."

Even killing a human being does not necessarily result in the loss of a person's hunting privileges. In 1981, the state of Vermont issued a hunting license to an eighteen-year-old youth who had shot and killed another hunter the previous year.

But times may be changing. In 1982, innovative legislation was passed in Pennsylvania that permitted the game commission of that state to revoke the hunting privileges of individuals who have been convicted of game law violations but have refused to pay fines imposed by courts and district magistrates. It is worth noting that this legislation was passed at a time when the Pennsylvania Game Commission was under fire by many hunters and nonhunters for its mismanagement practices, including its handling of the Clemson Island deer hunt.

A substantial percentage of the monies that are paid in fines for hunting violations filters back to the Pennsylvania game bureau. Since the average amount in fines owed by each illegal hunter is equal to the hunting license purchases of an individual over a ten to twenty–year period, it is easy to understand why the game commission decided to revoke some hunting privileges during a time of economic recession. Furthermore, with more than 2 million big- and small-game hunters in Pennsylvania, the loss of several hundred hunters a year will not put a serious dent in the game commission's hunting license revenue. Gerald D. Kirkpatrick, chief of law enforcement for the game commission, said that as of August 1982 offenders owed the commission approximately $250,000 in unpaid penalties. During the summer of 1982, the game commission revoked the hunting privileges of 485 state residents.

Prior to 1982, I had heard of only one case in which a nonfelon's hunting license had been revoked. That was in December 1981 when Jiri Bar of Monroe County, Pennsylvania was fined $6,000 and his hunting privileges were revoked when game commission officials found parts of more than thirty wild birds and mammals in his home. These included skins, skulls, and frozen and jarred meat of eleven bears and nineteen deer, plus parts of other animals and protected birds. Bar had shot the animals from the dining room window of his home. Most of the "game" animals had been shot out of season.

Naturally, the tendency of most state wildlife agencies to allow irresponsible hunters to retain their hunting privileges has fringe benefits. If a hunter is fined for a violation, this may discourage him from committing another or it may not. Either way, the wildlife agency receives money from a fine, from subsequent hunting license purchases by the illegal hunter, and perhaps from further fines for future violations by the same person. While hunting privileges are seldom revoked in most states, it is difficult in many states for a qualified person to obtain a license to rehabilitate injured wildlife. This is incongruous if not unethical.

Illegality on the Increase

Illegal poaching is not as uncommon as many people believe. In some parts of the United States and Canada, the nocturnal shooting of deer by spotlight is rampant. One such area is the eastern shore of Maryland. According to the Salisbury (Maryland) *Daily Times* (November

16, 1981), 194 people were arrested in that state during 1980 on charges of poaching deer. This was an increase from the previous year, when 171 had been arrested for jacklighting. Maryland state police said that there have been many cows, watchdogs, and horses killed by jacklighters who have shot at glowing eyes in the darkness without bothering to look at the rest of the animal. Chickens in pens have died from heart attacks, suffocation, or broken necks when they panicked after being caught in a bright ray of light at night. In one jacklighting case, a poacher fired at a deer with a high-powered rifle and missed. The slug tore through the side of a farmhouse and lodged in a bedroom wall just above the head of a sleeping farmer. The jacklighting problem in Maryland is aggravated by the fact that the wildlife department of that state has only two game wardens on patrol per county along the eastern shore and must rely on citizen complaints combined with occasional aircraft surveillance.

A study conducted in 1981 by John Cartier, a field editor for *Outdoor Life*, indicated that poaching and the illegal tagging of deer are on the increase nationwide. Cartier wrote that during the decade of the 1970s, these activities had increased 19.5 percent in the Prairie States, 34.3 percent in the Southeast, 59 percent in the South Central Region, 60.6 percent in the Northeast, 88 percent in the Intermountain States, 99.1 percent in the North Central region, and 112.1 percent in the Far West. Part of the reason for the increases in poaching, especially in western states, may be illegal trafficking in wildlife or parts thereof. There has been a dramatic upsurge in the illicit sale to Asian countries of ground and powdered antlers of deer and elk and the gall bladders of bears. Asians consider them to be potent aphrodisiacs and panaceas. Many traders from India, Pakistan, and other countries in this region pay high prices for these products.

Other forms of illegal hunting are on the increase:

—Illegal tagging is becoming common in New York State. This is when a hunter kills a buck, places his wife's or someone else's tag on it, and then continues to hunt. In 1982 New York State conservation officers apprehended several men in the town of Lindley with seven illegal deer and more than fifty extra tag and party permits in their possession.

—During the December 1981 deer season in Pennsylvania, conservation officers held a surprise road check in Clarion County. A total of 112 arrests were made for violations ranging from illegal deer to untagged deer to loaded guns in vehicles.

—Charles Alsheimer wrote in the Hornell *Evening Tribune* (December 15, 1981): "This past summer I asked an area banker's wife if she liked to hunt deer as much as her husband. She said,

'No, I don't hunt, but every year I'm a pretty good shot from nine miles away.' Just last week an individual from the southern part of the county told me he hadn't got his buck yet, but one guy who hunts with him had already taken three bucks."

In the autumn of 1983, Frank Everest, Jr., a member of the Virginia Commission of Game and Inland Fisheries, and a group of hunting companions (including Philip McGuire, assistant criminal enforcement director for the U.S. Bureau of Alcohol, Tobacco and Firearms) were collared by federal game wardens while hunting doves over a baited field near Manassas, Virginia. Baiting doves is a misdemeanor outlawed by the Migratory Bird Treaty Act. Everest paid a $100 fine and two months later resigned his seat on the game commission at the request of Governor Charles Robb.

In January 1983, Representative Russell Letterman, the chairman of the Pennsylvania house game committee, was fined twenty-five dollars for stopping his car along a highway and taking a shot at a doe—a shot that fortunately missed. Afterward, Letterman said, "I made a mistake. . . . I knew it was illegal, and I paid."

These incidents are not unusual. According to *The Conservationist*, Dennis O'Reilly, a New York State conservation officer, observed, "It's funny, people, normally well-adjusted people, get into the woods with a gun and they go a little nuts." O'Reilly should know. He has had more than a decade of experience enforcing game laws.

Undiplomatic Immunity

If some hunters have developed a readily discernible sense of self-importance, they are not entirely to blame. Despite myriads of game regulations, hunting is essentially a privileged activity that is exempt from many of the laws and codes of conduct that govern more peaceful pursuits.

For example, the wilderness guides of the New York State DEC, which feature maps of designated wilderness areas on state lands, issue the following conspicuous warning to campers and hikers:

REMEMBER—These are forbidden acts and punishable as violations. . . . Molesting or disturbing birds and their nests or other wildlife; committing a breach of the peace; behaving in such a manner as to be likely to endanger health, life, limb or property of others. . . .

Yet hunters may molest and disturb "game" birds with blasts from their shotguns during New York's "small game" hunting seasons. And it would be difficult to imagine a more blatant breach of the peace in a pristine wilderness area than sudden, loud gunshots. A hunter needn't be reckless or irresponsible to endanger the health, life, limb, or property of another person. The other person needs only to be in the path of flying lead as it whistles between the trees. Indecent language loudly used by hunters is not uncommon. And what could be more boisterous than a deer drive by a large group of "sportsmen?" By the same token, threats, abuses, and insults from hunters are not unheard of, particularly if an owner of a posted wildlife sanctuary discovers a group of them trespassing. I have known more than one such individual who has been threatened to be burned off of his land, and I once spoke with the owner of a sanctuary who had been shot at while patrolling his land.

An article by Gail Williams in the New Jersey *Courier-News* (December 15, 1980) described a confrontation between trespassing hunters and and members of Luke Dommer's Committee to Abolish Sport Hunting:

> Dommer has had a few tense moments at the wrong end of a gun.
>
> His animal welfare organization patrols a 212-acre wildlife preserve in West Milford [N.J.] during deer season every year. . . .
> One time, on a chilly morning last year, his group confronted 40 hunters trespassing in the refuge. An argument erupted when Dommer demanded to see their hunting licenses and a hunter trained his rifle on him.
>
> "It was pitch black out there and there was a lot of shoving going on," Dommer recalled in hushed tones. "Someone could have been murdered. . . ."

Most states, including New Jersey, require a hunter to present his hunting license to a landowner or to the landowner's authorized representative on demand. New York is no exception. The DEC folder that summarizes New York's "big game" hunting regulations states specifically: "A license to hunt, trap or fish does not give the holder any right to go on private property without permission of the landowner. . . . It is illegal to refuse to show your license to any person on request." But while it is easy to inscribe this legal technicality for official purposes, it is often very difficult to enforce. Some landowners whose acreage includes a substantial tract of rugged forest are not overanxious to confront a group of armed strangers (particularly since there is the possibility that they may have been fortified with bottled courage). And in the middle of the woods, miles from the nearest police or conservation officer, official regulations are difficult for a landowner to enforce. This is especially true if he is pitted against a large group of hunters.

"Thou Shalt Trespass"

As in New York, some state fish and wildlife agencies specifically note on literature distributed to hunters that it is illegal to hunt on posted lands without receiving the landowner's permission, and some states even add a touch of unintended humor. For example, the *Vermont Guide to Hunting* advises:

Check first with the landowner before hunting, and DON'T take your firearm with you to the door.

But while the fish and game departments of some states discourage hunters from trespassing on unposted private lands without obtaining a landowner's permission, those of other states, while not actively encouraging hunters to trespass on such lands, do little to discourage it. For example, the Minnesota trespass law prohibits hunters and ORV users from utilizing *agricultural* lands without owner, occupant, or lessee permission. Agricultural lands are described in the Minnesota game regulations booklet as those "containing plowed or tilled fields, standing crops or their residues, or lands with a maintained fence for the purpose of enclosing domestic livestock." However, in the case of nonagricultural lands, including the forestlands that cover the northeastern section of the state, the law stipulates only that (author's italics): "No person shall enter upon any land not his own . . . after being notified *not to do so,* either orally by the owner, occupant or lessee or by [no hunting or no trespassing] signs erected" by the owner, occupant or lessee. Most hunters view these posters with something less than enthusiasm. Therefore, in the interest of peacekeeping, many landowners who would like to erect them do not do so.

The owner of a wildlife sanctuary should not expect a great deal of moral support from his or her local game warden. Wardens will usually respond to complaints from the owners of lands that have been closed to hunting. But while wardens are *individuals,* some of whom are more preservationist-oriented than others, their jobs are to enforce *game laws*—whatever game laws happen to be at a given time. They are not on patrol primarily to protect those species of wildlife that would normally be unprotected had a sanctuary owner not established private protection. Furthermore, most wardens are hunters or have hunted in the past and are favorably disposed toward other hunters. Thus the owner of a sanctuary may learn that while his or her local conservation officer will usually enforce trespass laws without undue antipathy, his sympathies are with hunters who choose to hunt on lands where wildlife is legally protected. As one New York State conservation officer suggested to a group of deer hunters who had complained of newly posted lands in their traditional hunting territory, "maybe if you offered to shoot woodchucks next May the landowners would let you hunt deer next November."[10]

In most trespass cases, local judges tend to be lenient. In a typical New Jersey case, the owner of a private sanctuary encountered several hunters with loaded weapons. The hunters claimed that they were simply trying to retrieve their hunting dogs (which were nearby and whose barking had alerted the refuge owner). The landowner brought the hunters to court, but since they were local residents, the judge dismissed charges. In reality, if not on legal parchment, the odds are weighted heavily in favor of hunters and against those who would establish protection for wildlife on their land.

Legality and Morality: A Dichotomy

Naturally, I have been dealing with the worst of the "slob" element. There *is* a substantial percentage of hunters who respect landowners' rights, carry their refuse out of the woods, and scrupulously observe hunting regulations (biologically and ecologically destructive though these regulations often are). But there is also a substantial percentage of macho tough guys who may be found roaming forests and fields during hunting seasons. A chain is only as secure as its weakest link. Many hunters entertain the theory that they are entitled to hunt on posted property if the landowner is not at home, cannot be located, or does not appear to be in the vicinity. This is particularly true if land has recently been posted by a new owner and if hunters have regularly used this property for many years. (Or if posted property offers access to federal or state land or to unposted private acreage where hunting is permitted by the landowner).

The trespass problem may be partly a result of the legal concept that wildlife "belongs to the people" and is therefore public property. In reality, wildlife does not belong to anyone; wildlife (and human life) belong to *the land*. But not by traditional legal standards—standards that hunters do not want changed. According to hunter/outdoor writer John Madson ("Our Hunting Heritage," *Field and Stream*, September 1981): "Wildlife in North America is public property. No free-ranging wildlife belongs to any landowner. It is in the public trust. A game bird or animal becomes private property only when it is lawfully reduced to possession. . . ."[11] In other words, shot and duly claimed by a hunter.

Carried to its illogical conclusion, this means that a person may abuse wildlife on any public or private lands in any way that is legal.

At worst, it might infer that a person has no right to protect wildlife on his or her land because wildlife is public property; therefore "game" animals may legally be utilized by the public (*utilized* meaning hunted or trapped, *public* meaning hunters and trappers). At best, the public ownership principle, if taken literally, would allow hunters to pursue hunted animals from protected lands onto lands where hunting is permitted for the purpose of shooting them. Fortunately, this was not the way that the legal powers incorporated the public ownership principle into law. But this is how many hunters seem to interpret it.

The Exploitation Continues

The double standard that exempts hunting from the rules that govern other activities is not limited to state and local levels. The Wilderness Act of 1964 set aside 9.1 million acres of wild, undeveloped lands to be safeguarded in perpetuity. The act specifies (author's italics): "A wilderness, in contrast to those areas where man and his works dominate the landscape, is hereby recognized as an area where the Earth *and its community of life* are untrammeled by man. . . ." Yet virtually all national forestlands within the wilderness sytem are hunted lands. Hunting is regulated by the game bureaus of the states in which national forests are located. The only lands in the wilderness system where hunting is still prohibited are the national parks.

The U.S. Department of Agriculture Forest Service folder titled *Keeping the Wild in Wilderness* piously proclaims that one of the objectives of wilderness management is to "maintain plants and animals native to the area by protecting complete communities of plant and animal life." But near the end of the pamphlet the reader encounters the following passage:

> Congress specifically allowed certain other well-established uses to continue within the wilderness system. . . . Hunting and fishing are allowed under State and Federal laws and regulations.

In many wilderness areas it is illegal for a person to cut a living or dead tree or even pick a wildflower. Yet it is perfectly legal, in season and according to game regulations, to needlessly blast the life out of a wild creature. Hunting has become such a publicly accepted recreational practice that many people do not consider associated inconsistencies. In an article titled "Santanoni" in the September-October 1981 issue of *Adirondack Life*, Alan Darling described a state-maintained, 12,500-acre "nature preserve" in the high peaks area of the Adirondacks. Wrote Darling: ". . . The preserve has its own management program, designed

203

to protect its natural setting and unique wildlife." But later in the article, the reader learns that "hunting is permitted throughout the preserve, and Moose Pond is a favorite spot for deer hunting" (for seven or eight weeks a year, not including bow hunting season). But this is little wonder, since the "preserve" was purchased from private holdings partly with funds raised by Trout Unlimited and monies granted by the Federal Bureau of Outdoor Recreation!

A Dangerous Obsession

It is true that aspiring hunters in many states must now pass hunter training courses before they are eligible to be issued licenses.[12] It is also true that *some* fish and game clubs are actively attempting to convince "slob hunters" to reform their traditional habits. However, there remain a significant percentage of hunters who are unable or unwilling to reform. Part of the reason may be that, for these individuals, hunting has become much more than a leisurely pastime. This is evidenced by their reaction, and the identical reactions of many "responsible" hunters, to events that they feel may threaten their avocation. Hunters sometimes become very upset, even outraged, when they feel that their interests are in jeopardy. But what are the real reasons for their vitriolic paroxysms? If sport hunting were no more than a recreational pursuit among most of its participants, then why do many hunters vigorously protest to newspapers, legislators, fish and game bureaus, and the general public and why do they express indignation at public hearings and organizational conventions each time minor progress is made toward the protection of hunted wildlife?

If sport hunting were merely a recreational activity and no more, why should these hunters consider it a hardship to relinquish their pursuit if public hunting were to be abolished for biological, ecological, and social reasons—even if there would be no attempt to outlaw the public use of firearms? (Therefore the money that hunters had paid for guns, ammunition, and associated equipment would not have been lost.) Since it should be obvious to both hunters and nonhunters that sport hunting will not be legislated out of existence in the near future, the reaction of these hunters to the modest victories won by those who wish to protect wildlife becomes more puzzling.

Even if sport hunting were to be abolished, it need not result in the loss of nonlive target shooting, gun collections, or the ownership of guns for protection against crime. It would certainly not include the abolition of one's right to pursue wildlife with a camera or to track animals, backpack, camp, or hike through the woods! Again one wonders about the reasons behind the hostile reaction of many hunters to the prospect of restrictions against hunting if hunting is simply an outdoor pastime that, one might otherwise assume, could be easily discarded with an admission that social attitudes must progress. The key may be that for many people recreational hunting has become *compulsive* hunting. I do not believe that it would be unfair or unrealistic to speculate that for many people hunting has become an obsession, perhaps an uncontrollable obsession. This presents a potentially dangerous situation, because hunters in this frame of mind can pose a serious threat to wildlife sanctuaries and their owners.

Threats and Harassment: The Otises' Story

Consider the case of Clair and Gloria Otis. Their story was related to Robert Enstad, a reporter for the *Chicago Tribune*. In 1978 Clair was approaching retirement. He and Gloria loved animals, and they planned to move from the Chicago suburbs to a home in the country where they could pursue their dream of rural living in an atmosphere of peace and tranquillity. The Otises contacted a real estate broker, who took them to a farmhouse in the rolling hills of Green County in south-central Wisconsin. The Otises immediately fell in love with the house and the surrounding countryside and decided to purchase the farm. When Clair retired in the spring of 1979, the Otises moved to their "dream farm" of 130 acres, which was located in an area known as "Little Switzerland" because of the production of milk, honey, and Swiss cheese. The farms were neat and well-kept. Most of the people in the surrounding area were from families whose ancestors had built the original farmhouses and had passed ownership from generation to generation. The Otises' daughter, Sharon Benes, and her husband purchased a house across the road from the Otises' farm. They moved in with their three small children. Gloria bought a quarter horse to add to her pets—a cat and two dogs. The Otises went to work fixing fences, painting the house, and planting a large garden.

Then their dream farm began to turn into a nightmare. In order to protect wildlife on their farm they posted "No Hunting—No Trespassing" signs around their property. A neighbor warned them that this would lead to trouble with other neighbors, most of whom hunted. The Otises did not realize how prophetic his statement would prove to be. That autumn they asked several hunters to leave their property. Then the trouble began. The "No Hunting" signs were torn down, nails were thrown in their driveway, and trash was deposited on their front lawn many times during the middle of the night. Sharon Otis Benes was told to keep her children indoors during hunting seasons. When the retired couple went to the nearby town of Monticello, people shouted taunts and made obscene gestures. Finally, even the local police were reluctant to respond to the Otises' calls. Clair telephoned the county sheriff dozens of times, but little could be done. Clair told a reporter that he was not certain the Monticello fire department would respond to a fire on his property. The threats and abuse continued. No one offered sympathy. Finally, after many sleepless nights, the Otises decided that they could take no more. Clair called the real estate dealer who had sold him the farm and put a "for sale" sign in front of the house. Said Otis, "You just can't live under these circumstances."

Nightmare in Orange: The Buyukmihcis' Experience

The Otises' experience is not exceptional, as Hope and Cavit Buyukmihci (pronounced "Ja-vit Boo-yook-moo-chee") can relate. The Buyukmihcis, who are in their late fifties, own and maintain Unexpected Sanctuary on the edge of the pine barrens in rural New Jersey. Hunting and trapping are prohibited on the 300-acre refuge, and Hope and Cavit stringently enforce this regulation, sometimes arresting violators. During New Jersey's December deer season, members of the Buyukmihcis' wildlife protection group, The Beaver Defenders, help the owners patrol their property, which has been clearly posted against hunting and trapping. The Buyukmihcis, who are ethical vegans, are a proud couple who love Nature and believe that it is the obligation of people to respect all life. They have the courage of their convictions.

Hope and Cavit refuse to apply for or accept grants from state or federal agencies or from conservation organizations, partly because they prefer to pay as many of the sanctuary's expenses as possible and partly because government bureaus, and all but a few of the well-endowed wilderness and "wildlife" groups, favor hunting and trapping. Thus they rely on their incomes and the contributions of friends and a small number of supporters to pay increasing taxes and maintenance costs. *Never has a single tax dollar supported the refuge. Never has a hunter or trapper offered or paid one penny for the sanctuary's upkeep.* Yet the Buyukmihcis have repeatedly been targets of theft, vandalism, threats of physical harm, and vows to burn them out. There have been several mysterious fires on the refuge. (Fortunately, all were discovered by Hope or Cavit before they had burned more than an acre or two.) After the Buyukmihcis had extinguished one small blaze, they discovered a blackened gasoline canister with the remains of a homemade fuse amidst the charred underbrush. On one occasion, while patroling the sanctuary during deer season, Cavit was threatened by a hunter who pointed a loaded rifle at him. After Cavit delivered a brief, low-keyed discourse, the hunter apologized and left the premises. If Cavit had wished to have the hunter arrested (assuming that his identity could have been discovered), it would have been extremely difficult to win a court case in the absence of witnesses.

A Deadly Serious Business

It is important not to confuse cause and effect. People are not "slobs" because they hunt. The fact that some men are coarse and callous in demeanor is completely independent of the fact that some of them hunt. Nonetheless, it could be argued that sport hunting is an activity that *appeals* to indurate people. Perhaps no professional group is better acquainted with the personalities and temperaments of various types of individuals than the New York City advertising executives who try to persuade people to buy their client's products. Most of these ad men have been trained in psychology and are experts at exploiting human weaknesses. Therefore no one should be surprised by the headings of advertisements for guns and ammunition in hunting magazines: "Magnum Punch From Browning's Pump"; "On Target—Start to Finish"; "Unbelievable Force"; "The Deadliest Mushroom in the Woods" (showing a picture of a spent rifle cartridge in the image of a phallic symbol). If a person reads beneath the lines of this sex-ego-power hard-sell, he or she will detect a callous disrespect for life. Likewise, thumb through any of the hunting magazines and read the titles of some of the articles: "The Deadly Still-Hunt," "Putting Turkeys to Bed," "Land of the Trophy Bucks," and so on. Some might argue that this is merely sensationalism designed to entertain readers. But if it did not reflect the temperament of many hunters, less hunting equipment would be purchased and fewer hunting magazines would be sold.

An insensitivity to animals often develops at an early age. The day a ten- or twelve-year-old kills his first squirrel or rabbit, certain that it is fun and perfectly ethical, he begins to become hardened and unsympathetic to the value of nonhuman life—and sometimes human life. This insensitivity may become increasingly pronounced as he grows older. Hugh Fosburgh commented on this in his book *One Man's Pleasure* (William Morrow & Co., 1960). Fosburgh, one of whose pleasures happens to be hunting, spent a year writing and studying Nature at his family's 5,000-acre reservation in the Adirondack wilderness. He noted that:

> Every hunter starts out as a neophyte and there is only one way to progress from this stage and that is by experience—plenty

of it—and along the way every best-intentioned would-be hunter in the world is going to learn the hard way—by grisly mistakes.

Fosburgh believes that the wounding of deer could be solved by better hunter training and the outlawing of buckshot, shotguns, and semiautomatic weapons. He wrote that during the years he had been hunting, five hunters had been accidently killed in the forty square miles to the south of his family's reservation. In every case the weapon involved had been either a shotgun or a semiautomatic weapon. He contends that if there were wounded deer statistics, they would reflect the use of these types of weapons. (This was before relatively inaccurate, short-range muzzle-loaders became popular for deer hunting.) Fosburgh also feels that some "needless" cruelty would be ended if hunters were to wait until they were absolutely certain of a kill before pulling the trigger. Further, he believes that society should discard the notion that killing is sport: "The sport is in the hunting, and when the shooting starts it is a dead serious business that shouldn't be taken lightly. But it often is. . . ." And he concludes: "So long as there is deer hunting there is going to be horrible cruelty inflicted."

As with many of the more well-intentioned hunters, the most obvious solution to hunting cruelty escapes Fosburgh. It would be the development by our society of an environmental ethic that would include an empathy with nonhuman life and the realization that if hunting is not absolutely essential for survival when one is living primitively in the wilderness, one should not hunt.

The Question Is Academic

R. D. Lawrence, wildlife biologist and well-known author, has written many books about animals (including *Paddy*, which was mentioned earlier). At one time he was a subsistence hunter in the wilderness of Ontario, Canada. Lawrence wrote that it was often necessary to hunt moose and deer after the close of established seasons, because during hunting seasons the woods were usually unsafe. Drawing from his experience with sport hunters, he wrote the following (*The Zoo That Never Was*, Holt, Rinehart & Winston, 1981):

> It used to be that a few unprincipled men earned for all hunters a reputation that most of them did not deserve. In more recent times, the opposite is taking place; there are so many ignorant, brutal, lawless men stalking the forest in the hunting season that the good, careful hunters . . . are so greatly outnumbered that many of the ones I know personally have put their guns away,

disgusted with the annual carnage and feeling that it is no longer safe to enter the wilderness at this time of madness.

There is evidence that hunters are now seeking a more favorable image. For example the National Wildife Federation has published a manual titled *Advanced Hunter Education and Shooting Sports Responsibility,* by Delwin E. Benson, an extension wildlife specialist and advanced hunter education instructor at Colorado State University, and Rodd E. Richardson, a wildlife biologist with the U.S. Forest Service. It is intended for use as a textbook in training courses at universities, adult education centers, *secondary schools,* and fish and game clubs.

The manual consists of forty-three lessons. Special focus is placed on public attitudes about hunting. Among the subjects covered in this category are "the hunting controversy," "hunting ethics in America," "respect for resources and people," and "improving the hunter's image." According to the National Wildlife Federation, the manual is designed to accentuate "respect, responsibility, restraint, and resources." Will the manual have a profound effect upon the conduct of "slob" hunters? Perhaps, but we should not expect miracles. Particularly since most hunters consider wild animals to be insentient resources.

In summary, if a person considers each of my five principles to be a basic definition of a "slob hunter," then he or she will have to admit that slob hunters are a serious problem. But the question of how large a percentage of hunters are slobs or how many hunters can be lumped into this category may be academic. A strong case could be made, *and is being made,* that public hunting *itself* is biologically, ecologically, and socially destructive. And is it possible to pursue a destructive activity in a constructive fashion?

VI./PSEUDOETHICAL ARGUMENTS

THESE ARGUMENTS INFER THAT ETHICS SHOULD NOT BE A CONSIDERATION IN MAN'S TREATMENT OF NONHUMAN LIFE. THE ARGUMENTS CONTAINED IN THIS SECTION ARE OFTEN USED TO JUSTIFY THE KILLING OF BOTH WILD AND DOMESTICATED ANIMALS. THEY INCLUDE THE VIEW THAT KILLING IS AN ESSENTIAL PART OF NATURE'S PLAN; THAT HUMANS HAVE BEEN GIVEN DOMINATION OVER OTHER SPECIES BY A DIVINE CREATOR; AND THAT NONHUMAN ANIMALS, BEING GOVERNED BY INSTINCT, HAVE A VERY LIMITED SENSE OF PAIN. ANOTHER ARGUMENT ASKS AT WHAT POINT ON THE EVOLUTIONARY SCALE ONE IS TO DRAW A LINE IF THERE IS TO BE ETHICAL ACCOUNTABILITY FOR ONE'S CONDUCT TOWARD NONHUMAN ANIMALS. BECAUSE OF THE NATURE OF THESE ARGUMENTS, IT WILL BE NECESSARY TO EXAMINE SOME SUBJECT MATTER THAT IS NOT DIRECTLY RELATED TO HUNTING.

> *I always had trouble trying to understand why it was okay to destroy life just because it was different from your kind of life. You hear people talk about some god-given right to kill their fellow creatures. But the god they're talking about is the god man created to gratify his egoism and justify his violence.*
> —Luke Dommer, president of The Committee to Abolish Sport Hunting (From ''De-Bunker of Hunting Myths—A Profile of Luke Dommer,'' by Mortimer Frankel, *Agenda,* March-April 1984)

THE CRUELTY IN NATURE ARGUMENT

Hunters' Argument: PEOPLE WHO OPPOSE SPORT HUNTING ARE VIEWING THE WORLD THROUGH ROSE-COLORED GLASSES. NATURE IS RED IN TOOTH AND CLAW. ANIMALS DISPLAY NATURAL AGGRESSIVENESS TOWARD MEMBERS OF THEIR OWN SPECIES. PREDATORS DEMONSTRATE CRUELTY TOWARD THEIR PREY. THEREFORE, HUNTERS ARE SIMPLY FOLLOWING NATURE'S LAW OF ''KILL OR BE KILLED.''

Analysis: Early in 1983, a hunting-trapping-fishing columnist for an upstate New York newspaper gently admonished those who "dream of an imaginary Eden where the lion shall lie down with the lamb while benevolent man looks on indulgently." He then explained that in real life the lion would eventually become hungry and eat the lamb and, furthermore, if man did not shoot the lion, *he* would become the lion's next meal.

Those who use the "Cruelty in Nature" argument contend that since killing is apparently a "law of Nature," there is nothing wrong with hunting and trapping. But man's exploitation of nonhuman animals cannot be considered natural in this sense. It is a perversion of life-sustaining natural predation and natural selection, which, through evolution, leads to "the survival of the fittest." This term has traditionally been misused and abused. As Charles Darwin theorized, the survival of the fittest meant that those individuals that can best adapt to prevailing environmental conditions have the greatest chances of long-term survival. The plant-eaters that are the strongest, quickest, or most intelligent or have the sharpest senses are able to escape predators. Likewise, the predators that are strongest, quickest, or most intelligent or have the sharpest senses have the best chances of capturing prey. But the biological principle of survival of the fittest does not include warfare, mayhem, mass murder, or the needless slaughter of other species of animals for recreation, fur, or material wealth.

Many people have developed a sensationalized concept of Nature that is based more upon negative feelings than reality. For example, George Romanes, a onetime hunter and an acquaintance of Charles Darwin during the 1850s, characterized Nature this way: "We find teeth and talons whetted for slaughter, hooks and suckers moulded for torment—everywhere a reign of terror, hunger, sickness, with oozing blood and quivering limbs, with gasping breath and eyes of innocence that dimly close in deaths of cruel torture." It would be an understatement to term Romanes' remark an overstatement. To claim that a predator is cruel because it kills for survival is to reflect the anthropomorphism of which hunters, and others, sometimes accuse animal protectionists.

It is easy for a well-fed man or woman to recline in the comfort of a modern living room and criticize a badger for killing fox cubs or condemn a wolf for killing a newborn fawn. But the badger and wolf may have young of their own to feed. A person may develop a sympathy for a snowshoe hare that has been crippled in a narrow escape from a lynx. But the hare's wounds may eventually heal and it may live for months or perhaps years. Is it any less pitiful to think of the starving lynx shivering in subzero winds because the hare escaped? It is simply a matter of perspective.

While there is much individualism among members of each animal species, each species displays characteristics common to that species that have evolved over tens or hundreds of thousands of years. No two predaceous species, no two herbivorous species have identical habits. Each species is unique, and people have no justification for condemning a member of another species for acts that are necessary for its survival. Neither does a person have an ethical right to kill an animal simply because he or she does not like the way an animal of a certain species behaves.

Peter Matthiessen, in his book *The Snow Leopard* (Bantam Edition published in 1979), describes the langur, a large silver-brown primate that inhabits parts of Nepal. The dominant male, upon taking control of a group, may systematically kill all of the infants, thereby bringing the breeding females into estrus. They will subsequently mate with him and produce his offspring. Does this seemingly cruel practice give a human being a right to hunt or otherwise inflict pain or death upon a male langur, in effect punishing him for his behavior? This would be absurd, because it would be placing human ethical standards on the behavior of a nonhuman animal.

But wouldn't this mean that if a human being were to kill or torture another species of animal, ethics would not be a valid consideration because human ethics can not be interpolated to include our treatment of nonhuman species? This would not be the case, because human ethics apply to *human acts* but not to acts that occur outside the human realm. The male langur, for example, exhibits behavior that has characterized others of his sex and species for aeons. Trying to place human moral standards on the conduct of langurs would be as illogical as expecting every human being to behave exactly like a langur!

An Interspecies Dichotomy

In a sense, nonhuman animals behave morally within the context of their natural life-styles. It is moral behavior *for them* because they are acting as they must in order to survive as individuals and species and by acting as they do they are filling an ecological niche and contributing to the balance of Nature. Each species of animal has evolved behavioral patterns that aid individual and group survival. For example, the battles for mating rights between males of some species help to perpetuate the genetic characteristics of the strongest members of these species. Red squirrels establish territories and drive out intruders because if each squirrel did not have sufficient territory, some natural areas would become overcrowded with squirrels, resulting in a depletion of food over the most favorable habitat. This would also adversely affect animals that prey on squirrels, and both squirrels and predators might become non-existent in many areas.

But simply the fact that each species of animal has unique behavioral characteristics does not mean that these types of behavior can be applied to *human* conduct in a moral sense. First, we are a distinct species with our own physical, mental, and emotional attributes. Second, some types of behavior that might be necessary to create order and stability within an animal society or to insure the best genetic characteristics for future generations (i.e., the conduct of the dominant male langur) would be destructive to individuals and society if practiced by human beings. Furthermore, there would be no justifiable reason for a human male to behave like a male langur in the previously mentioned fashion, so this type of conduct would be unethical. We should treat other species of animals ethically because this means not to exploit them in ways that have nothing to do with our survival. As zoologists/ethologists Hugo and Jane van Lawick-Goodall wrote in *Innocent Killers* (London: Collins, 1970): "It is, in fact, only man who kills with complete awareness of the suffering he may inflict: only man, therefore, who can be guilty of deliberate torture."

There is an argument similar to the one being analyzed that is sometimes used as a justification for hunting. It is that we, as human beings, are either a part of the natural order or we are not. If we are, then we have a right to hunt because, by doing so, we are simply following the natural laws that apply to other species (i.e., predators). If we are *not* a part of the natural ecology, then we still may hunt because of the wide biological and mental gap that separates us from the so-called "lower animals."

The first part of this argument is invalid because, as previously explained, hunters cannot be compared to natural predators—either biologically or ecologically. The second part is equally invalid because it cites human superiority over nonhuman animals as a legitimate reason for hunting, while inferring that it is acceptable for humans to act like so-called "lower animals"! But these animals hunt only for survival.

Even if hunting were "natural" in the sense that for thousands of years people have hunted, the question that must be asked is, simply because hunting may be "natural" in the historical sense, does this mean that people *should* hunt? Human beings have free choice; people are *capable* of evolving to a higher level of consciousness that transcends established behavioral patterns when these patterns have been cruel and exploitive. We *can* develop feelings of compassion for both human and nonhuman life. The development of this environmental ethic would be a giant step up the evolutionary ladder for mankind.

When "Natural" Is Unnatural

Many philosophers and humanitarians have questioned the concept that human beings should behave according to some sort of "natural law." One of these was Dr. Christina Hoff, a professor of philosophy at Clark University in Worcester, Massachusetts. In a speech at a bioethics conference at Yale University in October 1980, Dr. Hoff questioned the view that man's domination over animals is natural. She explained that slavery and abuse of labor could be considered "natural," although certainly not ethical. She concluded, "It has become clear that these so-called 'laws' of nature cannot provide an adequate basis for a moral theory, if only because they may be cited to support almost any conceivable theory." It was Adolf Hitler who said that "Nature confers the master's right to the strongest. They must dominate!" Nature's laws are taken out of context when they are used as a justification for cruelty.

The late ecologist-author Edwin Way Teale wrote that Nature is impartial. It is neither malevolent nor munificent. But there is beauty in Nature just as there are examples of compassion within the nonhuman animal kingdom: the love of a mother and, among some species, both mother and father for their young; a devotion to a mate; and among social animals a concern for—and often a willingness to fight for—the safety of another member of the pack or colony.

When intraspecies battles occur, they are usually brief. Afterward, both victor and vanquished will return to more peaceful activities with little or no outward sign that their lives had been temporarily disturbed. Even fights between territorially motivated red squirrels seldom result in serious injuries. When a wolf or coyote is defeated in an altercation, it will expose its throat as a sign of submission. The victor will promptly cease his aggressive behavior and, having established his dominant position, will allow his opponent to rejoin the pack.

The Humane Rationalization

Some hunters have claimed that hunting by humans is less cruel than natural predation—that a deer will suffer less from one or two swiftly delivered, well-placed bullets than from the fangs of a wolf pack. Those who use this argument overlook the fact that wolves have a right to exist. As to whether it is inhumane for wolves to kill a deer, this depends largely upon whose point of view a person takes—that of a deer or that of a hungry wolf. The wolf does not kill to be wantonly cruel. The wolf kills for one reason—to eat. There is no dishonor in that. The wolf kills with its sharp teeth because these are the only tools at its disposal. We cannot be certain, but it would be logical to assume that

214

if there were a quicker and more humane method of dispatching its prey the wolf would use it.

Wolves have evolved as meat-eaters; their physiology has been designed for predation, and they do what they must in order to survive. When a wolf is satiated it does not kill again until it is driven by hunger. This is more than can be said of most *people* who hunt. Moreover, unless a deer is very weak or trapped in deep snow, it has a better chance to escape a wolf pack than to evade a hunter with a high-powered rifle, particularly a weapon that is mounted with a telescopic sight.

By what divine judgment has the human race been given the right to abuse other forms of sentient life for its selfish ends? If a bird or nonhuman mammal can be reduced to a statistic, then of what value is life—*any* life?

THE BIBLICAL ARGUMENT

Hunters' Argument: MAN HAS A MORAL RIGHT TO USE ANIMALS IN WAYS THAT BENEFIT HIM. IT IS WRITTEN IN GENESIS THAT ALL ANIMALS WERE CREATED FOR HIS USE. HE HAS BEEN GIVEN "DOMINION OVER THE FISH OF THE SEA AND THE FOWLS OF THE AIR."

Analysis: The "biblical" argument is seriously flawed—not to a person who does not use the Bible as a source of supreme authority, but to anyone who *does* and understands the Bible's message. One must consider the Bible in its total context, and it teaches that love and kindness are among the highest virtues. Further, *dominion* is often confused with *domination*. The former refers only to "supreme authority," while *domination* can mean "arbitrary or insolent sway."

The Bible teaches that God is omnipotent and a being of pure love. It infers that God is to man as man is to nonhuman animals. Therefore, if God loves man despite man's wrongdoing, why can't man display the same love and consideration toward the life forms over which *he* has "dominion"? Some people have asked, "Why love an animal that will not return your love?" The answer is that selflessness is the purest form of love. Unfortunately, some people are unwilling to love unless they receive some form of self-gratification as a result. This is the antithesis of the Bible's message.

If a person considers the Bible in its totality, he or she will inevitably conclude that, according to Scripture, it is God's plan that people establish a benevolent stewardship over the earth and its plant and animal life.[1] Not to do so would be a serious crime. A careful study of the Bible confirms this. For example, Christ said, "Consider the lilies of the field.

They toil not, neither do they spin, yet Solomon in all his glory was not arrayed like one of these." Christ also said, "Lift the stone and you will find me. Cleave the wood and I am there." These and other references to nature conflict with the view that the Bible is homocentric in its philosophical orientation.

There are many indications in the Bible of a divine plan for humane stewardship. Consider the portrayal of God in Job (12:10): ". . . In whose hand is the soul of every living thing." Psalms 50:10 reads: "For every beast of the forest is mine and the cattle upon 1000 miles" and verse 11: "All the fowls of the mountains and the wild beasts of the field are mine." The Bible teaches that people may learn a great deal from Nature: "But ask the beasts, and they shall teach thee and the fowls of the air, and they shall tell thee. Or speak to the earth, and it shall teach thee." (Job 12:7–8).

It should be emphasized, however, that proof-texting the Bible is often an inadequate method of obtaining biblical knowledge. Most religious scholars agree that the Bible is a collection of writings that represent a period of over 1,000 years and contain a wide variety of religious teachings. Most biblical philosophy shows a sequence of progressive development over a period of time, notwithstanding the common thread that binds it together. Thus many apparent contradictions and paradoxes are found in the Bible. If one is to understand the Bible's message, one must concentrate less upon individual passages and more on that common thread—its totality.

Transmigration and the Bierce Hypothesis

Some philosophers have suggested that there may be an afterlife for many species of birds and mammals. Others have speculated that the spirits of nonhuman animals may transmigrate along the evolutionary ladder and eventually become human beings. If this is true, then animals share a much closer spiritual kinship with us than is commonly believed, and in this case it would be imperative to include animals in a humane cultural ethic.

But if the spirits of dead animals progress along the evolutionary ladder, wouldn't a hunter be doing an animal a great service if he were to kill it and help it to achieve a better and possibly more fulfilling life? No, because if one were to use this rationale, one could also ask why not kill a *human being* if there is a beautiful afterlife? If this reasoning were valid, then there would be nothing wrong with killing another person. In fact, murder would be the greatest act of kindness because it would propel a person into a heavenly existence!

All plants and animals have a purpose in Nature. The fish, the grouse, the fox, the deer, the wolf, the dolphin—each is here to perform a necessary function. And who are we to pass judgment on other forms of life that share the earth with us and make it whole? It is written in Ecclesiastes: "For that which befalleth the sons of men, befalleth beasts; even one thing befalleth them, as one dieth, so dieth the other; yea, they have no pre-eminence above a beast; for all is vanity."

Ambrose Bierce had nothing to do with writing or interpreting the Bible. But this nineteenth-century American writer coined an interesting, if rather cynical, description of the human species. In his satirical *Devil's Dictionary*, he characterized man as a creature so lost in contemplation of what he *thinks* he is that he tends to overlook what he really ought to be. And he noted that among man's chief occupations is the extermination of animals, his own species included. Romans 8:6 put it another way: "To have your mind controlled by human nature results in death."

Does God condone cruelty? Not according to Isaiah 1:15: "When ye make many prayers I will not hear; your hands are full of blood." Likewise, Isaiah 66:2 states: "He that slayeth an ox is as he that slayeth a man." It is only one step from perpetrating violence and death against another species to perpetrating it against one's own species, and it is a relatively short step.

Christ said, "You shall know the truth and the truth shall make you free." One day wild creatures shall be free from man's tyranny.

THE PSEUDOSCIENTIFIC ARGUMENT

Hunters' Argument: BRUTALITY IS IN THE MIND OF THE BE-HOLDER. AN ANIMAL HAS NO EMOTION AND VERY LITTLE SENSE OF PAIN. MAN, WITH HIS INTELLIGENCE, DISPLAYS A VAST SPECTRUM OF EMOTIONS. ANIMALS, BY CONTRAST, ARE GOVERNED BY INSTINCT, AND WE MUST NOT INSIST THAT PEO-PLE TREAT THEM WITH COMPASSION AND RESPECT.

Analysis: This commonly used pseudoscientific argument is unscientific. Upon what basis does one conclude that animals cannot and do not experience some of the sensations and emotions that are commonly assumed to be the sole province of our species? Since nonhuman animals are unable to converse in words and phrases, we must base our contentions upon observation and intelligent deduction.

The "old school" of scientific thought, founded by seventeenth-century French philosopher and mathematician René Descartes, held that nonhuman animals are mindless automatons governed exclusively by cause and effect. Thus, if a hunter wounded a wolf with his blunderbuss and the wolf howled, it was not sensing pain but merely reacting instinctively to a cause and effect stimulus. The wolf's cry was a predetermined vocal response, like the sound of a stone when it is kicked.

Unfortunately, modern pseudoscientific thought has not progressed very far beyond Cartesianism. A commercial wildlife biologist might ask, "How do you know that animals sense pain and that they are capable of suffering? It has never been conclusively proven." But an animal protectionist would be justified in rephrasing this question and asking, "How do *you* know that nonhuman animals do *not* feel pain, and that they are *incapable* of suffering? It has never been proven that they do *not* suffer in painful or stressful situations!"

George Reiger ("The Truth About Bambi," *Field and Stream*, March 1980) claims that "wildlife sentimentalists feel justified in selecting those 'scientific truths' they like and rejecting as 'unproven' those that embarrass them." This may be true in some cases, but an ecologist might ask whether hunters are guilty of the same selective empiricism. A certain amount of skepticism is essential in the pursuit of knowledge. But skepticism can be, and often is, carried to unscientific extremes by even the most literate people. The scientific method (which is dutifully taught to potential wildlife biologists at colleges and universities) mandates that a person must not accept a logical conclusion unless it can be painstakingly demonstrated that there is no statistical possibility of error. A strict adherence to this procedure often results in a pseudoscientist disbelieving every probable hypothesis that has not been systematically proven. He or she *assumes the negative simply because the positive has not been validated by the scientific method.*

The Ego Factor

It has been my experience that most people—including self-styled pragmatists—are inclined to believe or disbelieve whatever flatters their ego. It is my opinion that many skeptical homocentrics, including most hunters, *do not want* to believe that animals share many of our human traits. (After all, it is easier to exploit what we depersonalize.) But there is nothing to be gained when an individual assumes on the basis of *scientific* evidence that people are not alone in their ability to experience a spectrum of emotions and sensory perceptions. I believe that birds and nonhuman mammals are sentient beings that deserve our ethical consideration, but I do not believe this simply because I have developed an empathy with animal life. I accept it on the strength of existing facts. A bit of thought will show that Descartes' mechanistic hypothesis is unsound.

Like man, nonhuman mammals have evolved highly developed central nervous systems. Pain is Nature's way of communicating the effects of sickness or injury. In the absence of pain, survival would become much more difficult. It may be true that some species of nonhuman animals are better equipped to withstand physical punishment than we are, due mainly to their protective layer of fur. We humans have no such protection. We have a thin epidermis, beneath which are myriads of sensitive nerve receptors. Other species of mammals, although not as highly developed as we are, are structured in basically the same fashion. To believe that nonhuman animals feel little or no pain would be to deny that they are complex living organisms with intelligence and well-structured nervous systems.

Some scientists would argue that pain is simply a result of impulses sent to the brain. Therefore, unless the brain has evolved to a very high degree, as is evidenced in human beings, it would not be possible to experience more than a small degree of pain. But philosopher-educator Peter Singer, in his excellent book, *Animal Liberation* (Avon paperback edition, published 1977), noted that a human baby is capable of sensing a high degree of pain despite its low level of conscious awareness. Singer also cited the example of severely retarded adults who are able to experience pain to a great degree despite their lack of intellect and inability to communicate. Are we to believe that when a raccoon's leg is seized by the steel jaws of a trap or a deer is felled by a hunter's bullet that these animals feel little or no pain? Descartes believed this. But Descartes' view that animals are mere *machina* was seriously flawed.

Intelligence and Emotions

Do nonhuman animals experience emotional sensations? Do they demonstrate love and selflessness? Some species of mammals, including some hunted and trapped species, mate for life (examples: foxes, beavers, wolves and coyotes).* They are kind parents and, like many other mammals and some birds, exhibit signs of sorrow at the death of a mate or their young. Beavers mourn their dead in a ritual in which all members of a lodge participate. One winter a friend wrote that a pair of wood ducks had been wintering on her partly frozen pond. Why hadn't they migrated farther south? Pellets from a hunter's shotgun had broken one

*Males of some other mammal species, such as the badger and ring-tailed cat, while not always monogamous, will sometimes help feed and care for their young. Male river otters often play with their pups and help train them to hunt and swim.

of the female's wings, and she was unable to fly. Despite this handicap, her mate would not leave her.

Farley Mowat, a Canadian naturalist and biologist, spent many months studying the habits of timber wolves in northern Manitoba. His findings are catalogued in his book *Never Cry Wolf* (Bantam Edition, published 1979).* With the aid of a periscopic telescope, he learned that wolves are excellent parents and will never leave their young alone. He found that wolves demonstrate great affection for their mates. When meeting after an absence, both male and female showed great joy at the reunion. Mowat learned that wolves will not kill unless they are hungry. When a family of foxes dug up food that a wolf had cached, the wolf pack simply watched them from a distance, seemingly amused.

Some species of mammals and birds exhibit signs of playfulness. Otters slide down snowy hillsides. Edwin Way Teale wrote of a ruby-throated hummingbird that continually rode the current of runoff from his lawn sprinkler—for no other reason, it seemed to him, than to experience a pleasurable sensation.

The Blind Instinct Theory Debunked

Despite evidence that birds and nonhuman mammals are intelligent creatures, most hunters—and many government wildlife biologists—believe that all animals are governed exclusively, or mainly, by instinct. But if this were true, no animals, with the exception of man, would be capable of learning. Like the lowly housefly, animals would be able to perform only those tasks that had been "precoded" into their genes by their predecessors.

If birds and mammals were governed only by instinct, they would be unable to adapt to a new environment. But this is not the case. Consider the tropical South American monk parakeet, an escapee to the United States from a docked ship that had transported a small number of these birds to New York City for sale as pets. Monk parakeets reversed their breeding season to correspond to that of northern-hemisphere birds *in a single season,* and many of them have found enough berries and seeds to survive winters in Pennsylvania. These foods were taken from plants that they *had never seen before!*

If the "blind instinct" theory were true, there would be no order among social animals—only chaos and anarchy, as is true of human societies that have no capable leaders and those that are ruled by a despot. The males of each species, programmed for dominance, would

---

*In 1983 a movie version of Mowat's book was produced by Walt Disney Studios. *Never Cry Wolf* starred Charles Martin Smith.

fight amongst themselves until all but the strongest were dead or severely incapacitated. The result would be the near-extinction of every species. Yet animal societies, as exemplified by those of penguins and Arctic seals, are peaceful and well ordered and each individual knows his or her niche in the social structure. The crocodile is one of the least-liked members of the animal kingdom. But crocodiles, when living in a group, display little intraspecies hostility. Two crocodiles will often peacefully share the same meal. These supposedly fierce reptiles allow tiny birds to perch within their powerful jaws. The birds pick small pieces of flesh food from between the crocodile's teeth.

Finally, if animal behavior could be explained exclusively in terms of instinct, each male or female of a species would react in *exactly* the same fashion to a given stimulus. There would be no room for variations. But this is not true. One can prove this simply by observing wildlife. For example, when a person approaches a family of young red squirrels, he or she may find that the first scurries for cover, the second stands its ground, the third advances cautiously, and the fourth retreats by stages. This demonstrates intelligence and individuality. The term "instinct" is an oversimplification, because members of each animal species originally had to *learn* the traits that characterize their species.

Star Charts and Innate Intelligence

But how were they learned? No one has given a satisfactory explanation of how swallows, robins, phoebes, and some species of migrating hawks are able to find their way back to the same nesting sites year after year from wintering grounds hundreds or thousands of miles away. Is this purely a result of instinct? A bit of thought will show that this would be a ridiculous assumption. It is believed that Canada geese, using a flyway a hundred miles or more from the Atlantic Ocean, may "hear" ocean waves that enable them to remain on a basically north-south flight path. Is this logical in human terms? It has been proven that geese are aware of positions of stars in the sky; this is how they are able to establish their bearings on nighttime migrations. They apparently sight on the North Star. Evidently, no one has thought to ask how geese, which to the best of our knowledge have never studied astronomy, can be aware of these things. Can this be explained by instinct? And if so, how did geese originally develop this method of navigation? Bird migration could be explained by an extra sense not present in humans. If this is true, it would indicate that nonhuman animals, while not having as great a capacity for *learning* as humans, use their intelligence in ways that we are unable to understand. This would destroy the widely held concept of human biological superiority over so-called "dumb animals," a concept that is embraced by most hunters and commercial wildlife biologists.

The term "dumb animal" is a misnomer. Each species has been gifted with attributes that are unique to that species and enable it to survive. In this sense, no species is superior to any other; all are equally adapted for survival in their unique ways. As a wise scientist once observed, there is no instinct without a certain amount of intelligence and no intelligence without a certain amount of instinct.

If birds and nonhuman mammals are intelligent beings who can experience pain and suffer—and the evidence supports this premise—then it would be as despicable to needlessly shoot an animal as to gun down a human being in cold blood. Moreover, if we accept the "pseudoscientific" hunting argument, we are condoning the oppression of nonhumans by humans largely on the assumption that man has preeminence over other animals because of his superior mental powers. But if superior intelligence were a justification for killing members of another species, then this would give extraterrestials who are much more intelligent than we are the moral right to kill *us* for food, for pleasure, or for any other reason.

Empathy is the key to understanding.

THE EVOLUTION ARGUMENT

Hunters' Argument: IF WE ARE TO BEHAVE ETHICALLY TOWARD ANIMALS, AT WHAT POINT DO WE DRAW THE LINE? HOW FAR DOWN THE EVOLUTIONARY SCALE DO WE GO? DO WE GIVE MORAL CONSIDERATION TO HOUSEFLIES, MOSQUITOES, AND COCKROACHES? WHAT CRITERIA DO WE USE FOR DETERMINING WHICH ANIMALS ARE TO BE INCLUDED WITHIN THE HUMAN SPHERE OF ETHICAL CONSIDERATION AND WHICH ARE NOT?

Analysis: Certainly we should include mammals. They are very intelligent and belong to the zoological group that includes our species. As previously noted, many species of birds also display signs of great intelligence, mating for life, migrating to the same locations each spring, demonstrating sorrow at the loss of a mate or offspring. So, at the least, warm-blooded creatures, birds and mammals, would receive ethical consideration. The ethical treatment of reptiles, amphibians, and fish would be more difficult to justify to hunters and other skeptics, although members of these zoological groups should not be harmed needlessly.

What about insects? Houseflies transmit diseases, and although they are an important link in the chain of life, it is understandable that a person might kill a fly that had entered his or her home. The killing of biting insects, such as mosquitoes and deerflies, is done mainly in self-defense. Likewise, most people would sympathize with a homeowner who destroys a hornets' nest that has been built above his or her doorway. But a person who kills houseflies for perverse pleasure, or saturates the surroundings with poison sprays in order to kill every biting insect (along with many nonbiting insects and birds), or shoots apart a hornets' nest that is hanging from a tree in the woods would be guilty of indefensible behavior. Even if insects are unable to experience physical sensations or emotions, they are an integral part of Nature and provide food for fish, frogs, snakes, and many species of birds.

But perhaps plants also have feelings. Some philosophers have suggested this. Certainly plants should be spared from needless harm. The unnecessary cutting of a tree, picking of a flower, or pulling of an edible plant without reason is wantonly destructive and disrespectful of Nature and the individual plant. But people must eat in order to live. We have been gifted with free will, and we can choose the lesser of evils when a choice becomes necessary. Plants lack a discernible nervous system and do not have a brain (as we tend to define it). If we must choose between killing an animal, which is susceptible to pain and which shares with us a conscious will to live, and killing a plant, which *may* have remote sensations of consciousness, then as rational individuals we must choose the latter. But neither should we take anything from Nature unnecessarily, whether it is the life of an animal, the life of a plant, or a nonliving object.

The question of where a person draws a line may be applied to hunting as it relates to other forms of animal exploitation. If a person hunts for nonessential reasons, then that individual helps to perpetuate an unjust system, one that includes *all* forms of animal abuse. Thus, whether consciously or not, the recreational hunter shares complicity with the trapper, the whaler, the dolphin killer, the killer of harp seal pups, the vivisectionist, the factory farmer, and many other animal exploiters. (Unless the hunter is actively attempting to curb these abuses. And this would be very unusual!)

It is not of such great importance where one draws a line regarding moral consideration for other species as it is for people to understand that even the most lowly forms of life have a purpose in Nature's plan. In the words of columnist Charles Maher: "Animal life has value—to animals if not to us—and every effort should be made to keep such life from being destroyed without real purpose."

PART THREE

Targeting the Issues

VII. / THE SOCIAL IMPLICATIONS

A DESCRIPTION OF SOME OF THE DESTRUCTIVE EFFECTS THAT HUNTING CAN HAVE UPON INDIVIDUALS AND SOCIETY, CONCLUDING WITH AN INSIGHT INTO ONE OF THE GROTESQUE SOCIAL CONSEQUENCES THAT HAS RESULTED FROM AN INSENSITIVITY TO LIFE—BOTH HUMAN AND NONHUMAN.

It's like a disease with some of them. They can't help themselves. I remember once I asked this old guy I had arrested again and again when the heck he was going to quit. He told me how he had gotten up one night and gone to the kitchen sink for a drink of water and there was snow on the ground and a big moon up over it and he saw some little creature run across, couldn't even tell what kind it was. "You know, I just wanted to get a gun and kill it so bad," he said.
—Warren Jenkins, a New Hampshire game warden who gave up hunting (quoted by Michael Knight in the *New York Times*, November 27, 1977)

THE INHUMANE EQUATION

Under no conditions can we afford to have our children given instruction which leads them to develop apathy or indifference to suffering or any form of pain. We must provide our children with planned learning experiences in caring for others and loving beyond themselves with compassion for all forms of life.
—Dr. Virgil Hollis, superintendent of schools for Marin County, California, from a 1979 speech (Courtesy of *The Beaver Defenders*)

News Items

—From the December 29, 1982 issue of *The Environment* (a publication of the New York State Department of Environmental Conservation): The DEC considers its most urgent priority on a list of public education plans to be an increased effort to reach young people by introducing them to hunting and fishing.[1] (For many years the DEC has sponsored an annual essay contest titled "Hunting Is Conservation" for youngsters in grades five through eight.)

—Dateline Littleton, New Hampshire: A farmer brings his six-year-old nephew on a mass elimination of woodchucks. After the farmer has shot each of the animals, the boy stuffs their carcasses into their vacant burrows.

—Dateline Williston, Vermont: A twelve-year-old girl is commended by a reporter for her many waterfowl, grouse, and rabbit kills. A news photo shows her kneeling and steadying a rifle in one hand and holding two dead Canada geese by their necks with the other. The cutline says "Annie Oakley."

—Dateline Richmond, Virginia (Autumn 1980): The U.S. Fish and Wildlife Service grants $52,000 of taxpayers' money to organized hunters in Virginia with the option to grant an additional $200,000 per year over the following five years for "Operation Respect." This is an attempt by hunters and wildlife officials to convince schoolchildren that game management is a sound practice. Included in the curriculum are courses in hunting techniques, trapping, and archery and a gun safety program for students twelve years old and older. Elementary-school children are warned about the biological fallacies in the Walt Disney movie *Bambi* and told that in real life Bambi's shooting would be a sound management practice. The project is cosponsored by the Virginia Game Commission.

—Dateline Mud Lake, Idaho (November 1981): Crowds of young people in their teens and preteens gather alongside adults for the Mud Lake "Bunny Bash." Rabbits, at a high point in their population cycle, had eaten farmers' crops. the previous summer. Many were later captured by farmers and confined to a large cage. Then the crowd gathered and the rabbits were released for the kill. People wielding tire irons, baseball bats, ax handles, and other weapons pursued the rabbits and bludgeoned most of them to death. Some boys and girls were no older than ten or eleven. The festivities included "bunny baseball" in which teenaged boys threw live rabbits into the air and swung bats at them, the object being to hit them over the top of a nearby fence.

CAUSE AND EFFECT

. . . Man has no effective way of living beyond or outside the kingdom of life. So whatever diminishes that kingdom diminishes him, both as a form of life and as a form of spirit.

—J. Hartt

There is increasing speculation that an insensitivity to animals may result in, or at least be related to, a dehumanization that becomes evident in violent, antisocial acts that are committed against people. This is particularly true when *children* develop a disrespect for the lives of animals. Studies by psychologists, sociologists, and educators indicate a link between childhood cruelty to animals and violent crimes as adults. D. Hellman, writing in the June 1966 issue of *The American Journal of*

228

Psychiatry, found that "violent crimes occur with twice the frequency with individuals that have had a history of cruelty to animals as compared with those who do not have cruelty to animals in their backgrounds." Robert M. Sanders, M.D., of the Department of Psychiatry at the University of Toronto, concluded the following in a report on the correlation between childhood cruelty to animals and adult social violence:

> One can draw an informed opinion based upon the information which is available . . . that . . . violence and criminality are reactively associated; that . . . there would appear to be some factor or factors which result in behavior which in childhood displays itself as cruelty to animals and in adolescence or adults brings about violence and criminality, directed towards society.

Sociologist Margaret Mead believed that children who display cruelty to animals are likely to "embark on a long career of episodic violence and murder." One of them was Albert De Salvo, the convicted "Boston Strangler," who had a history of sadistic behavior toward animals as a youth.

Senseless violence against people is sometimes a *direct result* of an insensitivity to the lives of animals. In May 1981, two twelve-year-old girls were brutally raped in Essex Junction, Vermont, by two young men, aged sixteen and fifteen. One of the girls was murdered. The elder assailant had witnessed a pig slaughter at a friend's farm a few weeks before. According to an article by Paul O'Neil and Christopher Whipple in the July 1982 issue of *Life* magazine, the assailant had "watched the bloody proceedings with fascination." He had told the girls, "You're gonna know what it's like to . . . get slaughtered like a pig."

The fifteen-year-old could not be tried as an adult under existing Vermont law. After 26,000 outraged people had signed a petition asking for a change in the state law, the Vermont legislature voted *unanimously* to lower the age to ten at which a person could be tried as an adult for certain felonies. Ironically, these were the same legislators who periodically pass laws encouraging the expansion of hunting and trapping, which result in the wounding and slow torture of countless animals. And it is the same legislature from which there has been scarcely a word of protest about the annual sixteen-day Vermont nightmare known as deer season.

Recreational hunting has apparently contributed to violent, antisocial acts. In Philadelphia, in 1980, a man who had had a domestic quarrel and had threatened to shoot his wife pointed a rifle from his window at advancing police and shouted, "I'm a hunter, and I never miss!" He didn't. He wounded two policemen before he surrendered. In Orroville, California, also in 1980, two young men, aged nineteen and twenty, murdered a deaf black man named Jimmy Campbell because they could find no animals to kill on a drunken hunting expedition. The Butte County Superior Court judge who sentenced them to twenty-five years to life in prison said that they had "demonstrated for some time their total disregard for the right of another to live." While these are isolated cases, they show what may happen to seriously disturbed people who have no compassion for animals—human or nonhuman.

Even if legal violence against animals were a substitute for illegal violence that would otherwise be directed at humans and even if this legal violence could be considered ethical, it would not be a legitimate reason for the continued existence of sport hunting. Violence-prone people are a potential threat to society, and they are equally dangerous whether they are walking the streets or stalking through the woods. Clair Otis, Cavit Buyukmihci, and many others have learned this the hard way.

TWILIGHT OF THE GODS

Until we stop harming all living things we are still savages.
—Thomas A. Edison

What may happen when an insensitivity to the value of life—human and nonhuman—results from extreme ignorance, an ignorance that has been tempered neither by humane teachings nor enlightened introspection? Consider a bizarre and chilling incident that took place in Colombia, South America, during the summer of 1972. It was reported in the *New York Times* (July 9, 1972):

> Evidence that untamed life on the prairies has changed little since the time of the conquistadores was provided in a courtroom here last week when a half-dozen cowboys charged with murder freely told in horrifying detail how they had lured 18 Indians to their ranch with the promise of a feast and massacred them for fun.
>
> "If I had known that killing Indians was a crime, I would not have wasted all the time walking just so they could lock me up," said 22-year-old Marcelino Jimenez, who hiked for five days to a police outpost after learning the authorities were looking for him.
>
> "From childhood, I have been told that everyone kills Indians," said another defendant, who added: "All I did was kill the little Indian girl and finish off two who were more dead than alive anyway."

Enrique Morin, the range boss who had engineered the massacre, explained his motive to reporters: "For me, Indians are animals like deer or iguanas, except that deer don't damage our crops or kill our pigs. Since way back, Indian hunting has been common practice in these parts."

Sixteen Indians were killed, but two managed to crawl away and describe the massacre to a priest. The priest then notified the authorities. The six cowboys and two female cooks were brought to trial but were acquitted on grounds of "invincible ignorance." Government officials, spokesmen for the Roman Catholic church, newspaper editors, and humanitarians were shocked. Their outcry caused the judge to order a new trial.[2]

Many American hunters and members of state wildlife agencies and game commissions who read the *Times* report were probably shocked that such ignorance and insensitivity still exists. But it is this insensitivity to the value of life that is responsible for the continuing slaughter of North American wildlife. The only difference between the massacre of Indians or other people and the wholesale killing of wolves, coyotes, woodchucks, or other "nuisance wildlife" or the pursuit and killing of deer by groups of hunters is that the latter acts are committed against another species, not against an ethnic race of our own species. But simply because a double standard exists, this does not mean that the standard is ethical.

If we are to establish an ethical system based upon a consistent universal standard we are faced with a clear choice: either we consider *all* intelligent life sacred or we consider *no* intelligent life sacred. And how much, much better it would be for all of us if we were to embrace a biocentric ethic!

VIII. / SEEKING SOLUTIONS

An ENUMERATION OF SOME OF THE FACTORS THAT PSYCHOLOGISTS HAVE SUGGESTED AS POSSIBLE MOTIVES FOR SPORT HUNTING, FOLLOWED BY A BRIEF SUMMARY OF THE ADVERSE EFFECTS OF PUBLIC HUNTING AND GAME MANAGEMENT AND A LIST OF RECOMMENDATIONS FOR REFORMING THE POLICIES OF STATE WILDLIFE AGENCIES AND GRADUALLY PHASING OUT RECREATIONAL HUNTING.

> *We and others indeed believe that along with the preeminence that* Homo sapiens *has achieved goes a very great moral responsibility—a stewardship if you will—upon which we must not turn our backs. Perhaps especially because we have the power to destroy them* we must respect the rights of our co-habitants of earth.
> —From *Extinction—The Causes and Consequences of the Disappearance of Species*, by Paul Ehrlich and Anne Ehrlich (Random House, 1981)

HUNTING HYPOTHESES

> *If one wantonly destroys one of the works of man, we call him a vandal. He faces the possibility of prosecution. But when one wantonly destroys another living thing we call him a sportsman, and if he kills often enough, that individual will be the recipient of awards and win the adulation and praise of many.*
> —Rabbi Sholom Stern, from a guest editorial titled "Hunters and Killers" in the Buffalo (N.Y.) *Courier-Express* (July 14, 1982)

There are hunting justifications other than those that I have analyzed. Most are shallow and simplistic. (Examples: the assertion that rights apply only to humans and cannot be allocated to animals; that hunting is an American tradition that stems from the constitutional "right to bear arms"; that hunting is simply a method of procuring food; that the primary objective of hunting is not killing, but communion with the natural world; that most hunters admire and respect their quarry; that it is a challenge to try to outsmart an animal, et cetera, et cetera.) Because of the ease with which any well-informed person can refute these arguments, they do not deserve further comment in this book.

Naturally, the validity of an argument depends upon whether one bases one's judgment upon a sound premise and whether all relevant facts have been considered. Prohunting arguments are based upon unsound premises and often evade major issues. Essentially, all of the prohunting rationalizations are little more than conscious or unconscious attempts to maintain credibility and dignity in the face of valid criticism. But if none of the prohunting arguments adequately explain people's reasons for recreational killing, then why *do* people hunt? Psychologists have proposed a number of theories, one of which, or a combination of which, may apply to some, or to all hunters.

1) Hunting is instinctive. In some parts of the world, prehistoric men hunted for survival and the impulse to kill for food has been passed from generation to generation. It remains a part of the male psyche even though hunting is no longer necessary.[1] More sophisticated and enlightened individuals have suppressed the urge to hunt and in place of hunting pursue other outdoor activities. Some of these people have become close to Nature as a result of camping, hiking, photography, snowshoing, ski-touring, backpacking, jogging, bird-watching, or Nature study, while others have excelled at amateur or professional athletics.

2) Hunting is a means of proving one's manhood. In primitive cultures, such as those in the interior of Africa, South America, and Indonesia, the customs of some tribes require an adolescent boy to kill an antelope, gazelle, or other animal before he will be accepted as an adult. After a youth has brought a dead animal into camp, the tribe may feast and celebrate, dancing around a fire in formal recognition of the youth's newly acquired manhood. (There is an interesting parallel in the venison, pheasant, grouse, or wild turkey dinners and associated dances that are held at some fish and game clubs. One reason for these activities is to attract new and presumably young members.)

3) People hunt in order to conform to peer or group norms. This may be particularly true in rural areas where tradition is a strong motivating force. Many of our mental attitudes were formed during our childhood. Young children learn, and usually believe, whatever they are taught. In closely knit societies, most people follow a life-style that they have been conditioned to accept. Many rural adults never acquire the depth of perception that is needed to question blindly accepted traditions. Consequently, as long as they are physically capable of hunting, they continue to hunt.

4) People hunt in order to overcome insecurity. Some hunters may subconsciously wish to punish animals to allay their own feelings of inferiority. Hunting allows a person who feels exploited to become an exploiter; a person on the lowest rung of the social

ladder is able to assert his dominance. In addition, the hunter's gun may become an extension of his personality. Its firepower and explosive noise may increase his self-confidence and induce a sense of superiority.

5) Some people may hunt partly because of a suppressed desire to punish animals for *what they imagine them to be*. The proverbial animal-hater would be included in this category. To him a big buck may be a "wary critter," a bear a "monster," a wolf "wicked," a bobcat "sneaky," a coyote "vicious," a fox a "hen-killer," a raccoon a sort of masked bandit that cannot be trusted, et cetera. These people may view animals as irrational beings that have no depth of feeling beyond an instinct for self-preservation and are incapable of suffering. In reality, these hunters may subconsciously *fear* Nature and, like those described in hypothesis number four, may need a high-powered weapon to achieve a sense of security.

6) Despite what has been perceived by some as man's technological mastery over Nature, there are those who believe that Nature is hostile and a threat to their physical well-being. As a result, Nature must be fought and defeated. There may be an element of conquest here. To these hunters might and right may be synonymous, and they may subconsciously view themselves as a Caesar, a Charlemagne, or an Alexander the Great.

7) For some men, hunting may be a form of violent sexual arousal or release. The hunter's rifle may become a phallic symbol, complete with the ejaculation of its bullet and the accompanying loud roar. There has been increasing speculation about this in recent years. Dr. John D. Copp, a California psychologist who once questioned waterfowl hunters about their reasons for hunting, wrote that hunters reported feelings of great elation after shooting a duck following a long, motionless, silent wait.[2] According to Copp: "They described the state immediately following a kill as . . . a kind of high. This heightened sense of arousal seemed to have a particularly pronounced effect among the younger hunters."

8) Hunting may be a means of releasing otherwise suppressed negative emotions—emotions such as hostility, anger, and aggression. Thus a person who has an unhappy or frustrated home life or who strongly dislikes his employer has the legal option to transfer his aggression onto an animal that is unable to retaliate.

9) At its lowest ebb, hunting may be a result of sadism. Sadism is caused by a complex interplay of psychological factors that create a sense of emotional pleasure from committing wantonly cruel acts. Sadism may be a motivating factor in a relatively small percentage of cases, but it is the most significant hunting hypothesis. There *are* hunters who pose a threat or potential threat to society—*not* because they hunt, but because of their insensitivity to the value of life. It is imperative that our society recognize the correlation

that often exists between violence directed at animals and violence directed at people.

10) Finally, some people may hunt because of a fear of their inner selves. The late author Hal Borland once speculated why many people do not seem to feel comfortable in the woods unless they are creating a loud disturbance. He had once believed that this was because they had become accustomed to noise and confusion. But he had changed his opinion. He wrote in *Countryman: A Summary of Belief,* (J. B. Lippincott, 1957, 1965) that perhaps some people fear solitude because they are afraid that they might meet themselves coming around a bend in a trail. It was Borland's theory that these people know, at least subconsciously, how little they can be trusted, but they are unwilling to openly confront their base motivations. Perhaps many people carry a shotgun or rifle into the woods because they are afraid that they might meet themselves behind a boulder or in a clump of bushes.

CONCLUSIONS: A REVIEW OF THE CAUSES AND SYMPTOMS OF WILDLIFE MANAGEMENT

The wildlife management philosophy of propagating and harvesting these beautiful and sentient creatures like a crop of potatoes is a shameful and vulgar perversion.
—Dr. William A. Ritchie, retired New York State archaeologist (From "Our World Alone?," an unpublished essay)

The evidence has been presented, and the current system of wildlife management stands accused on five counts: as a destructive practice biologically, ecologically, ethically, individually, and socially. A brief review of pseudoscientific wildlife management:

1) The *method* that is most often used to achieve objectives is to create greater imbalances of species within already imbalanced ecosystems. This is done by maintaining or contributing to a synthetic "balance" in which ecosystems are top-heavy with commonly hunted species. Large natural predators that would normally be found there are at very low population levels, if they exist at all.

2) The *procedure* that is employed to maintain this artificial balance is to use hunters as a substitute for native predators, despite the fact that this is a biologically and ecologically destructive practice.

3) The *purpose* of this procedure is threefold:

a) to maintain the traditional system of public hunting and hunter-subsidized state wildlife agencies;

b) to guarantee a flow of revenue for use by these agencies and for a small sector of the private economy;

c) to insure that each hunter is allowed to "harvest" his or her share of "surplus" game populations—a surplus that, if it exists at all in some locations, is most often a result of land and wildlife mismanagement.

The traditional homocentric values of our society, combined with profit-oriented life-styles, has resulted in an abuse of technology that characterizes today's wildlife management practices. The exploitation of wild animals is currently the most effective method of generating revenue from their use (abuse). However, these profits could be equalled or surpassed by the sale of products that would be purchased if greater numbers of people were to appreciate wildlands for their intrinsic values and utilize them as spiritual havens.

Under the present wildlife management system, funds for the restoration of endangered species are severely limited. At the same time, there are large sums of money available for the "study" and manipulation of hunted species and the manipulation of their habitat. The ensuing destruction results in the dispersion and deaths of many "nonfavored" animals. Since a disproportionate percentage of hunters' money has traditionally been used for the management of hunted animals, a vicious cycle has resulted whereby the killing continues, aided and abetted by revenue obtained from the purchase of hunting and trapping licenses, firearms, and ammunition. Most hunters apparently want their license and excise tax money to be used only in ways that will insure maximum sustained yields of "harvestable game." In states that have an income tax checkoff for nongame management, the money that is obtained is often spent for the manipulation of nongame wildlife that has a potential to provide hunters with future "harvestable surpluses." Even when legitimate *nongame* management is undertaken, it is usually done on hunted lands, sometimes as part of "comprehensive" programs that include the management of game species. And hunting is often used as an adjunct to nongame management. Furthermore, many bonafide nongame programs include methodology that is ecologically and ethically questionable.

It will be difficult to reform wildlife management, because wildlife officials and the politicians who support their programs occupy positions of power and power-holders usually try to prevent those with opposing viewpoints from sharing power with them. But the fatal flaw of game management may be that it is financed largely by special interest minority groups in each state. An informed and concerned electorate, comprised of people who are willing to contribute money to finance ecologically sound wildlife management programs, *could* constructively transform the present system. Given enough time, it *shall be* constructively transformed.

Constructive Outdoor Uses Evolve

There are already promising portents. David W. Lime, in an article titled "Wildlife Is for Non-Hunters, Too" (*American Journal of Forestry*, September 1976) revealed that: 1) more then 80 percent of visitors to wildlife areas in California during 1972 engaged in nonhunting activities; 2) during 1967–68, 84 percent of the visitors to the Adams Point Wildlife Management Area in New Hampshire came there for nonhunting recreation; 3) in 1974, hunting accounted for only 7 percent of the total use of 119 national wildlife refuges and 16 waterfowl production areas in the Upper Midwest. (Forty-six percent was for fishing and the remainder for bird-watching, hiking, picknicking, and other nonconsumptive outdoor activities. But between 1976 and 1985, hunting opportunities were expanded in many of these areas.)

Lime quoted a 1975 study that stated that during 1974 approximately $500 million had been spent by bird-watchers for birdseed, binoculars, camera equipment, and associated items while in 1970 only $180 million had been spent by waterfowl hunters.* Lime cited a number of factors that have contributed to an upsurge in the nonconsumptive enjoyment of wildlife. Among them were: a shrinkage in the accessible land base for hunters; a decline in the quality of hunting, caused in part by crowding; and an increased effort by opponents of hunting to solicit public support.

Public attitudes about the natural world are slowly changing. But enlightenment will not result in better conditions for wildlife unless laws are passed that reform wildlife management and protect all species of wild animals from exploitation.

RECOMMENDATIONS

The fish and game commissions, as presently constituted, must go. They must be removed, together with their entourage of public relations officials and biologists. They must be replaced by ecologists, but above all, by humanitarians.
—Cyril Toker, M.D., the late director of Friends of Animals Committee
for Humane Legislation

---

*A 1980 survey by the U.S. Fish and Wildlife Service indicated that as many as 92 million Americans participate in wildlife appreciation activities each year. In 1980, $14.7 billion was spent on nonconsumptive wildlife-related activities, equipment, and travel, including $517 million for birdseed and feeders.

What must be done? *If hunting is to be restricted, two broad goals must be achieved:* First, it will be necessary to stop the lengthening of hunting seasons and the establishment of new seasons on previously protected species. Then pressure must be placed upon legislators to *shorten* some hunting seasons and abolish those that are most destructive (for example, wolf hunting and spring turkey hunts). Second, the opening of new lands (i.e., state parks and national wildlife refuges) to hunting must be halted and increasing amounts of public land must be declared state or federal wildlife sanctuaries.

But before any of these scenerios are likely to occur, *there must be a shift away from the financing of state wildlife programs by hunters, trappers, and fishermen* and a gradual phasing in of public funding of state fish and game bureaus by general state tax revenues and monies that would be obtained from nonconsumptive users of state forests, state parks, and other public wildlands.[3] These funds might include revenue from public "use permits," which would be required in order to utilize state forests and parks; state taxes on camping and backpacking equipment, skies, snowshoes, binoculars, nature books, birdseed, et cetera; and the availability for public purchase of state nongame wildlife stamps. The money received from these sources would be used to purchase wildlife habitat that would be protected from hunting, trapping, and off-road vehicles.[4]

Form Ecological Advisory Boards

After the preceding measures had been enacted, each state would form a wildlife committee (in contrast to a "game commission"). In accordance with existing laws and more progressive future legislation, the committees' purpose would be to develop new and ecologically sound regulations governing the protection, or lack of protection, of each species of wild animal in their state. How would these committees be structured? Initially an eleven-member committee might consist of three ranking members of hunters' organizations, three ranking members of animal welfare-rights organizations; three ecologists of the Rachel Carson–Edwin Way Teale–Joseph Wood Krutch variety; and two impartial members who were not hunters, trappers, or fishermen. (Naturally this would require a change in the laws of most states, which now stipulate that members of game commissions hold a valid hunting and/or trapping and/or fishing license.) Committees would be directly responsible to *all* the people of their respective states. The diverse representation would probably result in some lively discussions, but at least the composition of the committees would be representative and democratic—both to people and, inasmuch as possible, to wildlife. Gradually, as public attitudes became more enlightened, greater emphasis would be placed upon protected status for all wildlife.

Isolate License-issuing Bureaus

The sale of hunting, fishing, and trapping licenses would be shifted from state wildlife departments to autonomous agencies whose sole purpose would be license issuance. These departments would not be connected in any way with the fish and wildlife bureaus of their states. The license issuing boards would have no political authority beyond this function; therefore hunters would not be able to influence wildlife policies by lobbying members of their wildlife department (or license issuing board). If necessary, Pittman-Robertson funds would supplement license fees to fund the licensing bodies, but P-R monies would no longer help to fund the operations of state wildlife departments, since under the present system, these monies provide an additional stimulus to issue as many licenses as conditions permit. Other federal funds, such as those for endangered species, would be used by state wildlife departments strictly for the nongame purpose for which they had been intended. There would be stipulations that would: 1) prohibit the future reclassification of any species aided by nongame funds into a "game" catagory, and 2) prohibit the purchase of hunted lands with nongame funds, including those obtained from the sale of state nongame wildlife stamps.

Ideally, by the time these steps had been taken, state wildlife agencies would be funded by general state tax revenues combined with funds obtained from users of state forests and parks and state taxes on nature books, hiking and camping gear, skies, snowshoes, bird-watching equipment, and birdseed, plus money from the sale of wildlife stamps. Hunting and trapping would be phased out in stages. Much more stringent hunter training would be required before anyone would be eligible to purchase a hunting license. Training programs would contain a comprehensive "game" species identification course that would include a thorough study of the physical characteristics of all hunted animals, including hunted waterfowl. These programs might be patterned after the rigid hunter training courses that are required in some European countries, such as West Germany, where more than a third of those who enroll usually fail to graduate.

Reduce Land Base Available for Hunting

The numbers of hunters that would be allowed to utilize public lands would be reduced by a process of issuing licenses only to those who had received progressively higher grades in hunter training programs. Initially, all who passed these courses would be allowed to hunt on their own land and consenting landowners' property. But a steadily declining percentage would be permitted to hunt on state and national forestlands and in those state parks where hunting is now practiced. (All national wildlife refuges would be protected as sanctuaries.)

A decline in the use of state lands by hunters would be ensured by the issuance of two types of hunting licenses. The first would allow the holder to hunt legal "game" on private land belonging to himself or a consenting landowner. As is now done in Connecticut, those who own ten or more acres of rural land would have the option to sign a form or forms that would allow a friend or friends (perhaps up to and including three in number) to hunt on their property. These forms would then be validated by the license issuing board. Any hunter who illegally trespassed on another person's land would be liable to receive a heavy fine. Heavy fines *and* jail sentences of up to six months would result if a person were to illegally hunt on public or private lands where wildlife were protected. The *killing* of wildlife on protected lands would be a felony and would be subject to even more stringent penalties.

The second type of license, which would be issued in steadily declining numbers, based upon hunter training performance, would allow the holder to hunt on unprotected public lands. Those who were issued these permits would already have or would be eligible for the issuance of the first type of license (for private land hunting). Hunting and trapping license fees would be much higher than they now are (in real dollars adjusted to future inflation). This would make hunting a privilege rather than a self-ordained and self-perpetuated "right." Excess funds that were collected by license-issuing bodies would be used to purchase wildlife habitat, most of which would be protected from consumptive uses—particularly in ecologically sensitive wild or wilderness areas. If more money were needed for the operations of a licensing agency, tax funds from that state's general treasury would be used.

Tighten Hunting Eligibility Requirements

The numbers of hunting licenses (permits) allowing the holder to hunt on unprotected public lands would be gradually reduced, while the issuance of hunting licenses to those wishing to hunt on unprotected private lands would be scaled down at a slower rate. Trapping would be eliminated when synthetic substitutes for fur became used exclusively. Hunting would be based upon individual need. An income line would be established. Native ruralites whose annual incomes were below this level, assuming that they could prove that they were "responsible" citizens who had successfully completed a hunter training course, would be eligible for the issuance of a hunting permit. This would allow them to hunt on their own land or on consenting landowners' property and on certain public forestlands in their region—areas where no critical habitat for any species existed.

If an individual who qualified could prove a need to hunt in order to live (as in the case of a wilderness homesteader), special privileges would be accorded, such as extended hunting seasons for deer and/or elk, caribou, moose, et cetera, provided that the hunted animals were plentiful in his or her region. In time, as people became more aware of their responsibility to protect other forms of life and gained a greater appreciation of the value of protected animals living in natural ecosystems, ruralites who had no need to hunt for subsistence would be phased out of consideration for permits. Eventually only those who lived primitively in wilderness areas (including native peoples) would be allowed to hunt and the number of "game" species would be greatly reduced. With the exception of these subsistence hunters, all hunting would be banned on state and federal lands. As public hunting was phased out, the number of people employed by license issuing boards in each state would be scaled down, along with the responsibilities of those who worked for these agencies. Vacancies on state wildlife committees would be filled by ecologists and humanitarians.

Special permits to shoot an individual animal or a very small number of animals might be issued to farmers or ranchers who experienced recurring problems. But a more humane solution would be for a representative of a wildlife department to suggest—and help to implement—nonlethal alternatives. If these failed, the biologist or conservation officer, as a last resort, would have the authority to shoot the animal(s). The killing of "nuisance wildlife" would be minimized if the federal government or state governments were to reimburse farmers for sizable losses of crops and livestock. Agriculturists would have to prove that damage had been caused by wildlife before they would be eligible for reimbursement. (Most experienced wildlife biologists are able to recognize animal damage.) Fraudulent claims, such as the self-destruction of part of a corn crop where the farmer claimed damage by raccoons, would be subject to heavy fines and imprisonment.

Naturally, the process that I have outlined would involve a series of slow, evolutionary steps. It is not the ideal method of banning sport hunting, which would be its outright abolition on all lands in the United States as a result of legislation passed simultaneously in each and every state. (In the case of deer and intensively hunted "game" birds, hunting would be gradually phased out over a period of five to ten years so as not to create temporary "population explosions" of these species, which would result from an abrupt cessation of hunting. Deer hunting would be scaled down using a formula by which two antlerless deer would be killed for every mature buck, thus helping to reestablish about a one-to-one sex ratio.) While a rapid abolition of sport hunting is not likely to occur, any steps that could be bypassed in the model that has been presented would be advantageous to wildlife and its environment. Ideally, in the absence of public hunting and trapping, most of the money obtained by state wildlife agencies and the U.S. Fish and Wildlife Service would be used to stem the decline and extinction of species and buy and protect natural habitat.

Pursue Ecologically Sound Policies

How would wildlife management be structured as public hunting is scaled down and eventually phased out? It would reflect a concern for the welfare of the greatest number of individual animals of all species normally found on public wildlands. The goal of wildlife management would be to insure, inasmuch as possible, ideal numbers of each of these species. This would be accomplished without resorting to ecologically destructive forms of habitat manipulation such as burning and large-scale logging. Management practices on public wildlands would include the reintroduction of large and medium-sized native predators such as timber wolves, panthers, and lynx, also bobcats and native species of foxes where their numbers were abnormally low in proportion to their prey.

If the population of a species or a number of species were to become abnormally low in a certain state or national forest, park, or refuge, whether this were due to nearby habitat destruction, air and/or water pollution, acid rains and snows, or the after-effects of fires, storms, et cetera, attempts would be made to increase the numbers of that species to a level compatible with a well-structured ecosystem—not to a level that would be compatible with the wishes of hunters or "harvest"-oriented game managers, as is currently the case. If there were a population decline due to normal cyclic factors, no form of management would be undertaken, since the species would eventually reestablish itself. Habitat would be manipulated only where the welfare of ecosystems depended upon it or where it was absolutely essential to maintain or increase the population of a threatened or endangered species.

Scale Down Management Activities

Manipulation of habitat on state and federal lands where commercial logging had been banned (ideally all government wildlands) might include reforestation

242

following fires, brush-clearing, very small-scale selective timber cutting (of ten acres or less) designed to open small areas of dense forests, the damming of a creek or stream, et cetera. The major emphasis would be upon the continued health of ecosystems. This would produce, inasmuch as possible, conditions favorable to the greatest number of animals of each species to be found in each natural area. However, *I can not reemphasize too strongly the importance of maintaining natural ecosystems whenever and wherever possible.* Nature is usually the best land and wildlife manager, and except where a serious man-made environmental disruption or rare natural disaster necessitated some form or forms of minor habitat manipulation or the stocking of wildlife, wildlands would be left undisturbed for the benefit of plants and animals and for use as spiritual havens by people who appreciate their intrinsic value. Ideally, people would live much more ecological life-styles that would include voluntary reductions in energy and "resource" use. *Established* biological controls would replace the use of pesticides.

There would also be a concerted public effort to clean up all sources of air and water pollution, including the coal-burning industries that are largely responsible for acid rains and snows in the northeastern states and southern Canada. Environmental contamination is a major factor in the decline and extinction of plant and animal species, and we must soon face up to this and begin cleaning up our environment, even though it will mean sacrifices, economic inflation, and lessened physical comfort. Ideally, there would also be a much-needed stabilization of the North American population by limiting families to no more than two children.

This is much more than a dream. With public enlightenment it may someday become a reality. In the future, if the training that is received by potential biologists at American colleges and universities emphasizes a love of wildlife and a spiritual kinship with the earth, increasing numbers of state wildlife officials will be preservation-oriented. Naturally, the scenarios that I have presented would depend upon an increasing awareness by the American people of their individual and collective responsibility to the natural world; an understanding based upon a selfless interest in the welfare of animals and a strong ethical commitment to the natural land. The pathway is clear. The only question that remains is whether we have the courage and the environmental sensitivity to do what is necessary.

IX. / TOWARD A MORE PERFECT WORLD

A SUMMATION, WHICH DEALS WITH ONE OF THE MAJOR LEGAL OBSTACLES TO THE DISCONTINUANCE OF SPORT HUNTING, WITH THE PROSPECT FOR REFORM AND SOME ENCOURAGING SIGNS OF A DEVELOPING BIOCENTRIC CULTURAL ETHIC.

> *Conscious change of direction toward the environmental ethic will . . . not be easy, for it will demand something that is foreign to us—humility.*
> —John A. Livingston (*One Cosmic Instant, Man's Fleeting Supremacy*, Houghton Mifflin Co., 1973)

NEEDED: AN EVOLUTION OF CONSCIOUSNESS

> *If there is no struggle there is no progress. . . . Power concedes nothing without a demand. It never did and it never will.*
> —Frederick Douglass, abolitionist (from an 1855 speech)

How much longer will the legalized slaughter of North American wildlife continue? For as long as the opponents of hunting are unable to place the issue where it belongs: in the mainstream of social and political consciousness. Clive Hollands, in his book *Compassion Is the Buglar* (MacDonald Publishers, Edinburgh, Scotland), wrote that animal rights must be a "political fight and not merely an undertaking of charitable work to alleviate the suffering of [a] few." The battle for the protection of all species of wild animals will also have to be a *legal* struggle. New laws will have to be passed and archaic laws abolished. The ways in which people *view* wildlife must also undergo constructive change.

The Property Concept

In 1842, the Supreme Court of the United States ruled that wildlife belong to the people, that, in effect, wildlife is held in trust for the

American public.* Some wildlife protectionists have used this as a basis for the abolition of public hunting. But those who use *existing* laws as a foundation for their opposition to wildlife exploitation do not understand the basic legal issue. By North American legal standards, wild animals are public *property*. It is this precept that allows hunters, trappers, and others to needlessly kill them. The essence of the property concept is that the owner or owners have the right to physical control of that property. Therefore, since wildlife legally "belongs to the people," individual members of the public (hunters) are allowed to "reduce hunted species to possession" by taking their lives. Until this legal principle is challenged and modified by an enlightened electorate, recreational hunting will continue to be a legal activity. (*No* individual, human or animal, can be accorded any form of legal rights as long as that individual is theoretically the property of a person or persons. It was for this reason that slaves in the pre–Civil War South were not protected by the Bill of Rights.)

The U.S. Supreme Court has declared that it is the duty of states to prevent the "extermination or undue depletion" of any species of wild animal. But this has been the only all-inclusive form of protection that the court has given to American wildlife. At the present time, all of the laws pertaining to hunting and hunted wildlife reflect the public ownership principle, which may be translated "hunter and trapper ownership." Perhaps the most extreme example of the ownership of wildlife by consumptive users is that many states allow a trapper to file *theft* charges against a person who has released an injured "target animal" from his trap. If laws such as this are to be changed, wild animals must first be legally recognized as *individuals* with the right to freely pursue their lives in reasonably natural surroundings.

THE ROAD AHEAD

I observe too many people in positions of power and influence who would rather destroy instead of protect our wildlife. People must realize, sooner or later, that we live in the same household together—our environment.
—Ralph Heath, Suncoast Seabird Sanctuary, St. Petersburg, Fla. (from a letter to the *St. Petersburg Times*)

When will strict laws governing the protection of American wildlife be passed and when will hunting be scaled down and phased out?

---

*This decision resulted from the case of *Martin v. Waddell*. The highest court ruled that wildlife is held in "trust for the benefit of the people" and not "for the benefit of private individuals as distinguished from the common good."

Probably not until one or more of the following have occurred:

1) When an increasing human population results in a serious depletion of wildlife habitat in most parts of the United States. When this has occurred, *all* species of wild animals will be seriously jeopardized. This has already happened in Great Britain, where animal rights is now becoming a national political issue. Let us hope and pray that North American legislators will recognize the urgency of protecting as much natural land as possible. Suburbanization does *not* automatically result in environmental awareness and a trend toward wildlife protection. As evidence, a traveler will notice a plethora of fish and game clubs dotting semirural areas on the outskirts of populated districts in densely settled Pennsylvania and southern New Jersey. There are also state game lands in Pennsylvania and New Jersey that are located near heavily developed areas.

2) When increasing percentages of people lose interest in recreational hunting as more constructive outdoor activities become established. A decline in hunting interest would slowly render hunting economically unprofitable.

3) When a majority of Americans become ecologically sensitive and understand the need for laws that would protect all species of wild animals from exploitation.

4) When vegetarianism becomes widely practiced, as it someday must, since it will be impossible to feed all of the world's people if grains that could be eaten by people are used to feed animals that are raised for human consumption, but that provide only a small fraction of the nutrients that they take in.

Empathy

There will not be a widespread concern for the welfare of the earth and the life that it supports until a majority of people have developed an empathy with the natural world. We have seen that many of those who call themselves conservationists are hunters. A "conservationist" is often a person who is concerned primarily about how shrinking natural lands and the extinction of some species of animals will affect *human* life, and consequently his or her *own life*. It is essential that we as a society develop an altruistic ethic that includes a respect for nature and a reverence for life.

Inevitably, public attitudes about nonhuman life will become more enlightened. Traditional concepts will be replaced by a biocentric and finally an ecocentric ethic. But sweeping reforms will not be achieved overnight. The restriction and eventual abolition of sport hunting is likely to occur in conjunction with other types of humane legislation (for example, laws that would eliminate vivisection and ensure humane livestock husbandry).

Henry Spira has said that power concedes nothing without a struggle. Those who love Nature and detest the slaughter of wildlife in North America and elsewhere must be prepared for a long and at times bitter and frustrating struggle. It is customary for a society to establish a set of cultural traditions and actively oppose attempts to modify and improve them. Throughout history, unethical institutions have usually been reformed by a slow evolutionary process. Reform movements have been, almost without exception, the products of a very few enlightened individuals.

THE DAWN OF A NEW ERA?

Someday sport-hunting will be considered no higher than slavery on the scale of social values.

—Edwin Way Teale

There have been humanitarians who have recognized man's affinity with Nature since the time of Saint Francis. And, like Saint Francis, many of them have tried to educate others. But because their views conflicted with prevailing social, political, legal, and religious concepts, they were unable to transform traditional attitudes and alter prevailing life-styles. Fortunately, unethical social practices such as sport hunting are no longer immune to constructive change. It is true that those who perpetuate these practices are armed with power. They have the support of the legal establishment and have large sums of money at their disposal. But, like corrupt politicians, unjust insitutions can be "removed from office," that is, they can be constructively changed and eventually abolished through the efforts of a well-informed public.

Doug Moss, a co-founder of Animal Rights Network, has recognized that this is the key to eventual victory. Said Moss: "We possess two vitally important factors—the truth, and a keen sense of moral justice, both of which, if used properly, serve as the foundation for the fight against the lies and disrespect of life possessed by the animal exploiters."

It must be emphasized that the abolition of recreational hunting should be sought *not* because this is an ideal that is compatible with what is commonly characterized as human nature. It is a goal that must be sought because sensitivity and empathy are noble qualities. A cultural ethic that includes a reverence for life would represent a higher set of values than any that have traditionally been embraced. A faith in the future hinges upon our free will and our ability to progress to a much higher ethical level.

A Promise for the Future

There is *hope*. Change is in the air, and although an awareness of our bond with nonhuman life is still in its early stages, enlightenment is beginning to permeate even the most immoveable bastions of insensitivity. This was evidenced when John Rundle, a member of the U.S. Forest Service stationed in the small mountain village of Rochester, Vermont, revealed that during the summer of 1980, six of the eight teenagers in his youth conservation group had expressed opposition to sport hunting. All of the young people in Rundle's group were from rural Vermont.

As with all hard-fought reforms, time, patience, knowledge, sincerity, and a belief in eventual victory are imperative. Tom Regan, a professor of philosophy at North Carolina State University and the author of *The Case for Animal Rights* (University of California Press, 1983) has said that every great movement goes through three stages: ridicule, discussion, and adoption. Recreational killing probably will not succumb swiftly, as a result of sweeping legislation. More likely it will die a natural death, slowly fading from sight as more humane public attitudes become established. But its fate is sealed.

Until that day when a majority in our society recognize their bond with all life we should remember the words of Rachel Carson[1]:

> Until we have the courage to recognize cruelty for what it is—whether its victim is human or animal—we cannot expect things to be much better in this world. . . . We cannot have peace among men whose hearts delight in killing any living creature. By every act that glorifies or even tolerates such moronic delight in killing we set back the progress of humanity.

Grey Owl, in *Tales From an Empty Cabin*, added a postscript to Carson's remarks when he wrote: "Kindness to animals is the hallmark of human advancement." A healthy society does not inflict violence on the powerless, and there can be no justification for a system that holds in contempt the lives of sentient beings. The great humanitarian, the late Dr. Henry M. Weber, may have said it best: "Sport-hunting has many defenders, but no defense."

APPENDIX:
WHAT YOU CAN DO

Conformism and inertia, not opposition, have always been the greatest obstacle to progress.
—Hans Ruesch (*Slaughter of the Innocent*, Bantam Books, 1978, and CIVITAS Publications, 1983)

As a wildlife protectionist, you can help to insure constructive changes in the management of American wildlife, changes that would restrict and eventually abolish sport-hunting. There are two ways that you can do this: by making personal commitments and by becoming directly involved with an animal protection group.

PERSONAL COMMITMENTS

Indirect Commitments

Hunted animals are killed in appalling numbers because of a large hunter population combined with a shrinking land base, due in part to the destruction of wildlife habitat. There are several methods by which you can help to curb this trend.

1) Limit your family to no more than two children. If you already have children, teach them to respect the earth and its plant and animal life.

2) Do not purchase unnecessary power-consuming luxuries. Many of these items waste a considerable amount of electricity and other natural resources. They also contribute to the destruction of wildlife habitat and the proliferation of new dams, atomic and fossil fuel plants, pipelines, transmission lines, and other sources of environmental contamination.

3) Recycle all reusable products. We are living in an age of disposable materials and planned obsolescence. A reversal of this wasteful trend would slow the rate of wildlife habitat destruction.

4) If you have garden space, grow some of your own food. If everyone with sufficient land were to establish a small vegetable patch and process some of their food, much wildlife habitat would be saved from clearing for agricultural use and the lives of many crop-consuming "nuisance" animals would be saved.

5) Become a vegetarian or, better still, a vegan (a vegan utilizes no animal or dairy products). A cow consumes ten to twenty times the amount of grain that is needed to nourish a person. An average chicken slaughterhouse uses 100 million gallons of water in a single day. In the words of Dr. George P. Cave, president of Trans-Species Unlimited: "Factory farming generates massive amounts of animal wastes which cannot be properly disposed of and are polluting our atmosphere and water supplies. Production of beef cattle results in overgrazing of land, cutting back of timber land, and accompanying erosion. Wildlife also suffers . . . from the destruction of habitat and from 'predator control' programs of ranchers."

Direct Commitments

1) Develop a greater sensitivity to Nature through hiking, photography, bird-watching, and other forms of Nature observation.

2) Educate yourself about wild animals and their habits. Read books that deal with wildlife in a sensitive fashion.

3) If you live in the suburbs or a semirural area, plant trees in your yard. Plant shurbbery around your property boundaries to attract birds. A mulch pile, particularly if there are bushes or small trees nearby, will attract rabbits, squirrels, and other small mammals.

4) Buy or build one or more bird feeders and fill them twice a day during cold weather with the kinds of seeds that are favored by resident species and winter migrants to your area.

5) Learn whether there is a qualified wildlife rehabilitator living in your area who can care for injured wildlife and young animals whose mothers have been seriously injured or killed. Some towns have ASPCA or Humane Society shelters for the care of wild animals and homeless dogs and cats.

6) If you own a large tract of wooded rural acreage, post it against hunting, fishing, and trapping. Or establish a wildlife sanctuary. This requires courage, but unless brave humanitarians exhibit this courage hunting on private rural lands will continue.

7) If you own more than thirty or forty acres of woodland and have no children, will your property to a person or organization that is willing to maintain it as a sanctuary and patrol it during hunting seasons.

8) Contribute money to private wildlife sanctuaries to help defray taxes and other expenses.

DIRECT ACTION

Individual Action

1) Educate yourself about hunting and its harmful biological and ecological effects. Subscribe to publications (including those of animal protection groups) that deal with wildlife from a nonconsumptive, ecological perspective. If possible, make the acquaintance of knowledgeable opponents of hunting and learn from them.

2) Write letters to the editors of newspapers expressing your views about wildlife preservation. Refute inaccurate claims made by hunters and wildlife officials in newspaper columns.

3) Write, call, or visit your state legislators and United States Congresspeople and Senators. This is *very* important because it is the only way that most citizens, acting independently, can help to enact laws that protect wildlife. Keep informed about pending wildlife legislation and know who sponsors each bill, who supports it, who opposes it, and when it is scheduled to be voted upon. Letters, telegrams, and telephone calls to legislators are all effective if a sufficient number of people support your views. Calls should be made at crucial times, if possible no more than a day or two before a vote. Whichever method or methods of communication you use, always support your views with substantive facts. *Do not use ethical arguments as a basis for your opposition to hunting bills.*

4) If you have experience in public speaking, a knowledge of biology and ecology, and a great deal of self-confidence, you may wish to debate hunters or wildlife officials on radio talk shows. A debate may also be a written exchange of views in a newspaper or magazine. A word of caution: wildlife officials are skilled public relations specialists, and face-to-face debates should not be attempted by the inexperienced or unprepared. Do your homework in advance and *do it well!*

GROUP INVOLVEMENT

If public hunting is to be curtailed, hunting opponents must work together to help pass restrictive measures. *Join an animal protection group,* preferably one that places a strong emphasis upon wildlife issues. (The names, addresses, and leaders of all of the major animal protection organizations, along with a brief description of the goals of each group, may be found in the annual *Encyclopedia of Associations* under the heading "Social Welfare Organizations." This reference book is available at most libraries.)

After you have joined an organization, become an active member.

251

Use your skills to help that group. Animal protection groups engage in a variety of activities:

1) PETITIONS—Almost anyone can collect signatures. Petitions submitted to legislators are a means of expressing public support or disapproval. While they usually do not achieve immediate results, they may influence legislators' future voting.

2) MONITORING LEGISLATION—If you live near a state capitol, you can keep informed about pending state wildlife legislation. You may be able to establish a communications network of preservationists. Some groups need a greater number of activists to monitor legislative developments, provide information for "action alerts," distribute educational leaflets and short pamphlets to politicians, and speak to legislators to express their views and those of their organization.

3) PUBLIC HEARINGS—Hearings that deal with proposed hunting legislation, such as the extension of a hunting season or the establishment of hunting in a state park, should be attended by as many wildlife protectionists as possible from the geographical region in which they are held. Attend these hearings, and encourage other preservationists to do likewise. Most hearings that deal with hunting legislation are attended by many hunters and only a small number of protectionists or none at all. The result is that most, or all, of the testimony given supports the expansion of hunting. Protectionists must attend hearings in large numbers and speak against proposed hunting legislation. (Advance notice of hearings usually appears in local newspapers and town halls.)

4) THE COURTS—On an increasing scale, legal suits are being filed in an attempt to halt newly legislated hunting seasons. Court battles involve a coordinated effort, and you may be able to help a group that has filed a suit if you are qualified to obtain information about the harmful biological and/or ecological effects that hunting would have on a potentially hunted species in an affected area.

5) DEMONSTRATIONS—Antihunting demonstrations are a show of unity, and while they are of little political value, they usually receive media coverage and acquaint people with the issues and the scope of the opposition to public hunting. You may be qualified to help coordinate demonstrations and provide advance publicity.

6) HUNT DISRUPTION—Peaceful disruption of hunting may sometimes be an effective tactic. The objective is to gain publicity and increased support for preservationism. Not all wildlife protectionists would agree that this is an appropriate tactic, and since there is an element of physical danger and possible legal consequences, it should not be attempted by novice activists. Hunt disruption has gained much publicity for the Hunt Saboteurs in Great

Britain and members of Greenpeace in British Columbia. But it must be well planned and very well coordinated to be effective.

7) COOPERATION—When you become active in an animal protection organization, seek cooperation with similar groups. If animal protection organizations are to achieve their goals, it will be necessary for all of them, including those whose leaders do not consider a ban on hunting to be among their highest priorities, to become more closely aligned. The hunting lobby *can* be defeated if dedicated wildlife protectionists work together.

8) HUMANE EDUCATION—If the group to which you belong does not strongly advocate humane education programs in public schools, suggest that its members actively seek to implement stronger humane education legislation and encourage stricter enforcement of existing laws. Write to your state legislators and get them involved. Work through your local PTA. In most of the twenty-two states that mandate some form of humane education, these programs are left to the discretion of individual teachers and principals. (Pennsylvania, a hunter-dominated state, stipulates that humane ed programs will include students only up to and including the fourth grade and may not exceed half an hour each week during the school term! Hunter training programs are now being offered to junior high school students in some Pennsylvania schools.) *No* state mandates the teaching of humane attitudes toward hunted animals, but New York State's humane ed program features a "conservation day" when state wildlife officials and game biologists often lecture to school children about wildlife management. Those incongruities must be corrected by public pressure.

STUDENT OPPOSITION AND ALTERNATIVES

If you are a college student majoring in wildlife science and you have chosen this curriculum because of an ethical commitment to wildlife, you might ask your wildlife biology and/or wildlife management professor some critical questions before you consider changing curriculums.

For example:

—Why isn't a much greater emphasis placed upon establishing an empathy with wild animals and their problems?
—Why are wild animals viewed principally as utilitarian entities to manipulate?
—Why do the professor and textbook disseminate information almost exclusively as a prerequisite for employment as a commercial biologist or wildlife manager, with little or no emphasis upon improving conditions for individual animals, single species, and

groups of species *for their own sake within natural or restored ecosystems?*

—Why is no emphasis placed upon the *ethical* implications of activities that adversely affect animals and natural lands?

—Why isn't a much greater emphasis placed upon man's responsibility to wildlife and its habitat and much less upon the consumptive exploitation of wildlife and the theoretical benefits that this creates for people?

—Are there ecologically sound alternatives to accepted wildlife management practices? (Answer: Of course!)

—Can students become involved in projects and compile reports about wildlife that are not directly related to subject material and the "accepted" procedures? (If the answer is "no" and your professor is adamant, do not be afraid to seek the support of those in higher positions—the departmental chairperson and, if necessary, the academic dean or college president.)

Above all, do not hesitate to ask, "Why?" Why are present methods of managing wildlife still considered sacrosanct by most wildlife biologists when they are incompatible with established natural processes? (If the answer is that game management is necessary to maintain high populations of some species for hunting, ask why this is done when public hunting and extensive habitat manipulation are biologically and ecologically destructive.)

It is important to be diplomatic. Depending upon the personality of a professor, it may be best to establish a rapport with him or her and gradually let him or her know that you are opposed to the present system of wildlife management. Unfortunately, not all wildlife professors appreciate student dissent, and you may be graded prejudicially even if you express your disagreement in an amiable fashion. If you are unable to obtain satisfaction through higher channels, you may have little choice but to change curriculums.

Alternative Research

If you are allowed to research and report upon alternative subjects, there are many areas that you could explore. For example:

—The importance of a certain species of large predator in the ecology (i.e., the timber wolf).

—The adverse effects of hunting on populations of hunted and nonhunted wildlife in a certain geographical area.

—An approximate calculation of the number of deer that are wounded during each bow hunting and/or gunning season in the state in which the college or university that you attend is located

254

and the adverse results upon the ecology and the intragroup structures of deer.

—Field comparisons of the habits, movements, and population characteristics of deer on hunted lands as opposed to those on adjacent protected lands. (For example, do deer seek sanctuary on the unhunted refuges?)

—The ecological absurdity of some game management practices (for example, pheasant stocking, managing deer at maximum population levels for hunting, bear hunting in areas where bear populations are very low, the hunting and trapping of rare or threatened animals, or the "control" of wolves and coyotes in a particular state or geographical area).

—The ethical responsibility and ecological necessity of maintaining natural or restored ecosystems in wild areas or in a specific wild area.

The wildlife science departments at many universities urge students to seek summer employment with government agencies. Even if these agencies are hiring you should explore alternative sources of employment. Is work available at a private wildlife refuge or with an animal protection organization? If not, could you volunteer your services while employed part- or full-time at a job that is not associated with wildlife or the environment?

Alternative Employment

When the time comes to seek permanent employment, does a wildlife protection group need a wildlife specialist? Are you qualified for employment with an organization such as Nature Conservancy? Is there a private wildlife sanctuary that needs a wildlife consultant or an environmental specialist? Or would you find it satisfying simply to be a general superintendent or help with various projects at a refuge? Even if the work were part-time, it would be rewarding and beneficial to animals and their environment.

Alternative employment *does* exist, and although it often does not include the high wages and material benefits that are found in commercial endeavors, students who are deeply committed to wildlife should consider these options. Only in this way will the quality and sensitivity of wildlife professionals be increased. And only in this way will conditions for wildlife be improved.

NOTES

Part I: Game Management: Root of an Evil

I. An Introduction to Wildlife Management

1. Kellert's findings are included in a three-volume set that totals more than 450 pages and has been reproduced by the National Technical Information Service of the U.S. Department of Commerce. An explanatory text accompanies the statistics. The survey included a random face-to-face sampling of 3,107 people from the continental United States and Alaska. While the results of the survey are of considerable interest, public attitudes about hunting and the attitudes of those who are opposed to hunting were not intensively investigated. In most cases "anti-hunters" were grouped under a separate heading, while birdwatchers, environmental protection organization members, wildlife protection organization members, and humane organization members were assigned their own classifications. Since the ratings of "anti-hunters" in the areas of knowledge about wildlife and approval of protection for endangered species was low, it is likely that most of Kellert's "anti-hunters" did not fit into any of the above organizational groupings. (Kellert's definition of *anti-hunter* was simply "those who said they were opposed to hunting for recreation, sport, or meat.")

2. Fifteen percent of those surveyed had hunted during the previous two years. About one-quarter of the respondents had hunted at some time during their lives. Eighty-five percent of those who hunted were male. More than half of those who had hunted during one period of their lives no longer did so. Approximately one-fifth of those who no longer hunted cited opposition to hunting as their reason for abstention. Other reasons given were no opportunity or time, personal health intervened, or spouse objected.

3. Kellert polled thirty-five people belonging to one or more of six "humane organizations" and seventy-one people belonging to one or more of six "wildlife preservation organizations." The number of these people, when compared to the total number of people that were polled, is approximately equal to the actual number of organization members as compared to the total U.S. population. Significantly, the leaders of only two of the "humane organizations," The Fund for Animals and the Animal Protection Institute, have expressed opposition both

257

to public hunting *and* to other forms of attempted wildlife "population control" (i.e., trapping, poisoning, the shooting of so-called "nuisance wildlife," and the killing done by game managers, government hunters, et cetera). *None* of the "wildlife preservation" groups that Kellert selected has ever officially opposed hunting, but by all indications, a significant percentage of those belonging to one of the groups, Defenders of Wildlife, are probably opposed. A second group, the World Wildlife Fund, is *unopposed* to recreational hunting and favors the attempted "control" of wildlife populations. A third organization, the National Wildlife Federation, is strongly prohunting and pro–game management. (Other "wildlife preservation" groups cited by Kellert were the National Audubon Society, the Cousteau Society, and the New York Zoological Society.)

4. Less than two weeks after newly elected New York governor Mario Cuomo had appointed Henry G. Williams as commissioner of the Department of Environmental Conservation in January 1983, Williams announced that he would attend the winter meeting of the Adirondack Conservation Council (a coalition of hunters' groups from the northern part of the state) to be held in Lake Placid that February. He made good on his promise. According to hunting-trapping-fishing columnist Bill Roden, who at one time was the director of the New York State Conservation Council (a key state hunter's organization): "It certainly is not his [Williams'] first meeting with sportsmen for if my recollection is correct, some years back he attended New York State Conservation Council meetings."

Compared to his predecessors, Williams is relatively progressive and open to public input. Nevertheless, on March 17, 1984, he attended the Adirondack Whitetail Deer Forum in Ticonderoga, New York. The annual forum, which brings together hunters, hunting columnists, hunting guides, taxidermists, hunting equipment dealers, et cetera, includes an exhibit of stuffed and mounted heads of trophy bucks shot during the previous hunting season.

Williams was Cuomo's second choice for DEC commissioner. His first choice had been Assemblyman Maurice Hinchey of Ulster County, who had declined the governor's job offer. Hinchey, a member of several powerful environmental resource committees during the course of his political career, has a long record of supporting hunting interests. Commissioner Williams's predecessors, including his immediate forerunners, Robert F. Flacke and Peter A. E. Berle, were equally adept at befriending hunters, attending "sportsmen's" meetings, and speaking at fish and game clubs around New York State.

5. The Adirondacks consist mostly of thickly wooded, rugged terrain, and since nearly half of the land within the Adirondack Park is state-owned, there is less likelihood of landowners posting their property than in the Southern Zone, which consists mostly of agricultural land.

6. Pittman-Robertson (P-R) funds are allocated by the federal government to the states on a 75-25 matching basis according to population, land area, and the number of hunting licenses sold in each state. P-R allocations are *not* based upon the number of guns and the amount of ammunition sold in a state. But it behooves state wildlife officials to persuade residents of their states to purchase firearms and ammunition. During fiscal 1980, the New York State Division of Fish and Wildlife received $14.5 million of a $15.7 million allocation for the "management" of fish and wildlife from hunting, fishing, and trapping licenses and from federal funds (including P-R revenue).

7. I have seen the remains of several deer that were killed by coyotes during severe winter conditions. In one case, a deer had apparently injured its leg on a heavy snow crust and was unable to escape. While there are higher coyote populations in some parts of the coyote's range than in others, these deer killings are the exception and not the rule. In most northern states in the coyote's range, coyotes help to keep deer active during autumn, winter, and early spring, leading to a reduction in highly browsed areas. During the winter of 1983–84, I heard of an unconfirmed case in the central Adirondacks where seven yarded deer had allegedly been killed by coyotes. (This was reported by a coyote hunter!) Cases such as these are very rare and would occur only during times of deep or heavily crusted snow. Coyotes have adapted to a wide variety of food, but they most often eat rabbits, snowshoe hares, red or gray squirrels, and other small mammals.

8. Wildlife biologists with the Maine Department of Inland Fisheries and Wildlife say that the deer herd in most areas of that state is in reasonably good condition and that there is a 75 to 80 percent pregnancy rate for does. This would indicate that there is more than enough browse to accommodate the existing number of deer and also that the deer have adjusted their birth rates to compensate for limited predation by coyotes, comparatively unlimited predation by hunters and other decimating factors. The Maine deer herd will not sink to near-extinction simply because of a low level of predation by coyotes. But the primary concern of officials of the Maine wildlife department is to increase the size of the deer herd to accommodate hunters and try to insure a maximum revenue yield for their department.

According to Maine state biologist Henry Hilton, speaking at the Hamilton County (New York) Coyote Forum on March 10, 1984, most of the predation on deer by coyotes occurs in the spring, when coyotes have pups to feed and fawns are available. Since most of the coyotes killed by hunters had been nonbreeding pups and subadults, Hilton said that the Department of Fisheries and Wildlife was planning some "coyote control measures" in the spring in areas of highest coyote populations. If breeding adults are killed, this means that many pups not old enough to fend for themselves will slowly starve unless a coyote pack is large enough so that "foster parents" will care for the pups.

Hilton did not mention whether "coyote control measures" in Maine would include aerial shooting or denning of pups. Denning is still practiced in some western states. A coyote den is located, and, with no route of escape, the pups are killed by one of several methods, including shooting, burning, drowning, gassing, clubbing, trapping, or poisoning (of baited meat).

9. Hunters' organizations obscured the issue, using the media to convince many people that the effort to end the moose hunt was simply the first step by "anti's" to abolish all hunting in Maine. But the fact that a full 40 percent of the Maine electorate voted to end the hunt indicates that the public is slowly developing an awareness of the significance of the hunting issue.

II. The Roots of Wildlife Exploitation

1. Many Indians were corrupted by the white men who wanted vast quantities of furs and other animal products, but this was not the Indians' nature or

tradition. Victor B. Scheffer, in his book *A Voice for Wildlife* (Scribners and Sons, 1974) noted that in 1832 a party of Sioux had brought 1,400 fresh bison tongues into a white men's encampment. They had left the bodies to rot. Scheffer wrote:

> The Indians were after whiskey, which they duly received, in trade for the tongues. That affair does not prove that the Indian was wasteful; it only proves that an individual possessed of a white man's gun and a white man's thirst was a modified Indian.

2. Leopold was critical of single species and limited multiple species fish and wildlife management in *A Sand County Almanac*, which he wrote shortly before his death and which was published after his death. Among his comments on the subject was the following:

> Damage to plant life usually follows artificialized management of animals—for example, damage to forests by deer. . . . Over-abundant deer, when deprived of their natural enemies, have made it impossible for deer food plants to survive or reproduce. . . . The composition of flora . . . is gradually impoverished, and the deer in turn are dwarfed by malnutrition. There are no stags in the woods today like those whose antlers decorated the walls of feudal castles.

While Leopold's ecological views progressed as he grew older, he never achieved a deep empathy with wild creatures or with ecosystems as Nature had developed them. He never advocated the reintroduction of rare, threatened, or endangered predators, he remained a hunter to the end, and he persisted in his mistaken belief that habitat manipulation is usually the key to benefiting wildlife and ecosystems.

3. A study by The Fund for Animals in Michigan concluded that there is an expenditure of many more BTUs of energy in the manufacture of a real fur coat than in the manufacture of a coat made from an equal amount of synthetic fur. Included in the fabrication of the genuine article are the manufacture of traps, cleaning and scraping of pelts, transportation of pelts, processing, and storage. There is also the time and effort that are required to trap a "fur-bearing" animal.

Part Two: Shooting Down the Myths

III. Pseudobiological Arguments

1. Twenty or thirty species of songbirds are a very small number of species to be found in a wooded area in the Southeastern United States. For example, a mature pine forest, which would include oaks and other hardwoods, would normally harbor at least five or six times this number during a twelve-month period.

2. Victor H. Cahalane, chief biologist with the National Park Service from 1936 to 1955, wrote in 1961 to the then director of the National Park Service, Conrad Wirth: "The sanctuary principle is a keystone in the basic concept of national parks. The principle was adopted because a natural animal community cannot be maintained for public benefit, education and enjoyment if hunting is

permitted. Where public hunting is a regular feature, animals become so wary that they are rarely seen by non-hunting visitors."

3. At first the Pennsylvania muzzle-loader season was held during January, a time when deer are in a weakened condition because of snow, cold temperatures, and reduced food supplies and are extremely vulnerable to stress. After the Pennsylvania Game Commission had received complaints about this practice (including protests from some hunters), the muzzle-loader season was pushed back. For a couple of years it was held during late December and early January, but by 1983 it was changed again so that it began in mid-December, directly following the regular firearms deer season.

4. In 1983 the New Hampshire Fish and Game Department did something almost unprecedented in the annals of modern deer management. It *reduced* the length of gun seasons for deer in part of the state. In that year, the department, some of whose members were alarmed at what appeared to be a decrease in the deer herd in parts of the White Mountains, shortened gun seasons in the state's Northern Zone to nineteen days while keeping seasons at their previous four and a half week length in the southern part of the state. Separate seasons for bucks only and deer of either sex were initiated in both zones. But the unusual two-week reduction in the length of the Northern Zone gun seasons was more than offset by the archery season, which lasted twelve weeks throughout the state, beginning on September 24 and finally concluding on December 15! Gun hunters who held an archery license could kill one deer with a muzzle-loader, shotgun, or rifle and an additional deer with a bow and arrow. Nothing of substance had changed. It was still Maximum Sustained Yield business as usual for the New Hampshire Fish and Game Department. After many hunters had complained about the shortened 1984 Northern Zone deer season, the New Hampshire Department of Fish and Game rose to the occasion, and in 1985 statewide gun seasons for deer were *five weeks* in length. Archery season extended from September 15 through December 16.

5. "Range carrying capacity" is a term that is used by commercial wildlife biologists mainly for the purpose of applying wildlife population and habitat information to game management. Theoretically, it is the point at which any further increase in a wildlife population, particularly that of a large species of ungulate such as the white-tailed deer, moose, elk, or caribou, will result in severe habitat destruction combined with malnutrition and die-offs due either to poor quality of insufficient food. Therefore it denotes the greatest population density of a species that a given type of habitat in a particular geographical area can support under a certain set of ecological conditions. However, there are such a large number of variables to consider, including habitat, topography, climate, weather factors, amount and availability of food, health of the herd, age factors, sex ratios, et cetera that even the most experienced wildlife biologist would have difficulty determining at what specific point a deer herd, or other wildlife population, has reached the carrying capacity of its range. Furthermore, there is such a large "gray area" between a healthy deer herd and a malnourished deer herd that the term "range carrying capacity" is devoid of substantive meaning. It has little significance in the real world, where events do not conform to imprecise terminology. The concept of a "range carrying capacity" is used more as an excuse to justify the killing of wildlife than as a specific and readily definable term.

6. Fosburgh cited "logging, negligible hunting, mild predation, and a succession of tolerable winters" as reasons for relatively high deer populations on the Baker Tract as compared to those on adjacent state land. Naturally, the final two factors would be true over the entire geographical area. As for negligible hunting, I would question whether this in itself is a long-term factor in determining the relatively high deer concentration on the private preserve. My experience has shown that deer instinctively seek areas of safety during hunting seasons. Evidence suggests that if a sizable area of favorable habitat has been closed to hunting, deer will seek refuge there, sometimes to the extent of permanently shifting their territories to this new location. Some deer may have a "sixth sense" that guides them to havens of safety, or they may simply know the areas that are most frequently utilized by hunters.

Many years during mid- or late November, when there is a light snow cover, I have noticed that groups of deer have created a series of trails on a thickly forested 265-acre property in my area that has been closed to hunting. The deer use these trails in a regular pattern. Often one or more of these trails come within 100 or 150 feet of Adriondack Forest Preserve Lands. But despite similar habitat on the unprotected state tract, deer tracks here at this time of the year are very sparse. (Both hunter utilization and annual deer "harvests" on this multi-thousand-acre state tract are relatively light, and during the six or seven week firearms deer season only mature bucks may be legally shot.) Soon after the conclusion of hunting seasons, most of the deer that had been using the protected acreage move back onto state land, resulting in a more equal distribution of deer and a lower concentration of deer on the refuge. (This would be the case throughout the year if there were no hunting.) Deer that remain in hunted areas during deer seasons often bed down during much of the day and forage mainly at night.

The tendency of deer to seek safe sanctuaries during hunting seasons carries a special danger. Not only are deer weakened by stress and the loss of critical fat reserves during the weeks of hunting pressure, but they may migrate into areas that contain inadequate or insufficient browse. During several years after the conclusion of the Adirondack deer seasons in early December, I have seen a small herd of deer wintering on the forested summit of the highest elevation in my vicinity. This mountaintop offers relative safety from hunters, who roam the lowlands. But deer are exposed to cold winds and lower temperatures than in the sheltered valley areas that they would normally favor. Moreover, there is an inadequate supply of high-quality browse on the summit. In many places footing is precarious. (One side of the mountaintop is a sheer rock wall.) Later in the winter, after having heavily browsed the sparse low-level twigs and buds of striped maple, mountain maple, and other favored saplings, these deer would migrate to sheltered valley areas. But by temporarily forcing the deer into a safe area of less than favorable habitat, hunters were *contributing to* potential malnutrition—exactly the opposite of hunters' claims that hunting reduces the incidence of deer starvation!

In the case of the extensive Baker Tract, is is very likely that deer from surrounding state land have, over a period of time, moved onto the protected tract, thus helping to create a consistently higher deer population there. If hunting were scaled down on state land adjacent to the tract, the deer in the protected area would probably disperse and more stable, lower deer populations would be the rule throughout the area.

The migration of deer to safe sanctuaries was given additional credibility by Richard Coble in an article titled "Habitat and Management of White-Tailed Deer," which appeared in the April 1983 issue of *Deer and Deer Hunting*. Coble wrote that one summer a pair of fawns had grazed each day in a field near his garden, often approaching to within a few yards as he worked. But he added: "About a week before deer season opened in November, however, they evidently reacted to a built-in warning system and departed for more secure quarters. We never did see the mother."

7. Two interesting sidelights to the Great Swamp deer hunts: First, the *Elks Magazine* of September 19, 1975 carried a quote from George E. Gage, at that time the manager of the Great Swamp National Wildlife Refuge. Gage's remarks were from a letter that he had written in response to an inquiry from the magazine about the first deer hunt at the refuge, in December 1974. Gage wrote: "None of the deer examined during the hunt was starving. Analysis of urine glucose and protein levels failed to confirm malnutrition. Of the 63 deer examined, only six were in poor-to-moderate condition based on evaluations of the various fat reserves. The remaining 57 deer had moderate-to-excellent quantities of fat. . . . They were generally in good condition, certainly far from the point of starvation." Gage stated that "during the period of August 1973 to August 1974 a minimum of 12 deer died as a result of starvation and disease" in the refuge. A total of 137 had died from all causes (including illegal hunting, cars, dogs, et cetera), and 14 of these had died from unknown causes.

The second interesting point: According to a biologist who has followed the story of deer hunting as it has unfolded at the Great Swamp, the original environmental impact statement suggested three annual hunts to determine whether the "management" plan designed by commercial biologists would be effective in significantly reducing the size of the deer herd. Not surprisingly, it was during the fourth year after the initial hunt that the deer herd in the swamp began to increase. Equally unremarkable was the fact that, even during the first three seasons, hunting failed to achieve the purported goal, which was to reduce the size of the herd to a posthunt level of about 250. The year 1983 marked the tenth annual deer hunt at the Great Swamp.

8. The hunting of "bucks only" differs from the hunting of bucks and a certain percentage of antlerless deer in that, despite a small ratio of bucks to does where the latter form of hunting is undertaken, game managers calculate annually how many does and fawns can be removed, taking habitat conditions and other factors into account. Thus there is less chance of a depletion of browse and a greater chance of high reproductive rates among surviving does year after year and thus more deer for hunters' guns each autumn. Naturally, where there are high buck "harvests" combined with protection of does, there are fewer bucks to mate with available does and thus lower reproductive rates than would be true where bucks and a certain percentage of does were removed, resulting in more browse for surviving deer.

9. During the 1978 deer hunt in Vermont, two brushfires were set in different parts of the state by overly desperate hunters who were attempting to drive deer out of the woods. Both fires burned out of control, charring a total of more than thirty acres.

10. DEC officials had claimed that bears had been raiding dumps, eating farm crops, and breaking into camps. There were some isolated cases, but as far as I have been able to learn, these incidents were as infrequent as during

any other year. This explanation, designed for public consumption, is typical of the justifications that are commonly given by wildlife officials for the extension of hunting seasons and the initiation of new ones.

11. Throughout the Adirondacks and Catskills, as well as in other designated areas of New York State, it is legal to hunt deer and bear *with a pistol!* State wildlife agencies receive P-R funds from the sale of handguns, but this may have changed by the time you read this. Late in 1982 a bill was introduced by U.S. Representative Martin A. Russo of Illinois that would transfer the excise tax on handguns (about $30 million a year) to a fund that would aid the victims of crime. As of this writing, Russo's bill has gained only limited public support and has provoked the vocal opposition of groups such as the National Rifle Association, the National Wildlife Federation, the Wildlife Management Institute, and The Wildlife Legislative Fund. As of the spring of 1984, P-R monies collected from the sale of handguns are still helping to fund the destruction of wildlife and its habitat.

12. The latter practice, like most activities undertaken by state fish and game agencies, is far from biologically or ecologically sound. It is done not to benefit aquatic life but to benefit fishermen. The lower Great Lakes tributaries, are sluggish and silty and unsuitable for salmon spawning. Moreover, Lake Ontario is heavily polluted, so fish must be restocked each year.

13. Interestingly, Will deserves some of the credit for New York State's eagle and peregrine falcon restoration programs. As of this writing, Will is considering and is expected to accept a job offer from Ducks Unlimited, as a regional director.

14. Game managers and commercial biologists in New York State were proving more adept at increasing deer populations through the use of deer management permits than their less experienced counterparts in Vermont. Part of the reason had to do with less severe winters and more abundant forage in parts of southern and southwestern New York, which includes many brushy, immature woodlands along with orchards and lands that have been planted with agricultural crops.

15. Biologists employed by the New York State Division of Fish and Wildlife do not know the exact number of deer killed per season in the state any more than they know the exact size of the deer herd. Since only about 65 percent of hunters in New York report their kill, the "harvest" estimation is a complicated computerized process based upon average reporting rates and the number of deer brought to official checking stations around the state. This is termed the "calculated take" by the DEC. It was fully described by William Sarbello in an article in the January-February 1981 issue of *The Conservationist* titled "Numbering the Take." (The term "take" is the DEC's benign substitute for "kill.") Concluded Sarbello: "When calculated take information is coupled with biological data and both are collected over a period of time the foundation is laid for managing one of the healthiest deer herds in the nation."

16. You may remember that 1974 was a year of gasoline "shortages," high inflation, and the threatened and actual layoffs of state employees in some states as a result of budget cuts.

17. The increase in Connecticut's deer population was no doubt partly due to the changes in reproductive behavior that usually accompany hunting.

18. Deer permits for people owning less than ten acres of land are issued by computer on a quota basis. This permit quota system for hunting both bucks and does, combined with limits on the numbers of hunters utilizing each state

forest or game management area, is unusual. But in view of the large number of resident hunters and the limited amounts of land open to hunting in Connecticut, wildlife officials have little choice but to restrict the number of permits that they issue. However, the Department of Environmental Protection has developed a system that allows Wildlife Unit employees to have the best of both worlds. A hunter must hold a small game license to enter the lottery for a state land deer permit. This makes the purchase of a small game license much more attractive. Since there are too many hunters in Connecticut (with the potential for creating ultra high-intensity hunting pressure) to make the issuance of unlimited numbers of big game licenses practical, the DEP is assured of a greater supply of revenue simply by requiring that a potential deer hunter purchase a small game hunting license as a prerequisite for the possible issuance of a state land permit. Those wishing to hunt on private land not belonging to themselves or their lineal descendants must obtain written permission from the landowner(s). Numbers of permits issues are based upon the acreage held by each landowner.

19. This figure is low compared to the 28,274 Maximum Sustained Yield deer that were killed on Pennsylvania highways during 1978, following an unusually severe winter. Some years the number of deer killed by automobiles in Pennsylvania has been higher.

20. The extent to which state wildlife officials are often willing to go in order to increase the populations of white-tailed deer is exemplified by a 1981 decision of the New York State Division of Fish and Wildlife to study the feasibility of selective timber cutting by DEC personnel on state lands in the Adirondacks and Catskills in order to increase browse for deer. Apparently the plan had both the endorsement of state wildlife officials and the backing of the Adirondack Conservation Council. The proposal was especially noteworthy because state forestlands in the Adirondack and Catskill Parks are guaranteed "forever wild" by an amendment to the New York State Constitution. In order to cut timber on these protected lands, it would be necessary to amend the state constitution. To do this, a proposal would have to be written into a bill, which would have to be passed by both houses of the state legislature and then resubmitted to the legislature after an intervening election. If adopted by each house by a majority vote, the bill would have to be submitted to the voters for their approval or disapproval. If a majority of voters approved the measure, it would become part of the constitution on January 1 of the following year.

In 1982, a bill was passed by the New York State legislature that would have provided $80,000 to the Division of Fish and Wildlife for a preliminary study. The appropriation was vetoed by then governor Hugh Carey as unnecessary and extravagant. This came at a time when officials of the Division of Fish and Wildlife were claiming that funds allocated to their department were insufficient to carry out existing programs. The timber cutting proposal is likely to be reintroduced in future sessions of the New York State legislature, in all likelihood by antienvironmental politicians who oppose the constitutional "forever wild" provision.

21. Game management may increase the incidence of rabies in other ways. According to Ted Williams ("A Disease Most Awful," *Audubon*, July 1984), an outbreak of rabies in the Mid-Atlantic states had apparently resulted from the stocking of Florida raccoons near the Virginia–West Virginia border. The animals had been ordered by sportsmen's clubs from wild animal dealers, and two of

the shipments contained raccoons that had died of rabies. Williams wrote that the virus now carried by Mid-Atlantic raccoons is identical to that found in the southeastern states; it is not the same as that carried by bats or skunks in the Virginia–West Virginia region.

22. In fairness it must be said that Rue's book, which contains dozens of excellent photographs taken by the author, is a well-written, painstakingly researched work—at least those parts that deal with the physical characteristics and behavioral patterns of North American deer. Unfortunately, many nonhunters assume that because commercial wildlife biologists and some hunters are knowledgeable about the habits of a certain species or a group of species, they are correct in their belief that hunting is necessary to keep some wildlife populations in balance with their food supplies. Rue is not a biologist, but he is a hunter, and for many years he was the chief gamekeeper at the Coventry (New Jersey) Hunt Club, which maintains its own gamelands upon which white-tailed deer are found.

The Deer of North America is the type of text that is used in wildlife science courses at colleges and universities, and Rue's book may be used for this purpose at some educational institutions.

IV. "Nuisance Wildlife" and Pseudoecological Arguments

1. As is true of deer in states such as Michigan, habitat manipulation is sometimes responsible for raids on crops by birds or wild mammals. After game managers at the Horicon National Wildlife Refuge in Wisconsin had altered the habitat to attract geese, large flocks raided farm fields near the refuge. The habitat manipulators then drained ponds and hazed geese with airplanes and motorboats to chase them away. When the geese dispersed to other nearby grain fields, wildlife managers supplied farmers with noisemakers, which were not particularly effective.

2. One or more of these factors may have been responsible in 1982 when a raccoon raided the pens of whooping cranes at the International Crane Foundation at Baraboo, Wisconsin. Having gained entrance through the nylon netting that roofed the crane pens, the raccoon killed four of the cranes on successive nights. The raids resulted in efforts to make the pens coon-proof. Predictably, they also resulted in a series of nocturnal coon hunts with dogs. These forays may or may not have eliminated the offending animal, but they *did* eliminate other raccoons. Since the hunts occurred in mid-June, they no doubt resulted in the deaths of more than one mother raccoon and the slow starvation of baby coons too young to forage for themselves.

3. The cougar population, like that of other predators, usually fluctuates in response to the populations of prey species. While it is true that some mountain lions have preyed on sheep in the Southwest, the cougar's principal prey is the mule deer and mountain goat. As a rule, cougars leave their mountain habitat only when natural food is scarce.

4. In New York State, for example, there are now about 650,000 deer and 700,000 deer hunters. In New Hampshire, a rural state, there are estimated to be 40,000 deer and 70,000 deer hunters.

5. Some scientists would dispute this. However, it is believed that *Australopithecus*, uncovered in East Africa by anthropologist Mary Leakey in 1975, lived primarily on fruits and vegetables. This early homonid has been dated as

having lived 3.75 million years ago. Later homonids such as *Homo erectus* (which lived 2 million years ago) are not believed to have constructed hunting tools. In fact, the first remnants of spears have been located in Spain and Germany and are dated as having been constructed about 250,000 years ago. Naturally, there is disagreement among anthropologists as to how many of the homonids now known to have existed were actually forebears of *Homo sapiens*. Human organs are continually evolving, and the ideal diet for a twentieth-century human would probably not have been the ideal diet for early homonids. But evidence supports the view that modern humans are not biologically equipped to be meat-eaters.

6. An innovative bill proposed by New Jersey state representative D. Bennett Mazur and five other members of the Garden State Assembly was introduced during the 1984 session of the Garden State legislature. It would mandate that any lands in that state that are purchased with nongame and/or endangered species funds could not be used for hunting and/or trapping. If this bill were passed, in the face of stiff opposition from prohunting legislators and officials of the New Jersey Department of Fish, Game and Wildlife, it might clear the way for the use of nongame and endangered species funds to benefit animals and ecosystems in that state. Regrettably, since nongame and endangered species funds are presently in short supply, the lands that would be purchased would probably be relatively small parcels of several hundred acres or less.

This was true of a 212-acre tract in West Milford, New Jersey. This property, formerly owned by the late conservationist Fred Ferber, was acquired by the state for back taxes after Ferber's death. A bill authored by New Jersey state senator James Vreeland and passed into law in 1981 established a wildlife sanctuary on this parcel in accordance with the wishes of Ferber's friends and family. (Ferber was an avid wildlife protectionist.) Animals may be released here for their well-being. But since wild animals have territorial boundaries that overlap property lines, some of the animals that would be given "refuge" here and also on *potential* nongame lands would stray onto adjacent public and private lands where hunting is permitted. Game officials are well aware of this, and this is the only flaw in an otherwise excellent proposal. The fact remains that as long as state game bureaus are funded by hunters and as long as hunting is permitted and encouraged on most public lands, members of target species living on these lands and some of those living on adjacent protected lands will be exploited.

7. Species endangerment is one of the many justifications that game officials use as leverage for their hunting and trapping programs. As long as a traditional *game* species has *not* become endangered, then usually it may be legally hunted. But "sufficient" animal population levels are a faulty basis for hunting—both pragmatically and ethically. Consider the bobcat. The bobcat population in a particular area can never exceed the limits of its food supply, and in most wild areas of the bobcat's range, there are more than enough jackrabbits, snowshoe hares, red squirrels, gray squirrels, mice, et cetera to support a relatively stable, if nonoptimum, bobcat population along with the other middle- and upper-level carnivores that would normally inhabit these regions. Yet any legal action that would seek to prohibit or restrict bobcat hunting and/or trapping, if it is to succeed, must use a *low bobcat population* as a primary argument. Game officials are saying, in effect, that unless or until it can be proven that the bobcat population in their state is critically declining and seriously threatened, they will continue to allow hunters and trappers to kill them.

This reasoning is not only nonecological, it is nonsensical, except by a Machiavellian economic standard. Why should maximum sustained yield hunting and trapping continue until a species is endangered? Animal populations are regulated by Nature, and while controlled hunting often increases animal populations—*if* these populations are well established—this population increase usually does not occur when members of a species are scattered sparsely over a wide area. This is true of the bobcat in many regions.

The "sufficient population" rationale also poses an important ethical question: why should the lives of individual animals be assigned greater value when members of their respective species decline in numbers? And why should a concern for saving these lives increase under these conditions? Is not the life of a white-tailed deer or ruffed grouse equally as valuable as the life of a whooping crane or bald eagle? Moreover, who are we to determine who shall be killed and who shall not? The logic is absent in a system in which the killing or harassment of a member of at least one species (Florida's endangered manatee) is punishable by a fine of up to $20,000 or one year in jail, while it is considered a criminal act to release a legal target animal from a trap or, in many states, to interfere with the conduct of a legal hunt.

The restoration of endangered species, like other aspects of utilitarian wildlife management, is based upon the premise that the problem is not that individual animals are being killed, but simply that too many members of certain species are dying.

8. The U.S. Fish and Wildlife Service has a basic *federal* endangered species list, which, in general, includes species that the federal government considers endangered throughout all or most of their range. But each state has *its own* separate endangered species list. In general, these state lists include most or all species that appear on the federal lists. But state lists vary between states (as do the "threatened," "rare," and "special concern" lists). A species that may be on the "endangered" (or other classification) list in one state may not be classified as such in an adjacent state. Moreover, each state has its own classifications of game and nongame species and species that are considered "nuisance wildlife."

9. Since the black duck closely resembles its cousin the hen mallard, the Fish and Wildlife Service and state game agencies, before the 1983 waterfowl seasons, distributed to waterfowl hunters more than a million illustrated leaflets that explained how to distinguish between the two species. The cost of preparing and disseminating these fliers must have amounted to a five-figure sum. This was money that *could* have been used to help determine the reasons for the decline of the black duck population and perhaps help to stem the decline. As of this writing, commercial biologists still do not know the reasons for this decline. (Naturally, federal wildlife officials have not yet suggested closed seasons on the black duck.)

10. In the words of Gerald D. Kirkpatrick, chief of the Division of Law Enforcement of the Pennsylvania Game Commission: "The hunting hours for the spring turkey season are designed to have hunters out of the woods by 12:00 noon in order to keep hen disturbance at a minimum. . . . Only bearded turkeys are legal. This regulation has kept the accidental killing of beardless turkeys to a bare minimum. All in all, the spring season has been a super success of the highest degree."

11. According to A. W. Schorger (*The Wild Turkey*, University of Oklahoma Press, 1966): "As the hen lies prone on the ground, the big tom hops on and stamps on her, raising each foot forward with a treading action, literally walking and jumping all over her back in the roughest manner. The weight ratio is two to one against her, yet she actually courts this treatment. In this preliminary nuptial action the male vigorously stamps on his mate from 20 to 40 times or even more and usually continues for at least five minutes. After this the hen tilts forward on her wishbone, raises her tail and the actual caress takes place."

12. Since hunters and wildlife officials do not seem to learn from the mistakes of the past (particularly when pleasure and/or profit are motivating influences), some states and geographical areas within states that do not presently have turkey hunting seasons may be the scenes of turkey hunts in the near future. According to the 1982–83 *Progress Report* of the New York State Division of Fish and Wildlife (Spring Edition), two major objectives of that department are to assure:

1) complete wild turkey population establishment efforts in selected areas of potential range by 1983, and also to
2) quadruple the statewide turkey harvest by 1992.

The report writer claimed that by 1992 "the spring harvest [in New York State] could be as high as 10,400 birds."

13. Wildlife population counts, while usually having a reasonable degree of accuracy, are educated estimates, unreliable within about ten percentage points above or below the estimate. The only "official" wildlife population statistics available are those issued by state wildlife agencies and the U.S. Fish and Wildlife Service, and for journalistic research purposes one usually has no choice but to assume that their figures are reasonably accurate. But they are sometimes grossly *inaccurate*. (For example, the New York State DEC's initial deer population estimates at Harriman Park.)

14. A prime example of game management practices that have upset ecosystems *and* destroyed habitat for many native species are the projects undertaken by Ducks Unlimited. In Canada this organization has caused the flooding of 1.4 million acres to create duck breeding habitat. Many small mammals were drowned in the affected areas, and many other mammals were forced to flee to other, perhaps less favorable, locations. A booklet published by Friends of Animals claims that as many as *8 million* animals may have been drowned as a result of these water containment projects.

15. This was one part of a three-part rider attached to the Endangered Species Act, which was reauthorized by Congress and signed by President Ronald Reagan in September 1982. Authored by Representative John Breaux (D-La.), the Sportsman's Bill or "Common Sense Amendments" also included: 1) A reversal of the Defenders of Wildlife Bobcat Suit. This would have required reliable population estimates before state game agencies could initiate or extend bobcat hunting or trapping seasons. It would also have prohibited the transportation of bobcat pelts in interstate commerce. (It is legal, as of the spring of 1984, to deal in the *international* export of bobcat pelts.) 2) Members of harvest-oriented state game agencies were given greater authority in the determination of rare, threatened, or endangered species in their respective states. This is a

very dangerous precedent because many species that are very low in number over most parts of their range may be more abundant in a favorable habitat in one geographical area, which may be centered in a single state.

V. Conservation Arguments and Hunters' Practices

1. Dr. Stephen Kellert, in his 1980 study, *Attitudes of the American Public Relating to Animals*, found that of a sampling of those people belonging to hunters' groups, only 7 percent were also members of environmental organizations while 15 percent belonged to wildlife preservation groups. By contrast, 22 percent of those surveyed who belonged to wildlife preservation groups also belonged to environmental groups, while *57 percent* of those in environmental protection groups belonged to wildlife preservation groups. No doubt the fact that none of the "wildlife preservation" organizations that were cited by Kellert have officially expressed strong opposition to public hunting had some bearing on the percentage of hunters belonging to these groups. About one-quarter of those in environmental protection organizations and a fifth of those in wildlife preservation groups belonged to hunters' organizations.

2. The Animal Welfare *Comsearch Printout* (published by the Foundation Center, 79 Fifth Avenue [at 16th Street], New York, N.Y. 10003) is an annual report that lists the grants that have been awarded to conservation and humane organizations during a particular year. The 1979 edition listed, among others, the following gifts:

—$10,500 from the Bingham Foundation in Ohio to the National Wildlife Federation for a *strip-mining project*! Also $50,000 from the Atlantic Richfield Foundation in California (no purpose given).
—$1,600,000 from the Max C. Fleischmann Foundation in Nevada to Ducks Unlimited for a new national headquarters.
—$50,000 from the Scaife Foundation in Pennsylvania to Trout Unlimited for an executive director.

3. State fish and wildlife bureaus are sometimes funded partly by general state tax revenues. This is a little-known fact, and it is particularly true when these agencies are divisions of state natural resource departments. According to the Hornell, New York *Evening Tribune* (Outdoor Section, Spring and Summer 1978): "In addition to the Conservation Fund of $15.4 million for the 77–78 license year, fish and wildlife programs are supported by $7.3 million of general tax revenue spent for such activities as capital development, land acquisition, construction and operation and maintenance of department buildings, facilities and equipment. So for every three dollars allocated to fish and wildlife programs, two come from the Conservation Fund and one from general tax revenues."

During fiscal 1974–75 (a period of high inflation), the New York State legislature allocated to the State Division of Fish and Wildlife, *in addition* to an appropriation from the general fund (author's italics), "the sum of one dollar *for each hunting, trapping and fishing license sold.*" Existing funds were deemed insufficient to cover the division's expenses. (Source of information: 55 *McKinney's Consolidated Laws*, Section 83 State Finance Laws).

State tax money is still used to promote game management in New York and some other states. During the 1981–82 fiscal year, for example, more than

$11.3 million in New York State tax dollars were funneled out of the state treasury to help fund a $30 million expenditure of the state Division of Fish and Wildlife. (This was an increase of $1.8 million from a $9.5 million tax allocation during fiscal 1980–81.) Since only about 15 percent of New York Staters hunt and/or trap, about $9.6 million of nonhunting taxpayers' dollars helped to fund the Fish and Wildlife Department's operations during fiscal 1981–82. This included:

—$3.6 million in capital construction funds used for fish and wildlife management (of a total expenditure of $17.5 million).
—*In addition*, $1.4 million of general use state tax money funded fish and wildlife management *and* game law enforcement (of a total *combined* expenditure of $22.5 million).

Perhaps the most incredible tax dollar allocation was the funneling of $346,000 from the state treasury for pheasant propagation and stocking (total cost: $1,363,000). About $294,000 of this (21.5 percent of the total) came from the pockets of nonhunters. This is another example of how nonhunters' tax money subsidizes recreational hunting—on the state level. (Source of statistics: *1981–82 Fiscal Report New York State's Fish and Wildlife Program*, prepared by the New York State Conservation Fund Advisory Council.* Nonhunters' tax allocations are my estimates.)

4. In the spring of 1984, the New York State DEC allocated $40,000 from voluntary state income tax contributions for a wildlife veterinarian. Among the other tax-gift funded programs that year were $114,000 for maintenance and improvement of public use facilities (including hunter access sites); $65,000 for the introduction of prohunting and trapping manuals into public schools; $32,000 for movies to be used in schools (mostly prohunting and trapping films); $50,000 continued funding for a landowner relations and assistance specialist (who advises rural property owners how to improve conditions for game birds and hunted mammals on their land and assists in formulating plans for hunter access onto their property); also $61,000 for habitat manipulation in state wildlife management areas.

5. Kellert, in his 1980 study of Americans' attitudes about animals, found that while hunters scored moderately high in their general knowledge about wildlife, most hunters ranked low in their approval rate for the protection of endangered species.

6. In 1982, in return for higher hunting, fishing, and trapping license fees in New York State, hunters were granted an eleven-member "Conservation Fund Advisory Council" whose travel expenses are paid by the DEC. Ten members are political appointees, while the eleventh is chosen by the governor upon recommendation by the state Division of Fish and Wildlife. The only criteria for membership on the council is that an appointee hold a New York State hunting and/or trapping and/or fishing license. The council's function is to monitor the expenditures of the state wildlife department and submit an annual financial report so that consumptive users of wildlife can exert pressure on state legislators and state wildlife officials if and when they believe that the department's funds are being used in ways that do not promote their interests. Members of the Advisory Council serve three-year terms. As of this writing, Advisory Council

*See note 6.

Chairman Robert A. Boice is in his third term as president of the New York State Conservation Council. He is also a state delegate to the National Wildlife Federation and a member of the National Rifle Association. Gerry Pendas, the Advisory Council's vice-chairman, is president of the Adirondack Conservation Council and the Saratoga County Council of Fish and Game Clubs.

Since the New York State Bureau of Audit and Control has traditionally overseen the expenditures of the Division of Fish and Wildlife, the Conservation Fund Advisory Council is essentially a special interest duplicate agency, part of a continuing effort by hunters to gain a tighter stranglehold over the New York State Division of Fish and Wildlife, and the first step toward a game commission in New York State.

7. During the autumn of 1983 and thereafter, there was increasing support by some members of the Adirondack Conservation Council for the New York State Division of Wildlife to allow hunters to kill *two* deer during the Northern Zone bowhunting season. (Hunters are allowed to "harvest" one deer of either sex by bow and arrow in this area of low deer populations.)

8. James T. Tanner, in his book *The Ivory-Billed Woodpecker* (The National Audubon Society, 1942, and Dover Books, 1966), noted that while cutting of mature trees in the southeastern United States and a subsequent reduction in the number of grubs upon which this large bird fed were the primary reasons for its endangerment during the early 1940s, live-target shooting by hunters had been, and still was, a factor in its continued decline. This had been particularly true on the Singer Tract, a large area of virgin timber in northeastern Louisiana. Tanner offered the following advice for the protection of the ivory-bill: "Any refuge where ivory-bills are to be protected should be patrolled by efficient wardens to keep out hunters of any kind. Where there are only a few birds in an isolated area, those few must be completely protected to insure their continued existence, for the loss of one or two individuals may be the beginning of the end. . . . The seemingly innate desire of most hunters to kill and examine a spectacular bird is a constant threat." Tanner suggested that refuges should require permits for all visitors. These would help game wardens monitor the location of people within the refuges and discourage illegal poaching.

Unfortunately, in many parts of the United States, particularly in isolated rural areas, hunting has changed little in the forty years since Tanner wrote his book. Today, the hunting of legal "game" species is still allowed at the Catahoula National Wildlife Refuge, only forty miles from the Singer Tract, where the last known ivory-bills were seen. The species is believed to be near extinction. (The Singer Tract is not far from the home territory of Representative John Breaux who assured the proponents of the 1982 Endangered Species Act reauthorization that hunting does not contribute to the extinction of any species of animal.)

Hunting *indirectly* contributes to species extinction—sometimes on national wildlife refuges. On January 23, 1984, a whooping crane was found dead on the Bosque Del Apache National Wildlife Refuge in New Mexico. Its death was attributed directly to lead shot poisoning. Hunting is permitted on the refuge.

9. In some states, almost anyone who can look down the barrel of a rifle or shotgun is eligible for a hunting license. In 1982 the state of Georgia issued a deer hunting license to an eighty-eight–year–old man who was almost totally deaf and had to use a cane as a walking aid. The man became lost overnight, but managed to hobble out of the woods, rifle in hand, the following morning while a search party combed nearby terrain.

10. In fairness to game wardens, it must be pointed out that their job is difficult and often dangerous. Michael Knight of the *New York Times*, quoting a 1977 study, wrote that America's state and federal game wardens, which at that time numbered 6,000, are eight times as likely to be assaulted with guns as any other law enforcement agents. Knight chronicled the experiences of Warren Jenkins, a New Hampshire game warden. In 1975, Jenkins surprised a band of poachers who had illegally killed a deer. One of the poachers shot Jenkins, and he was left deep in the woods. Fortunately, he was rescued. According to Knight: "Other poachers have shot at him, pointed guns in his face, and tried to run him over with cars. Earlier this month (November 1977), one fired a shotgun six times at his house."

11. Apparently, Madson bases his contentions on a combination of an 1842 U.S. Supreme Court ruling, which declared that wildlife is held in trust for all people and a decision by the Supreme Court of Minnesota (*State v. Rodman*) in which the court ruled that the state is entitled to make laws regulating the times and manner in which wild animals can be killed. This decision included the observation that the state may "impose limitations upon the right of property in such game after it has been reduced to possession. Such limitations deprive no person of his property, because he who takes or kills game has no previous right to property in it, and when he acquires such right by reducing it to possession he does so subject to such conditions and limitations as the legislature has seen fit to impose." However, the court also declared that "the ownership of wild animals, so far as they are capable of ownership, is in the state, not as proprietor but in its sovereign capacity, as the representative and for the benefit of all its people in common."

12. According to John G. Mitchell (*The Hunt*, Alfred A. Knopf, 1979, 1980): ". . . In more than half of the states, safety training remains strictly voluntary; and in only eighteen of the states with either mandatory or voluntary programs is wildlife identification a part of the regular curricula. Which may explain why some hunters cannot see much difference between a moose and a human being."

VI. Pseudoethical Arguments

1. Kellert's study of American's attitudes toward animals indicated that people who attend church most frequently have the greatest dominionistic, utilitarian, and negativistic feelings toward animals. Likewise, those who attend church least frequently—or not at all—are most likely to view animals in a positive, humane manner. They are more likely to consider animals ecologically important and believe that, as human beings, they have an ethical responsibility to other forms of life. While there were notable variations among individuals, this was the trend that Kellert found. This would tend to confirm the high degree of biblical misinterpretation about humane stewardship.

Part Three: Targeting the Issues

VII. The Social Implications

1. State wildlife officials are not always able to implement plans for the indoctrination of children. In 1982 animal protection groups, led by Friends of Animals, forced the temporary postponement of a scheme by the New Jersey Department of Fish, Game and Wildlife that would have used Pittman-Robertson

funds to incorporate hunter-trapper education into that state's public school system. After preservationists had gained the support of the New Jersey PTA, state wildlife officials withdrew their proposal. But late in 1983 it was resurrected as part of "Project Wild," an elementary ecology course. If it is not defeated it may be in effect by the time you read this. Proposed funding included 50 percent from voluntary income tax contributions and 50 percent from hunting, fishing, and trapping license fees. State game bureaus in *many* states are now attempting to incorporate hunter-trapper training into their schools, and some have succeeded. (As previously noted many junior high schools and high schools in rural Pennsylvania now offer these courses.)

But some states, such as New York, have developed more sophisticated methods of indoctrinating youngsters. The New York State Department of Environmental Conservation operates four "environmental education" camps in different parts of the state. Life at Camps Colby, DeBruce, and Rushford is described in a DEC flier as an idyllic experience where twelve-to-fourteen–year–old boys and girls can engage in philosophical contemplation of the natural world by "writing inspired nature poetry and sitting along a flowing stream listening to the sounds of Nature." But the camps also "develop new skills in . . . hunting, fishing, and trapping during courses offered by certified instructors." Youngsters may fish in a lake artifically stocked with trout. Another DEC camp brochure proclaims that "wildlife management [goes] hand in hand with those [activities] which develop the youngsters' appreciation of the natural world." The brochure includes a drawing of a DEC hunting safety instructor teaching a boy how to shoot a rifle. In addition to required fish and wildlife management courses at the more "advanced" Rogers Ecology Workshop (for young men and women ages 15–17), a student may choose elective courses in fishing, archery and bow hunting, fly tying, trapping, animal skinning, habitat manipulation, and animal-skin study and taxidermy preparation.

2. South American Indians are suffering many abuses partly because they are widely regarded to be biologically inferior. A report in the September 1982 issue of *World Press Review* titled "Saving the Jungles—Humanity's Stake in a Vanishing Resource" alleged that Indians had been massacred in Brazil because of the drive to clear Amazonian lands for agricultural development—primarily beef cattle raising. According to the article, "desire for land, coupled with exagerated fears of Indian fierceness and a widespread belief that they are sub-human, have led to many atrocities. A 1968 Brazilian government investigation found that Cintas Largas (Surui) Indians in the northern Matto Grosso had been bombed from the air with dynamite, and that most of the Beicos-de-Pau tribe had died after its food had been laced with arsenic."

Readers may recognize some close parallels between these incidents and the wolf and coyote "control" practices of the U.S. Fish and Wildlife Service and the Alaska Fish and Game Department.

VIII. Seeking Solutions

1. In recent years, increasing numbers of women have joined the ranks of American hunters. An article by Albert L. Hershey in the Buffalo, New York *Courier-Express* (November 15, 1981) quoted New York State hunting safety instructor Fran Lounsbury, who said that eight of twenty-two persons in his most recent class were women, as were sixteen in an earlier class. According to

Lounsbury, most of the women apparently were interested in hunting because their husbands hunted. However, recreational killing did not appeal to all of the women who had graduated from his class. One twenty-five–year–old said, "I honestly don't know if I could ever shoot an animal. I like to target shoot, but I don't know if an animal is the kind of target I want."

By the autumn of 1981, it was estimated that about 9 percent of American hunters were women.

2. In the autumn of 1979, Copp distributed questionnaires to 100 duck and goose hunters at the Delevan National Wildlife Refuge northeast of San Francisco. One of the questions on the sheet was "Why do you hunt?" According to an article in the *Los Angeles Times,* six answers predominated: 1) to get outside; 2) to escape from frustrating or boring work; 3) to escape from routine or stifling family life; 4) to socialize with other men of similar interests; 5) to master a difficult skill; 6) to overcome the challenge of nature. Naturally, these are superficial reasons and do not reflect inner motivations. But Copp found that escape and release were common themes. Of the 100 hunters questioned, not one mentioned killing for food as a principal reason for hunting.

3. It is true that the U.S. Fish and Wildlife Service is funded mainly by federal tax money. It is equally true that many federal game management programs are similar to those of state wildlife agencies. Therefore, one might ask, would direct tax funding of state wildlife agencies lead to constructive policy changes? The answer is that it would. Except in the cases of waterfowl hunting, predator control, and "nuisance wildlife" control programs, the Fish and Wildlife Service is not as beholden to special interest groups as are state wildlife bureaus. Furthermore, federal wildlife policies are determined by a central authority: the Fish and Wildlife Service is an entity; it is not a group of autonomous units. It is much more difficult to pinpoint the attitudes of 260 million Americans than to gauge the opinions of much smaller numbers of people in individual states. State wildlife officials would be obliged to consider the opinions of preservationists and ecologists in their respective states if their agencies were funded by general tax revenues and by fees paid by nature enthusiasts, including users of state forests and parks. It would be logical to conclude that as state wildlife departments evolved into more ecologically based units, the U.S. Fish and Wildlife Service would do likewise.

4. Additional money for wildlife programs might be acquired through voluntary tax checkoffs, as is now done in some states. However, in its present form this system does little or nothing to allow wildlife protectionists a voice in determining wildlife policies. Game bureaus continue to be funded mainly by hunting, fishing, and trapping license revenue, and the tax donation is an anonymous system. Therefore, how can anyone determine the ecological views of those who have donated part of their tax refund? Consumptive users of wildlife are issued licenses as proof that they have paid money to a game bureau, and wildlife officials can point to the numbers that are sold as "proof" of widespread support for their programs.

IX. Toward a More Perfect World

1. Interestingly, Ms. Carson worked as an editor of publications for the U.S. Fish and Wildlife Service during World War II.

INDEX

United States Fish and Wildlife Service, United States Forest Service, and United States National Park Service)

United States Fish and Wildlife Service, 35, 68, 72, 131, 132, 136, 139, 148, 152, 153, 179, 181, 228, 268, 274, 275 (See also individual programs)

United States Forest Service, 172, 179

United States National Park Service, 135, 136, 137, 260

University of Maine, 40

University of Minnesota, 44

University of Vermont, 39, 40

University of West Virginia, 40

Utah Division of Wildlife Resources, 149

V

van Lawick-Goodall, Hugo
  Innocent Killers (Coauthored by Jane Van Lawick-Goodall), 213

Vermont deer disaster, 86–96

Vermont Deer Prospects Report, 1978, 49, 89

Vermont Department of Fish and Game, 86, 92, 94, 96

Vermont Guide to Hunting, The, 53

Virginia Game Commission, 228

Vogt, Bill
  "The Kaibab Comes to New Jersey," 43

Voles, 76

Volunteer, The, 16

Voyageurs National Park, 172

W

Washington State Department of Game, 120, 155

Waterfowl hunting
  adverse effects, 68–69
  (See also Hunting, waterfowl)

Watt, James, 130, 136

Weasal, 63, 140

Weber, Henry M. (M.D.), 9, 248

Weiss, John, 115

Wentz, W. Alan, 42

Wetlands for Wildlife, 167, 169

What They Say About Hunting, 19, 167

Whooping crane, 272

Wich, Kenneth F., 19–22, 25

Wigard, Lani, 114–15

Wilbrecht, John E., 9

Wilderness Act of 1964, 183, 203

Wilderness Society, The, 166

Wildlife for Tomorrow, 8, 22

Wildlife Legislative Fund of America, 4, 161, 264

Wildlife Management Areas (New York State), 99

Wildlife Management Institute, 4, 40, 44, 167, 174, 264

Wildlife Mismanagement, 51

Wildlife population estimates, 269

Wildlife Society, The, 4, 44, 45, 167

Wild turkey (See Turkey, wild)

Will, Gary B., 48, 102–103, 264

Williams, Henry G., 258

Wilson, Steven C., 58

Wind Cave National Park, 137

Windeatt, Phillip
  The Hunt and the Anti-Hunt, 143

Winkler, William G. (M.D.), 122

Wirth, Conrad, 260

Wolf (See Timber wolf)

Women, in New York State hunter training programs, 274

Woodcock
  biological deformities, 178–79

Woodpecker, ivory-billed, 272

World Press Review, 274

World Wildlife Fund, 168, 258

Y

Yellowstone National Park, 80

Yosemite National Park, 59

Z

Zinc phosphide, 137